2024 Low Carb

Keto

Cookbook for Beginners

2000 Days Easy, Delicious & Low Sugar Keto Diet Recipe Book - Your Solution to Shedding Excess Fat | Includes 30 Day Meal Plans

Sadiyah Nojood Kouri

Discover Your Special Bonus Now!

Scan the QR code below to claim your bonus before you begin reading.

Table of Contents

Introduction

➢ Welcome to a culinary voyage where flavor meets fitness, and indulgence meets vitality. Say hello to the Keto Cookbook, your passport to a lifestyle that celebrates deliciousness without compromising on health.

Crafted with a blend of passion and precision, this cookbook is your roadmap to navigating the vibrant world of the ketogenic diet—a lifestyle embraced by millions for its transformative effects on health and wellness. Rooted in the essence of simplicity and taste, our recipes are tailored to suit the fast-paced American lifestyle, ensuring that busy individuals can effortlessly integrate keto goodness into their daily routines.

What sets the ketogenic diet apart is its focus on high-fat, low-carb ingredients that trigger ketosis—a metabolic state where your body becomes a fat-burning powerhouse. But let's be real: sticking to any diet can be challenging, especially when faced with the temptation of convenience foods and carb-heavy delights.

Fear not, for our cookbook is your culinary compass, guiding you through a world of delectable dishes that not only meet but exceed your keto aspirations. From hearty breakfasts to savory dinners, from on-the-go snacks to decadent desserts, we've curated a tantalizing array of recipes that cater to every palate and preference.

But we offer more than just recipes. Dive deep into the heart of keto living with expert insights on meal planning, smart ingredient swaps, and practical tips for staying on track. Discover the joy of cooking with wholesome, nourishing ingredients that fuel your body and invigorate your spirit, all while fitting seamlessly into your busy lifestyle.

So, whether you're a keto newbie eager to explore new flavors or a seasoned enthusiast in search of culinary inspiration, join us on this journey to wellness through food. Embrace the freedom to savor the foods you love, guilt-free, and unlock the door to a life filled with boundless energy and vitality.

It's time to reclaim your health, reignite your passion for cooking, and embark on a culinary adventure like no other with the Ultimate Keto Cookbook. Let's cook up a storm, nourish our bodies, and embrace a lifestyle that celebrates the harmony of flavor and fitness, one delicious bite at a time.

Unlocking the Power of the Ketogenic Diet: Your Comprehensive Guide

What is the Keto Diet?

The ketogenic diet, commonly known as the keto diet, has surged in popularity as a low-carbohydrate, high-fat eating plan. Its fundamental aim? To shift your body's primary fuel source from carbohydrates to fats. By drastically cutting carbs and upping fat intake, the keto diet drives your body into a metabolic state called ketosis.

In a typical diet, carbs reign supreme, broken down into glucose for energy. But in ketosis, your body adapts, breaking down stored fats into ketones for fuel. These ketones become your body's primary energy source, including for the brain.

Key Principles and Guidelines

Central to the keto diet is strict carb limitation, typically hovering around 20-50 grams per day or 5-10% of total daily calories. This limitation forces your body to tap into fat stores for energy, leading to significant fat loss.

The keto diet is celebrated for its weight loss prowess, curbing appetite and stabilizing blood sugar levels. Lower carb intake reduces insulin levels, facilitating efficient fat burning and noticeable weight loss, especially in body fat.

Beyond the scale, the keto diet boasts health benefits. It improves insulin sensitivity, aiding those with type 2 diabetes or at risk. It also lowers triglycerides, boosts HDL cholesterol, and reduces blood pressure. Additionally, ketosis fuels mental clarity and focus, enhancing cognitive function.

What to Eat on Keto

Your keto plate stars high-quality fats like avocados, nuts, seeds, olive oil, and coconut oil. Moderate protein portions from meat, poultry, fish, and eggs fill your plate, while low-glycemic veggies such as leafy greens, broccoli, cauliflower, and zucchini round out your meal.

Tailoring the Keto Diet

The keto diet isn't one-size-fits-all. Consulting healthcare pros or dietitians before diving in ensures personalized guidance and proper nutritional fulfillment.

In Conclusion

The keto diet is a transformative eating plan that shifts your body's energy source to fats. Its potential benefits span weight loss, improved insulin sensitivity, and heightened mental clarity. With proper knowledge and focus on whole, nutrient-dense foods, the keto diet promises long-term success and holistic health.

Benefits of the Keto Diet

The ketogenic diet offers a myriad of potential advantages that extend far beyond mere weight loss. Here's a comprehensive look at the key benefits associated with embracing a well-structured ketogenic lifestyle:

1. Weight Loss: Perhaps the most renowned benefit of the ketogenic diet is its unparalleled ability to facilitate weight loss. By curtailing carbohydrate intake and ramping up fat consumption, the body undergoes a metabolic transformation, tapping into stored fat as its primary energy source. This metabolic shift can lead to substantial weight loss over time. Additionally, the ketogenic diet often induces a sense of satiety, curbing hunger pangs and cravings, thereby bolstering adherence to a calorie deficit and aiding in weight management.

2. Enhanced Energy and Mental Clarity: Many adherents of the ketogenic diet report heightened energy levels and sharpened mental clarity. This phenomenon stems from the efficient utilization of ketones, which furnish a steady stream of energy to the brain. The absence of blood sugar spikes and crashes, common with high-carbohydrate diets, may contribute to heightened focus, concentration, and cognitive function.

3. Blood Sugar Regulation: The ketogenic diet has shown promise in regulating blood sugar levels, making it particularly beneficial for individuals grappling with insulin resistance, prediabetes, or type 2 diabetes. By minimizing carbohydrate intake, the diet helps stabilize blood glucose levels, mitigating the need for copious amounts of insulin. This can translate to enhanced glycemic control and potentially lower the risk of diabetes-related complications.

4. Alleviated Inflammation: Chronic inflammation is implicated in a host of health ailments, spanning from cardiovascular disease to diabetes and certain autoimmune disorders. Emerging research suggests that the ketogenic diet exerts anti-inflammatory effects, potentially dampening inflammation markers in the body. By adopting a ketogenic eating pattern rich in nutrient-dense, anti-inflammatory foods, individuals may experience a reduction in inflammation and its associated health benefits.

5. Improved Heart Health: Contrary to earlier assumptions, studies indicate that a well-structured ketogenic diet can foster positive effects on heart health. It may lead to reductions in triglyceride levels, elevation of high-density lipoprotein (HDL) cholesterol (the "good" cholesterol), and improvements in other markers linked to cardiovascular well-being. Notably, the quality of fats consumed on a ketogenic diet plays a pivotal role in its heart health benefits, underscoring the importance of prioritizing healthy fats from sources such as avocados, nuts, seeds, and olive oil.

6. Enhanced Metabolic Function: The ketogenic diet is associated with enhancements in various metabolic parameters. It can heighten insulin sensitivity, a pivotal factor in maintaining healthy blood sugar levels and forestalling insulin resistance. Additionally, the diet has been shown to ameliorate markers of metabolic syndrome, including abdominal adiposity, blood pressure, and fasting insulin levels. These favorable changes can contribute to overall metabolic health and a diminished risk of chronic diseases.

7. Potential Therapeutic Applications: Beyond its role in weight loss and metabolic optimization, the ketogenic diet holds promise in managing a spectrum of medical conditions. Extensively studied as a therapeutic modality for epilepsy, especially in children, the ketogenic diet often yields substantial reductions in seizure frequency. Preliminary investigations suggest potential benefits in neurodegenerative disorders like Alzheimer's and Parkinson's disease, as well as polycystic ovary syndrome (PCOS). However, further research is imperative to elucidate the full spectrum of therapeutic applications of the ketogenic diet.

It's crucial to recognize that the ketogenic diet may not be suitable for everyone, and individual responses can vary widely. Consulting with a healthcare professional, particularly if you have underlying health conditions, before embarking on a ketogenic journey or implementing significant dietary modifications is highly advisable. A personalized approach and diligent monitoring can ensure that the diet aligns with your unique needs and aspirations, fostering optimal health and well-being.

Who Benefits from the Keto Diet

The ketogenic diet presents advantages for various groups, including:

1. **Individuals with Obesity:** The keto diet aids weight loss by curbing hunger and enhancing satiety.

2. **Those with Type 2 Diabetes:** Improved blood sugar control and reduced insulin resistance are key benefits for managing type 2 diabetes.

3. **People with Neurological Disorders:** Therapeutic benefits, notably for epilepsy and Alzheimer's disease, are observed with the keto diet.

4. **Individuals with Polycystic Ovary Syndrome (PCOS):** Hormonal imbalances associated with PCOS, like insulin resistance and high androgen levels, may improve with the keto diet.

5. **Athletes:** Endurance athletes may find the keto diet advantageous as it enhances fat utilization and decreases reliance on carbohydrates for energy.

However, it's crucial to consult a healthcare professional before embarking on the keto diet, as it's not suitable for everyone and may pose risks.

Who Should Approach with Caution or Avoid the Keto Diet

While beneficial for some, the keto diet may not be suitable for all:

1. **Those with Certain Medical Conditions:** Individuals with liver or pancreatic disease, gallbladder disease, or a history of pancreatitis should exercise caution.

2. **Pregnant or Breastfeeding Women:** Adequate nutrient provision for fetal development and milk production may be compromised on the keto diet.

3. **Individuals with a History of Eating Disorders:** The strict dietary constraints of keto may trigger disordered eating patterns.

4. **Those with a History of Kidney Stones:** Increased fat intake could heighten the risk of kidney stone formation.

5. **Children:** Due to increased carbohydrate needs for growth and development, the keto diet may not be suitable.

Prior consultation with a healthcare professional is imperative before initiating any dietary or lifestyle changes, especially if there are underlying medical conditions or concerns.

Tips for Embarking on the Keto Journey

Starting the keto diet can be daunting, but these tips will ease your transition:

1. **Research and Plan:** Prioritize research and meal planning to ensure adequate nutrient intake and adherence to recommended macronutrient ratios.

2. **Gradual Carb Reduction:** Ease into the diet by gradually reducing carb intake over a few weeks to minimize "keto flu" symptoms and ensure a smoother transition.

3. **Opt for Healthy Fats:** Emphasize healthy fats like avocado, olive oil, nuts, and seeds to fuel your keto journey.

4. **Hydration Is Key:** Stay hydrated to prevent dehydration and constipation, both common concerns on the keto diet.

5. **Monitor Ketone Levels:** Keep tabs on your ketone levels through urine strips or blood tests to verify ketosis and maintain optimal levels.

6. **Navigate Social Situations:** Plan for social events and dining out by researching menus or bringing keto-friendly snacks to stay on track.

7. **Seek Professional Guidance:** Consider consulting a healthcare professional to assess if the keto diet aligns with your needs and receive personalized guidance.

Remember, the keto diet isn't a one-size-fits-all solution. Consulting a healthcare professional before starting is crucial to ensure proper nutrient intake and hydration while on the diet.

CHAPTER 1 Breakfasts

Cranberry-Orange Scones

Prep time: 5 minutes | Cook time: 22 minutes | Makes 8 scones

- 2 cups (8 ounces / 227 g) blanched almond flour
- ⅓ cup erythritol
- ½ teaspoon baking powder
- ¼ teaspoon sea salt
- ¼ cup coconut oil, melted
- 2 tablespoons orange zest
- ½ teaspoon vanilla extract
- 1 large egg
- ½ cup (2 ounces / 57 g) cranberries, fresh or frozen

1. Preheat the oven to 350ºF (180ºC). Line a baking sheet with parchment paper. 2. In a medium bowl, combine the almond flour, erythritol, baking powder, and sea salt. 3. In a small bowl, whisk together the melted coconut oil, orange zest, vanilla, and egg. Stir the wet mixture into the almond flour mixture, pressing with a spoon or spatula, until a uniform dough forms. (The dough should be pliable and dense, but not crumbly; add a little more coconut oil, a teaspoon at a time, if it's very dry.) Stir and press the cranberries into the dough. 4. Place the dough onto the lined pan and form a disc shape, about 1 inch thick and 6 inches in diameter. Cut into 8 wedges, like a pie or pizza. Move the pieces about 1 inch apart. Bake for 18 to 22 minutes, until golden. 5. Cool completely on the pan to firm up. (Scones will fall apart if you move them before cooling.)

Per Serving:

calories: 232 | fat: 21g | protein: 6g | carbs: 9g | net carbs: 4g | fiber: 5g

Kale Frittata with Crispy Pancetta Salad

Prep time: 20 minutes | Cook time: 15 minutes | Serves 4

- 6 slices pancetta
- 4 tomatoes, cut into 1-inch chunks
- 1 large cucumber, seeded and sliced
- 1 small red onion, sliced
- ¼ cup balsamic vinegar
- Salt and black pepper to taste
- 8 eggs
- 1 bunch kale, chopped
- Salt and black pepper to taste
- 6 tablespoons grated Parmesan cheese
- 4 tablespoons olive oil
- 1 large white onion, sliced
- 3 ounces beef salami, thinly sliced
- 1 clove garlic, minced

1. Place the pancetta in a skillet and fry over medium heat until crispy, about 4 minutes. Remove to a cutting board and chop. 2. Then, in a small bowl, whisk the vinegar, 2 tablespoons of olive oil, salt, and pepper to make the dressing. 3. Next, combine the tomatoes, red onion, and cucumber in a salad bowl, drizzle with the dressing and toss the veggies. Sprinkle with the pancetta and set aside. 4. Reheat the broiler to 400ºF. 5. Crack the eggs into a bowl and whisk together with half of the Parmesan, salt, and pepper. Set aside. 6. Next, heat the remaining olive oil in the cast iron pan over medium heat. Sauté the onion and garlic for 3 minutes. Add the kale to the skillet, season with salt and pepper, and cook for 2 minutes. Top with the salami, stir and cook further for 1 minute. Pour the egg mixture all over the kale, reduce the heat to medium-low, cover, and cook the ingredients for 4 minutes. 7. Sprinkle the remaining cheese on top and transfer the pan to the oven. Broil to brown on top for 1 minute. When ready, remove the pan and run a spatula around the edges of the frittata; slide it onto a warm platter. Cut the frittata into wedges and serve with the pancetta salad.

Per Serving:

calories: 584 | fat: 44g | protein: 30g | carbs: 15g | net carbs: 12g | fiber: 3g

Cinnamon Crunch Cereal

Prep time: 5 minutes | Cook time: 12 minutes | Serves 6

- 3½ cups (14 ounces / 397 g) blanched almond flour
- ½ cup erythritol

- ➢ 2 teaspoons ground cinnamon
- ➢ ½ teaspoon sea salt
- ➢ 2 large eggs, beaten
- ➢ 1 teaspoon vanilla extract
- ➢ Cinnamon Coating:
- ➢ ½ cup erythritol
- ➢ 1 tablespoon ground cinnamon
- ➢ 2 tablespoons coconut oil, melted

1. Preheat the oven to 350ºF (180ºC). 2. In a large bowl, stir together the almond flour, erythritol, cinnamon, and sea salt. 3. In a small bowl, whisk together the eggs and vanilla. Add to the flour mixture and mix well until a dough forms. 4. Place the dough between two large greased pieces of parchment paper, at least 20 × 14 inches in size. Use a rolling pin to roll the dough out into a very thin rectangle, about 1/16 inch thick. It will tend to form an oval shape, so just rip off pieces and reattach to form a more angular shape. You can split the dough into two or more smaller batches if you can't get it to roll thin enough between your 20 × 14-inch pieces of parchment, or don't have a pan that large. 5. Place the bottom piece of parchment paper onto an extra-large baking sheet, at least 20 × 14 inches in size (or two 10 × 14-inch pans, if you've split your dough into smaller batches). 6. Cut the dough into ½-inch-wide strips. Rotate the pan 90 degrees and cut the dough strips into ½-inch-wide strips again, so you are left with ½-inch squares. You don't need to separate the squares; just cutting the dough is sufficient. 7. Transfer the pan(s) to the oven and bake for 8 to 12 minutes, until golden brown and crispy. 8. Meanwhile, make the cinnamon coating: In a large zip-seal bag, combine the erythritol and cinnamon and shake to mix. 9. When the cereal is finished baking, remove from the oven and cool at room temperature to crisp up. 10. Brush the cereal on both sides with melted coconut oil. Then break apart the squares and add to the bag with the cinnamon-erythritol mixture. Shake to coat. Store in an airtight container in the pantry.

Per Serving:

calories: 446 | fat: 39g | protein: 16g | carbs: 26g | net carbs: 7g | fiber: 19g

Super Breakfast Combo

Prep time: 10 minutes | Cook time: 0 minutes | Serves 1

- ➢ Chocolate Fat Bombs:
- ➢ 1 tablespoon coconut butter
- ➢ 2 teaspoons coconut oil

- ➢ 1 teaspoon cocoa powder
- ➢ ½ teaspoon confectioners'-style erythritol, or 1 drop liquid stevia
- ➢ Matcha Latte:
- ➢ 1 cup (240 ml) boiling water
- ➢ 2 tablespoons collagen peptides or protein powder
- ➢ 1 tablespoon coconut butter, coconut oil, or nut butter
- ➢ 1 teaspoon erythritol, or 2 drops liquid stevia
- ➢ 1 teaspoon matcha powder
- ➢ ½ teaspoon maca powder (optional)
- ➢ ¼ teaspoon chaga powder or ashwagandha powder (optional)
- ➢ 1¼ cups (300 ml) full-fat coconut milk, hot

1. To prepare the fat bomb, place all the ingredients in a bowl and either set out in the sun to melt or microwave for 20 to 30 seconds. Once the coconut butter has melted, whisk thoroughly and transfer to a paper muffin liner, a silicone mold, a plastic container—anything will do. Place in the freezer for 5 minutes, or until hardened. 2. Meanwhile, place the boiling water, collagen, coconut butter, sweetener, matcha, and maca and chaga, if using, in a 20-ounce (600-ml) or larger mug. Whisk until the ingredients are incorporated and the lumps are gone, about 1 minute. Stir in the hot coconut milk. 3. Serve the latte with the chilled fat bomb.

Per Serving:

calories: 740 | fat: 65g | protein: 26g | carbs: 12g | net carbs: 2g | fiber: 9g

No-Crust Spinach Quiche

Prep time: 10 minutes | Cook time: 35 minutes | Serves 6

- ➢ 4 tablespoons butter, divided
- ➢ 1 onion, diced
- ➢ 2 garlic cloves, minced
- ➢ 2 cups fresh spinach, chopped
- ➢ Salt and freshly ground black pepper, to taste
- ➢ 10 eggs
- ➢ 1 cup heavy (whipping) cream
- ➢ 2 cups shredded cheese (Colby-Monterey Jack is good), divided

1. Preheat the oven to 375ºF (190ºC). 2. Grease a large round baking

dish with 2 tablespoons of butter. 3. In a medium skillet over medium heat, combine the onion, garlic, spinach, and remaining 2 tablespoons of butter. Season with salt and pepper. Sauté for 4 to 5 minutes and remove from the heat. 4. In a large bowl, whisk the eggs and cream. Add the spinach and 1 cup of cheese and mix to combine. Pour the mixture into the prepared baking dish and season with more salt and pepper. Top with the remaining 1 cup of cheese. Bake for about 30 minutes or until the eggs are set. Cool slightly, slice, and serve. Refrigerate leftovers in an airtight container for up to 1 week.

Per Serving:

calories: 483 | fat: 43g | protein: 21g | carbs: 4g | net carbs: 4g | fiber: 0g

Pizza Pâté

Prep time: 10 minutes | Cook time: 0 minutes | Makes 2½ cups

- ➢ 1 cup (190 g) chopped pepperoni
- ➢ ¾ cup (120 g) raw almonds, soaked for 12 hours, then drained and rinsed ½ cup (120 ml) melted coconut oil
- ➢ ⅓ cup (80 ml) tomato sauce
- ➢ ¼ cup (17 g) nutritional yeast
- ➢ 2 teaspoons apple cider vinegar
- ➢ 2 teaspoons onion powder
- ➢ 1 teaspoon garlic powder
- ➢ ¼ teaspoon finely ground gray sea salt
- ➢ 1 tablespoon finely chopped fresh basil

1. Place all the ingredients except the basil in a high-powered blender or food processor. Blend or pulse until smooth, about 1 minute. 2. Add the basil and pulse until just mixed in.

Per Serving:

calories: 144 | fat: 13g | protein: 5g | carbs: 3g | net carbs: 1g | fiber: 1g

Green Monster Smoothie

Prep time: 3 minutes | Cook time: 0 minutes | Serves 1

- ➢ 1 cup ice
- ➢ 1 cup chopped fresh spinach
- ➢ ½ cup fresh raspberries
- ➢ 2 (1-gram) packets 0g net carb sweetener
- ➢ 1 cup unsweetened almond milk (or dairy alternative milk of your choice)

1. Pulse all ingredients in a food processor or blender 30–60 seconds until ice is blended.

Per Serving:

calories: 67 | fat: 3g | protein: 3g | carbs: 10g | net carbs: 4g | fiber: 6g

Hashed Zucchini & Bacon Breakfast

Prep time: 10 minutes | Cook time: 15 minutes | Serves 1

- ➢ 1 medium zucchini, diced
- ➢ 2 bacon slices
- ➢ 1 egg
- ➢ 1 tablespoon coconut oil
- ➢ ½ small onion, chopped
- ➢ 1 tablespoon chopped parsley
- ➢ ¼ teaspoon salt

1. Place the bacon in a skillet and cook for a few minutes, until crispy. Remove and set aside. 2. Warm the coconut oil and cook the onion until soft, for about 3-4 minutes, occasionally stirring. Add the zucchini, and cook for 10 more minutes until zucchini is brown and tender, but not mushy. Transfer to a plate and season with salt. 3. Crack the egg into the same skillet and fry over medium heat. Top the zucchini mixture with the bacon slices and a fried egg. Serve hot, sprinkled with parsley.

Per Serving:

calories: 440 | fat: 39g | protein: 15g | carbs: 10g | net carbs: 7g | fiber: 3g

Broccoli & Colby Cheese Frittata

Prep time: 15 minutes | Cook time: 20 minutes | Serves 4

- ➢ 3 tablespoons olive oil
- ➢ ½ cup onions, chopped
- ➢ 1 cup broccoli, chopped
- ➢ 8 eggs, beaten
- ➢ ½ teaspoon jalapeño pepper, minced
- ➢ Salt and red pepper, to taste
- ➢ ¾ cup colby cheese, grated
- ➢ ¼ cup fresh cilantro, to serve

1. Set an ovenproof frying pan over medium heat and warm the oil. Add onions and sauté until caramelized. Place in the broccoli and

cook until tender. Add in jalapeno pepper and eggs; season with red pepper and salt. Cook until the eggs are set. 2. Scatter colby cheese over the frittata. Set oven to 370ºF and cook for approximately 12 minutes, until frittata is set in the middle. Slice into wedges and decorate with fresh cilantro before serving.

Per Serving:

calories: 426 | fat: 34g | protein: 23g | carbs: 8g | net carbs: 6g | fiber: 2g

Egg Tofu Scramble with Kale & Mushrooms

Prep time: 10 minutes | Cook time: 25 minutes | Serves 4

- ➢ 2 tablespoons ghee
- ➢ 1 cup sliced white mushrooms
- ➢ 2 cloves garlic, minced
- ➢ 16 ounces firm tofu, pressed and crumbled
- ➢ Salt and black pepper to taste
- ➢ ½ cup thinly sliced kale
- ➢ 6 fresh eggs

1. Melt the ghee in a non-stick skillet over medium heat, and sauté the mushrooms for 5 minutes until they lose their liquid. Add the garlic and cook for 1 minute. 2. Crumble the tofu into the skillet, season with salt and black pepper. Cook with continuous stirring for 6 minutes. Introduce the kale in batches and cook to soften for about 7 minutes. Crack the eggs into a bowl, whisk until well combined and creamy in color, and pour all over the kale. Use a spatula to immediately stir the eggs while cooking until scrambled and no more runny, about 5 minutes. Plate, and serve with low carb crusted bread.

Per Serving:

calories: 309 | fat: 23g | protein: 21g | carbs: 6g | net carbs: 5g | fiber: 2g

Vegetable-Beef Hash with Nested Eggs

Prep time: 5 minutes | Cook time: 35 minutes | Serves 4

- ➢ 2 tablespoons good-quality olive oil
- ➢ ½ pound grass-fed ground beef
- ➢ ½ red bell pepper, diced
- ➢ ½ zucchini, diced
- ➢ ¼ onion, diced

- ➢ 2 teaspoons minced garlic
- ➢ 1½ cups low-carb tomato sauce
- ➢ 1 tablespoon dried basil
- ➢ 1 teaspoon dried oregano
- ➢ ⅛ teaspoon sea salt
- ➢ ⅛ teaspoon freshly ground black pepper
- ➢ 4 eggs

1. Cook the beef. In a large deep skillet over medium-high heat, warm the olive oil. Add the beef and, stirring it occasionally, cook until it is completely browned, about 10 minutes. 2. Make the sauce. Add the bell pepper, zucchini, onion, and garlic to the skillet and sauté for 3 minutes. Stir in the tomato sauce, basil, oregano, salt, and pepper, bring it to a boil, and cook for about 10 minutes. 3. Cook the eggs. Make four wells in the beef mixture using the back of a spoon. Crack an egg into each well, then cover the skillet, reduce the heat to medium-low, and simmer until the eggs are cooked through, about 10 minutes. 4. Serve. Divide the mixture between four bowls, making sure to include an egg in each serving.

Per Serving:

calories: 275 | fat: 19g | protein: 18g | carbs: 8g | net carbs: 6g | fiber: 2g

Sausage Breakfast Stacks

Prep time: 10 minutes | Cook time: 15 minutes | Serves 2

- ➢ 8 ounces ground pork
- ➢ ½ teaspoon garlic powder
- ➢ ½ teaspoon onion powder
- ➢ 2 tablespoons ghee, divided
- ➢ 2 large eggs
- ➢ 1 avocado
- ➢ Pink Himalayan salt
- ➢ Freshly ground black pepper

1. Preheat the oven to 375°F. 2. In a medium bowl, mix well to combine the ground pork, garlic powder, and onion powder. Form the mixture into 2 patties. 3. In a medium skillet over medium-high heat, melt 1 tablespoon of ghee. 4. Add the sausage patties and cook for 2 minutes on each side, until browned. 5. Transfer the sausage to a baking sheet. Cook in the oven for 8 to 10 minutes, until cooked through. 6. Add the remaining 1 tablespoon of ghee to the skillet. When it is hot, crack the eggs into the skillet and cook without disturbing for about 3 minutes, until the whites are opaque and the

yolks have set. 7. Meanwhile, in a small bowl, mash the avocado. 8. Season the eggs with pink Himalayan salt and pepper. 9. Remove the cooked sausage patties from the oven. 10. Place a sausage patty on each of two warmed plates. Spread half of the mashed avocado on top of each sausage patty, and top each with a fried egg. Serve hot.

Per Serving:

calories: 533 | fat: 44g | protein: 29g | carbs: 3g | net carbs: 3g | fiber: 5g

Heart-Healthy Hazelnut-Collagen Shake

Prep time: 5 minutes | Cook time: 0 minutes | Serves 1

➢ 1½ cups unsweetened almond milk
➢ 2 tablespoons hazelnut butter
➢ 2 tablespoons grass-fed collagen powder
➢ ½–1 teaspoon cinnamon
➢ ⅛ teaspoon LoSalt or pink Himalayan salt
➢ ⅛ teaspoon sugar-free almond extract
➢ 1 tablespoon macadamia oil or hazelnut oil

1. Place all of the ingredients in a blender and pulse until smooth and frothy. Serve immediately.

Per Serving:

calories: 345 | fat: 32g | protein: 13g | carbs: 8g | net carbs: 3g | fiber: 5g

Green Eggs and Ham

Prep time: 5 minutes | Cook time: 10 minutes | Serves 2

➢ 1 large Hass avocado, halved and pitted
➢ 2 thin slices ham
➢ 2 large eggs
➢ 2 tablespoons chopped green onions, plus more for garnish
➢ ½ teaspoon fine sea salt
➢ ¼ teaspoon ground black pepper
➢ ¼ cup shredded Cheddar cheese (omit for dairy-free)

1. Preheat the air fryer to 400°F (204°C). 2. Place a slice of ham into the cavity of each avocado half. Crack an egg on top of the ham, then sprinkle on the green onions, salt, and pepper. 3. Place the avocado halves in the air fryer cut side up and air fry for 10 minutes, or until

the egg is cooked to your desired doneness. Top with the cheese (if using) and air fry for 30 seconds more, or until the cheese is melted. Garnish with chopped green onions. 4. Best served fresh. Store extras in an airtight container in the fridge for up to 4 days. Reheat in a preheated 350°F (177°C) air fryer for a few minutes, until warmed through.

Per Serving:

calories: 401 | fat: 30g | protein: 21g | carbs: 12g | net carbs: 6g | fiber: 9g

Turkey Sausage Breakfast Pizza

Prep time: 15 minutes | Cook time: 24 minutes | Serves 2

➢ 4 large eggs, divided
➢ 1 tablespoon water
➢ ½ teaspoon garlic powder
➢ ½ teaspoon onion powder
➢ ½ teaspoon dried oregano
➢ 2 tablespoons coconut flour
➢ 3 tablespoons grated Parmesan cheese
➢ ½ cup shredded provolone cheese
➢ 1 link cooked turkey sausage, chopped (about 2 ounces / 57 g)
➢ 2 sun-dried tomatoes, finely chopped
➢ 2 scallions, thinly sliced

1. Preheat the air fryer to 400°F (204°C). Line a cake pan with parchment paper and lightly coat the paper with olive oil. 2. In a large bowl, whisk 2 of the eggs with the water, garlic powder, onion powder, and dried oregano. Add the coconut flour, breaking up any lumps with your hands as you add it to the bowl. Stir the coconut flour into the egg mixture, mixing until smooth. Stir in the Parmesan cheese. Allow the mixture to rest for a few minutes until thick and dough-like. 3. Transfer the mixture to the prepared pan. Use a spatula to spread it evenly and slightly up the sides of the pan. Air fry until the crust is set but still light in color, about 10 minutes. Top with the cheeses, sausage, and sun-dried tomatoes. 4. Break the remaining 2 eggs into a small bowl, then slide them onto the pizza. Return the pizza to the air fryer. Air fry 10 to 14 minutes until the egg whites are set and the yolks are the desired doneness. Top with the scallions and allow to rest for 5 minutes before serving.

Per Serving:

calories: 428 | fat: 28g | protein: 32g | carbs: 11g | net carbs: 7g | fiber:

4g

Turmeric Scrambled Eggs

Prep time: 5 minutes | Cook time: 5 minutes | Serves 2

- ➢ 3 large eggs
- ➢ 2 tablespoons heavy cream (optional)
- ➢ 1 teaspoon ground turmeric
- ➢ Salt, to taste
- ➢ Freshly ground black pepper, to taste
- ➢ 1 tablespoon butter

1. In a small bowl, lightly beat the eggs with the cream. Add the turmeric, salt, and pepper. 2. Melt the butter in a skillet over medium heat. When it just starts to bubble, gently pour in the egg mixture. Stir frequently as eggs begin to set, and cook for 2 to 3 minutes. 3. Remove from the heat, taste and add more pepper and salt if needed, and serve.

Per Serving:

calories: 213 | fat: 18g | protein: 10g | carbs: 2g | net carbs: 2g | fiber: 0g

Cauliflower & Cheese Burgers

Prep time: 10 minutes | Cook time: 35 minutes | Serves 6

- ➢ 1½ tablespoons olive oil
- ➢ 1 onion, chopped
- ➢ 1 garlic clove, minced
- ➢ 1 pound cauliflower, grated
- ➢ 6 tablespoons coconut flour
- ➢ ½ cup gruyere cheese, shredded
- ➢ 1 cup Parmesan cheese
- ➢ 2 eggs, beaten
- ➢ ½ teaspoon dried rosemary
- ➢ Sea salt and ground black pepper, to taste

1. Set a cast iron skillet over medium heat and warm oil. Add in garlic and onion and cook until soft, about 3 minutes. Stir in grated cauliflower and cook for a minute; allow cooling and set aside. 2. To the cooled cauliflower, add the rest of the ingredients; form balls from the mixture, then, press each ball to form burger patty. 3. Set oven to 400°F and bake the burgers for 20 minutes. Flip and bake for another 10 minutes or until the top becomes golden brown.

Per Serving:

calories: 260 | fat: 18g | protein: 16g | carbs: 11g | net carbs: 7g | fiber: 4g

Almond Flour Pancakes

Prep time: 5 minutes | Cook time: 10 minutes | Serves 6

- ➢ 2 cups (8 ounces / 227 g) blanched almond flour
- ➢ ¼ cup erythritol
- ➢ 1 tablespoon baking powder
- ➢ ¼ teaspoon sea salt
- ➢ 4 large eggs
- ➢ ⅔ cup unsweetened almond milk
- ➢ ¼ cup avocado oil, plus more for frying
- ➢ 2 teaspoons vanilla extract

1. In a blender, combine all ingredients and blend until smooth. Let the batter rest for 5 to 10 minutes. 2. Preheat a large, very lightly oiled skillet over medium-low heat. (Keep oil very minimal for perfectly round pancakes.) Working in batches, pour circles of batter onto the pan, 2 tablespoons (⅛ cup) at a time for 3-inch pancakes. Cook 1½ to 2 minutes, until bubbles start to form on the edges. Flip and cook another minute or two, until browned on the other side. 3. Repeat with the remaining batter.

Per Serving:

calories: 355 | fat: 31g | protein: 12g | carbs: 12g | net carbs: 5g | fiber: 7g

Jerky Cookies

Prep time: 10 minutes | Cook time: 6 hours | Serves 18

- ➢ 1 pound (455 g) ground beef (10% fat)
- ➢ 2 tablespoons coconut aminos
- ➢ 1 teaspoon smoked sea salt
- ➢ 1 teaspoon ground black pepper
- ➢ ½ teaspoon garlic powder
- ➢ ½ teaspoon red pepper flakes

1. Place 2 oven racks as close to the middle of the oven as possible. Preheat the oven to 170°F (77°C) and line 2 baking sheets with parchment paper or a silicone baking mat. 2. Place all the ingredients in a medium-sized bowl and combine with your hands until well mixed. 3. Scooping a heaping tablespoon of the meat mixture into your palm, roll it into a ball, and then flatten it into a 2-inch (5-cm)

round. Transfer to a prepared baking sheet and repeat with the remaining mixture. 4. Bake the cookies for 6 hours, flipping them over halfway through cooking. From time to time, rotate the pans from one oven rack to the other to ensure even baking. The cookies are done when they are chewy like jerky. 5. Transfer the cookies to a cooling rack and allow to cool for 30 minutes.

Per Serving:

calories: 47 | fat: 2g | protein: 8g | carbs: 1g | net carbs: 1g | fiber: 0g

Diner Pancakes

Prep time: 10 minutes | Cook time: 28 minutes | Makes eight 5- to 6-inch pancakes

➤ ¼ cup plus 2 tablespoons coconut flour
➤ ¼ cup finely ground golden flax meal
➤ 1 teaspoon baking powder
➤ ¼ teaspoon pink Himalayan salt
➤ ¼ cup (½ stick) unsalted butter, melted but not hot
➤ ½ teaspoon vanilla extract
➤ 15 drops of liquid stevia
➤ 6 large eggs
➤ ¾ cup unsweetened coconut milk or almond milk
➤ For serving:
➤ Butter
➤ Sugar-free maple syrup

1. In a small mixing bowl, whisk together the coconut flour, flax meal, baking powder, and salt. Set aside. 2. Put the melted butter, vanilla extract, and stevia in a large mixing bowl. While whisking, add the eggs one at a time. Continue whisking for 60 to 90 seconds, until the mixture is airy and fully combined. 3. Add the milk to the egg mixture and whisk to combine. 4. Add the dry ingredients to the wet ingredients in 2 batches, whisking until fully combined. Allow the batter to sit for 5 minutes before cooking. 5. Heat a nonstick skillet over medium-low heat. Grease the pan with coconut oil spray. 6. Using a ¼-cup measuring cup, scoop up some of the batter and pour it into the center of the skillet. If the batter does not spread out on its own, use a spoon to spread it out until it is 5 to 6 inches in diameter. (Note: You can make the pancakes any size you want; just keep in mind that changing the size will affect the yield and possibly the cooking time.) The pancake is ready to flip when bubbles start to form on the surface, about 3 minutes. Flip and cook for another minute, until golden brown on both sides. 7. Repeat this process with the remaining batter, making a total of 8 pancakes. Grease the pan after each pancake. To keep the pancakes warm while the rest are cooking, place them on a baking sheet in a 200°F oven. 8. Serve the pancakes warm with butter and sugar-free maple syrup. 9. Allow to cool before storing in a sealed container in the refrigerator for up to 5 days. Reheat in a preheated 200°F oven for 15 minutes or in the microwave for 30 seconds. Sadly, these pancakes do not freeze well.

Per Serving:

calories: 298 | fat: 24g | protein: 13g | carbs: 9g | net carbs: 3g | fiber: 6g

Bacon Tomato Cups

Prep time: 10 minutes | Cook time: 25 minutes | Serves 6

➤ 12 bacon slices
➤ 2 tomatoes, diced
➤ 1 onion, diced
➤ 1 cup shredded cheddar cheese
➤ 1 cup mayonnaise
➤ 12 low carb crepes/pancakes
➤ 1 teaspoon dried basil
➤ Chopped chives to garnish

1. Fry the bacon in a skillet over medium heat for 5 minutes. Remove and chop with a knife. Transfer to a bowl. Add in cheddar cheese, tomatoes, onion, mayonnaise, and basil. Mix well set aside. 2. Place the crepes on a flat surface and use egg rings to cut a circle out of each crepe. Grease the muffin cups with cooking spray and fit the circled crepes into them to make a cup. 3. Now, fill the cups with 3 tablespoons of bacon-tomato mixture. Place the muffin cups on a baking sheet, and bake for 18 minutes. Garnish with the chives, and serve with a tomato or cheese sauce.

Per Serving:

calories: 474 | fat: 42g | protein: 18g | carbs: 6g | net carbs: 4g | fiber: 2g

Quick Keto Blender Muffins

Prep time: 5 minutes | Cook time: 25 minutes | Makes 12 muffins

➤ Butter, ghee, or coconut oil for greasing the pan
➤ 6 eggs
➤ 8 ounces (227 g) cream cheese, at room

temperature
- 2 scoops flavored collagen powder
- 1 teaspoon ground cinnamon
- 1 teaspoon baking powder
- Few drops or dash sweetener (optional)

1. Preheat the oven to 350ºF (180ºC). Grease a 12-cup muffin pan very well with butter, ghee, or coconut oil. Alternatively, you can use silicone cups or paper muffin liners. 2. In a blender, combine the eggs, cream cheese, collagen powder, cinnamon, baking powder, and sweetener (if using). Blend until well combined and pour the mixture into the muffin cups, dividing equally. 3. Bake for 22 to 25 minutes until the muffins are golden brown on top and firm. 4. Let cool then store in a glass container or plastic bag in the refrigerator for up to 2 weeks or in the freezer for up to 3 months. 5. To serve refrigerated muffins, heat in the microwave for 30 seconds. To serve from frozen, thaw in the refrigerator overnight and then microwave for 30 seconds, or microwave straight from the freezer for 45 to 60 seconds or until heated through.

Per Serving:

1 muffin: calories: 120 | fat: 10g | protein: 6g | carbs: 1g | net carbs: 1g | fiber: 0g

Classic Cinnamon Roll Coffee Cake

Prep time: 10 minutes | Cook time: 45 minutes | Serves 8

- Cake:
- 2 cups almond flour
- 1 cup granulated erythritol
- 1 teaspoon baking powder
- Pinch of salt
- 2 eggs
- ½ cup sour cream
- 4 tablespoons butter, melted
- 2 teaspoons vanilla extract
- 2 tablespoons Swerve
- 1½ teaspoons ground cinnamon
- Cooking spray
- ½ cup water
- Icing:
- 2 ounces (56 g) cream cheese, softened
- 1 cup powdered erythritol

- 1 tablespoon heavy cream
- ½ teaspoon vanilla extract

1. In the bowl of a stand mixer, combine the almond flour, granulated erythritol, baking powder and salt. Mix until no lumps remain. Add the eggs, sour cream, butter and vanilla to the mixer bowl and mix until well combined. 2. In a separate bowl, mix together the Swerve and cinnamon. 3. Spritz the baking pan with cooking spray. Pour in the cake batter and use a knife to make sure it is level around the pan. Sprinkle the cinnamon mixture on top. Cover the pan tightly with aluminum foil. 4. Pour the water and insert the trivet in the Instant Pot. Put the pan on the trivet. 5. Set the lid in place. Select the Manual mode and set the cooking time for 45 minutes on High Pressure. When the timer goes off, do a quick pressure release. Carefully open the lid. 6. Remove the cake from the pot and remove the foil. Blot off any moisture on top of the cake with a paper towel, if necessary. Let rest in the pan for 5 minutes. 7. Meanwhile, make the icing: In a small bowl, use a mixer to whip the cream cheese until it is light and fluffy. Slowly fold in the powdered erythritol and mix until well combined. Add the heavy cream and vanilla extract and mix until thoroughly combined. 8. When the cake is cooled, transfer it to a platter and drizzle the icing all over.

Per Serving:

calories: 313 | fat: 27g | protein: 9g | carbs: 7g | net carbs: 4g | fiber: 3g

Vegetable and Cheese Bake

Prep time: 7 minutes | Cook time: 9 minutes | Serves 3

- 3 eggs, beaten
- ¼ cup coconut cream
- ¼ teaspoon salt
- 3 ounces (85 g) Brussel sprouts, chopped
- 2 ounces (57 g) tomato, chopped
- 3 ounces (85 g) provolone cheese, shredded
- 1 teaspoon butter
- 1 teaspoon smoked paprika

1. Grease the instant pot pan with the butter. 2. Put eggs in the bowl, add salt, and smoked paprika. Whisk the eggs well. 3. After this, add chopped Brussel sprouts and tomato. 4. Pour the mixture into the instant pot pan and sprinkle over with the shredded cheese. 5. Pour 1 cup of the water in the instant pot. Then place the pan with the egg mixture and close the lid. 6. Cook the meal on Manual (High Pressure)

for 4 minutes. Then make naturally release for 5 minutes.

Per Serving:

calories: 237 | fat: 18g | protein: 14g | carbs: 6g | net carbs: 4g | fiber: 2g

Cauliflower Avocado Toast

Prep time: 15 minutes | Cook time: 8 minutes | Serves 2

➢ 1 (12 ounces / 340 g) steamer bag cauliflower
➢ 1 large egg
➢ ½ cup shredded Mozzarella cheese
➢ 1 ripe medium avocado
➢ ½ teaspoon garlic powder
➢ ¼ teaspoon ground black pepper

1. Cook cauliflower according to package instructions. Remove from bag and place into cheesecloth or clean towel to remove excess moisture. 2. Place cauliflower into a large bowl and mix in egg and Mozzarella. Cut a piece of parchment to fit your air fryer basket. Separate the cauliflower mixture into two, and place it on the parchment in two mounds. Press out the cauliflower mounds into a ¼-inch-thick rectangle. Place the parchment into the air fryer basket. 3. Adjust the temperature to 400ºF (204ºC) and set the timer for 8 minutes. 4. Flip the cauliflower halfway through the cooking time. 5. When the timer beeps, remove the parchment and allow the cauliflower to cool 5 minutes. 6. Cut open the avocado and remove the pit. Scoop out the inside, place it in a medium bowl, and mash it with garlic powder and pepper. Spread onto the cauliflower. Serve immediately.

Per Serving:

calories: 305 | fat: 23g | protein: 16g | carbs: 13g | net carbs: 7g | fiber: 6g

Duo-Cheese Omelet with Pimenta and Basil

Prep time: 10 minutes | Cook time: 10 minutes | Serves 2

➢ 3 tablespoons olive oil
➢ 4 eggs, beaten
➢ Salt and black pepper, to taste
➢ ¼ teaspoon paprika
➢ ¼ teaspoon cayenne pepper
➢ ½ cup asiago cheese, shredded
➢ ½ cup cheddar cheese, shredded
➢ 2 tablespoons fresh basil, roughly chopped

1. Set a pan over medium heat and warm the oil. Season eggs with cayenne pepper, salt, paprika, and black pepper. Transfer to the pan and ensure they are evenly spread. Top with the asiago and cheddar cheeses. Slice the omelet into two halves. Decorate with fresh basil, to serve.

Per Serving:

calories: 770 | fat: 68g | protein: 33g | carbs: 3g | net carbs: 2g | fiber: 1g

Bacon-Jalapeño Egg Cups

Prep time: 5 minutes | Cook time: 25 minutes | Makes 6 egg cups

➢ For The Bacon:
➢ 6 bacon slices
➢ 1 tablespoon butter
➢ For The Eggs:
➢ 2 jalapeño peppers
➢ 4 large eggs
➢ 2 ounces cream cheese, at room temperature
➢ Pink Himalayan salt
➢ Freshly ground black pepper
➢ ¼ cup shredded Mexican blend cheese

To Make The Bacon: 1. Preheat the oven to 375°F. 2. While the oven is warming up, heat a large skillet over medium-high heat. Add the bacon slices and cook partially, about 4 minutes. Transfer the bacon to a paper towel–lined plate. 3. Coat six cups of a standard muffin tin with the butter. Place a partially cooked bacon strip in each cup to line the sides. To Make The Eggs: 1. Cut one jalapeño lengthwise, seed it, and mince it. Cut the remaining jalapeño into rings, discarding the seeds. Set aside. 2. In a medium bowl, beat the eggs with a hand mixer until well beaten. Add the cream cheese and diced jalapeño, season with pink Himalayan salt and pepper, and beat again to combine. 3. Pour the egg mixture into the prepared muffin tin, filling each cup about two-thirds of the way up so they have room to rise. 4. Top each cup with some of the shredded cheese and a ring of jalapeño, and bake for 20 minutes. 5. Cool for 10 minutes, and serve hot.

Per Serving:

calories: 159 | fat: 13g | protein: 9g | carbs: 1g | net carbs: 1g | fiber: 0g

Double-Dipped Mini Cinnamon Biscuits

Prep time: 15 minutes | Cook time: 13 minutes | Makes 8 biscuits

- 2 cups blanched almond flour
- ½ cup Swerve confectioners'-style sweetener or equivalent amount of liquid or powdered sweetener
- 1 teaspoon baking powder
- ½ teaspoon fine sea salt
- ¼ cup plus 2 tablespoons (¾ stick) very cold unsalted butter
- ¼ cup unsweetened, unflavored almond milk
- 1 large egg
- 1 teaspoon vanilla extract
- 3 teaspoons ground cinnamon
- Glaze:
- ½ cup Swerve confectioners'-style sweetener or equivalent amount of powdered sweetener
- ¼ cup heavy cream or unsweetened, unflavored almond milk

1. Preheat the air fryer to 350°F (177°C). Line a pie pan that fits into your air fryer with parchment paper. 2. In a medium-sized bowl, mix together the almond flour, sweetener (if powdered; do not add liquid sweetener), baking powder, and salt. Cut the butter into ½-inch squares, then use a hand mixer to work the butter into the dry ingredients. When you are done, the mixture should still have chunks of butter. 3. In a small bowl, whisk together the almond milk, egg, and vanilla extract (if using liquid sweetener, add it as well) until blended. Using a fork, stir the wet ingredients into the dry ingredients until large clumps form. Add the cinnamon and use your hands to swirl it into the dough. 4. Form the dough into sixteen 1-inch balls and place them on the prepared pan, spacing them about ½ inch apart. (If you're using a smaller air fryer, work in batches if necessary.) Bake in the air fryer until golden, 10 to 13 minutes. Remove from the air fryer and let cool on the pan for at least 5 minutes. 5. While the biscuits bake, make the glaze: Place the powdered sweetener in a small bowl and slowly stir in the heavy cream with a fork. 6. When the biscuits have cooled somewhat, dip the tops into the glaze, allow it to dry a bit, and then dip again for a thick glaze. 7. Serve warm or at room temperature. Store unglazed biscuits in an airtight container in the refrigerator for up to 3 days or in the freezer for up to a month. Reheat in a preheated 350°F (177°C) air fryer for 5 minutes, or until

warmed through, and dip in the glaze as instructed above.

Per Serving:

calories: 187 | fat: 17g | protein: 5g | carbs: 8g | net carbs: 5g | fiber: 3g

Jalapeño and Bacon Breakfast Pizza

Prep time: 5 minutes | Cook time: 10 minutes | Serves 2

- 1 cup shredded Mozzarella cheese
- 1 ounce (28 g) cream cheese, broken into small pieces
- 4 slices cooked sugar-free bacon, chopped
- ¼ cup chopped pickled jalapeños
- 1 large egg, whisked
- ¼ teaspoon salt

1. Place Mozzarella in a single layer on the bottom of an ungreased round nonstick baking dish. Scatter cream cheese pieces, bacon, and jalapeños over Mozzarella, then pour egg evenly around baking dish. 2. Sprinkle with salt and place into air fryer basket. Adjust the temperature to 330°F (166°C) and bake for 10 minutes. When cheese is brown and egg is set, pizza will be done. 3. Let cool on a large plate 5 minutes before serving.

Per Serving:

calories: 486 | fat: 37g | protein: 29g | carbs: 5g | net carbs: 3g | fiber: 1g

Ham and Vegetable Frittata

Prep time: 10 minutes | Cook time: 27 minutes | Serves 4

- 2 tablespoons butter, at room temperature
- ½ cup green onions, chopped
- 2 garlic cloves, minced
- 1 jalapeño pepper, chopped
- 1 carrot, chopped
- 8 ham slices
- 8 eggs, whisked
- Salt and black pepper, to taste
- ½ teaspoon dried thyme

1. Set a pan over medium heat and warm the butter. Stir in green onions and sauté for 4 minutes. 2. Place in garlic and cook for 1 minute. Stir in carrot and jalapeño pepper, and cook for 4 more

minutes. Remove the mixture to a lightly greased baking pan, with cooking spray, and top with ham slices. 3. Place in the eggs over vegetables and ham; add thyme, black pepper, and salt for seasoning. Bake in the oven for about 18 minutes at 360ºF. Serve warm alongside a dollop of full-fat natural yogurt.

Per Serving:

calories: 239 | fat: 16g | protein: 19g | carbs: 5g | net carbs: 4g | fiber: 1g

Bacon, Spinach, and Avocado Egg Wrap

Prep time: 10 minutes | Cook time: 10 minutes | Serves 2

- 6 bacon slices
- 2 large eggs
- 2 tablespoons heavy (whipping) cream
- Pink Himalayan salt
- Freshly ground black pepper
- 1 tablespoon butter, if needed
- 1 cup fresh spinach (or other greens of your choice)
- ½ avocado, sliced

1. In a medium skillet over medium-high heat, cook the bacon on both sides until crispy, about 8 minutes. Transfer the bacon to a paper towel−lined plate. 2. In a medium bowl, whisk the eggs and cream, and season with pink Himalayan salt and pepper. Whisk again to combine. 3. Add half the egg mixture to the skillet with the bacon grease. 4. Cook the egg mixture for about 1 minute, or until set, then flip with a spatula and cook the other side for 1 minute. 5. Transfer the cooked-egg mixture to a paper towel−lined plate to soak up extra grease. 6. Repeat steps 4 and 5 for the other half of the egg mixture. If the pan gets dry, add the butter. 7. Place a cooked egg mixture on each of two warmed plates. Top each with half of the spinach, bacon, and avocado slices. 8. Season with pink Himalayan salt and pepper, and roll the wraps. Serve hot.

Per Serving:

calories: 336 | fat: 29g | protein: 17g | carbs: 5g | net carbs: 2g | fiber: 3g

Bacon and Mushroom Quiche Lorraine

Prep time: 10 minutes | Cook time: 37 minutes | Serves 4

- 4 strips bacon, chopped
- 2 cups sliced button mushrooms
- ½ cup diced onions
- 8 large eggs
- 1½ cups shredded Swiss cheese
- 1 cup unsweetened almond milk
- ¼ cup sliced green onions
- ½ teaspoon sea salt
- ¼ teaspoon ground black pepper
- 2 tablespoons coconut flour

1. Press the Sauté button on the Instant Pot and add the bacon. Sauté for 4 minutes, or until crisp. Transfer the bacon to a plate lined with paper towel to drain, leaving the drippings in the pot. 2. Add the mushrooms and diced onions to the pot and sauté for 3 minutes, or until the onions are tender. Remove the mixture from the pot to a large bowl. Wipe the Instant Pot clean. 3. Set a trivet in the Instant Pot and pour in 1 cup water. 4. In a medium bowl, stir together the eggs, cheese, almond milk, green onions, salt and pepper. Pour the egg mixture into the bowl with the mushrooms and onions. Stir to combine. Fold in the coconut flour. Pour the mixture into a greased round casserole dish. Spread the cooked bacon on top. 5. Place the casserole dish onto the trivet in the Instant Pot. 6. Lock the lid, select the Manual mode and set the cooking time for 30 minutes on High Pressure. When the timer goes off, do a natural pressure release for 15 minutes, then release any remaining pressure. Open the lid. 7. Remove the casserole dish from the Instant Pot. 8. Let cool for 15 to 30 minutes before cutting into 4 pieces. Serve immediately.

Per Serving:

calories: 433 | fat: 29g | protein: 32g | carbs: 7g | net carbs: 5g | fiber: 2g

Chunky Cobb-Style Egg Salad

Prep time: 5 minutes | Cook time: 10 minutes | Serves 6

- 8 cups water
- 1 dozen large eggs, room temperature
- ¼ cup mayonnaise, homemade or store-bought
- 2 tablespoons chopped fresh chives
- 2 tablespoons chopped fresh dill
- 2 tablespoons minced shallots or red onions
- 12 slices cooked bacon, chopped

- ➤ Sea salt and ground black pepper, to taste
- ➤ Microgreens, for serving
- ➤ Sliced cucumbers, for serving (optional)

1. Fill a large pot with the water and bring to a boil. Fill a large bowl with ice water. 2. Place the eggs in the boiling water and cook for 10 minutes. Transfer the eggs to the ice water and chill for 10 minutes. This will keep them from turning green around the yolks. 3. Peel the eggs, place them in a large bowl, and mash them with a potato masher or large fork. Mix in the mayonnaise, chives, dill, and shallots. Stir in the bacon so it is evenly distributed. 4. Season with salt and pepper to taste and serve over microgreens and with sliced cucumbers on the side, if desired.

Per Serving:

calories: 498 | fat: 46g | protein: 20g | carbs: 2g | net carbs: 2g | fiber: 0g

Bacon Crackers

Prep time: 10 minutes | Cook time: 20 minutes | Makes 60 crackers

- ➤ 13 strips bacon (about 13 ounces/370 g), preferably thick-cut

1. Preheat the oven to 400°F (205°C) and line a rimmed baking sheet with parchment paper or a silicone baking mat. 2. Cut the strips of bacon into roughly 2-inch (5-cm) squares, about 6 per strip. Place the squares on the prepared baking sheet, leaving a small gap between crackers. 3. Bake the crackers until crisp, about 15 minutes if using regular bacon or 20 minutes if using thick-cut bacon. 4. Allow the crackers to cool on the baking sheet for 10 minutes. Transfer to a serving plate and enjoy.

Per Serving:

calories: 258 | fat: 25g | protein: 8g | carbs: 1g | net carbs: 1g | fiber: 0g

Burger Skillet

Prep time: 5 minutes | Cook time: 20 minutes | Serves 4

- ➤ 2 pounds (907 g) ground beef
- ➤ 2 garlic cloves, minced
- ➤ 1 teaspoon dried oregano
- ➤ 1 teaspoon kosher salt
- ➤ ½ teaspoon black pepper
- ➤ 3 cups fresh baby spinach

- ➤ 1½ cups shredded cheese (Cheddar or Pepper Jack)
- ➤ 4 large eggs

1. Preheat the oven to 400°F (205°C). 2. In an ovenproof skillet (cast iron works well), brown the ground beef. When it is just cooked, in about 5 minutes, push the meat to the edges and add the garlic. Sauté for about 1 minute, then stir into the meat. Add the oregano, salt, and pepper, and stir well. 3. Begin adding the spinach one handful at a time, adding more as it wilts. As soon as all the spinach is incorporated, remove the pan from the heat. Stir in ½ cup of the cheese. 4. Spread the meat evenly in the skillet, then create four depressions in the top of the meat and gently crack an egg into each depression. Sprinkle the remaining cheese on top. 5. Transfer the skillet to the oven. Bake 10 minutes. The egg whites should be set and the yolks still runny. Leave in oven for a few minutes longer for firmer yolks, if desired. Scoop out each of the servings and transfer to plates.

Per Serving:

calories: 414 | fat: 30g | protein: 32g | carbs: 4g | net carbs: 3g | fiber: 1g

Spaghetti Squash Fritters

Prep time: 15 minutes | Cook time: 8 minutes | Serves 4

- ➤ 2 cups cooked spaghetti squash
- ➤ 2 tablespoons unsalted butter, softened
- ➤ 1 large egg
- ➤ ¼ cup blanched finely ground almond flour
- ➤ 2 stalks green onion, sliced
- ➤ ½ teaspoon garlic powder
- ➤ 1 teaspoon dried parsley

1. Remove excess moisture from the squash using a cheesecloth or kitchen towel. 2. Mix all ingredients in a large bowl. Form into four patties. 3. Cut a piece of parchment to fit your air fryer basket. Place each patty on the parchment and place into the air fryer basket. 4. Adjust the temperature to 400°F (204°C) and set the timer for 8 minutes. 5. Flip the patties halfway through the cooking time. Serve warm.

Per Serving:

calories: 150 | fat: 12g | protein: 4g | carbs: 7g | net carbs: 4g | fiber: 3g

Creamy Almond Coffee Smoothie

Prep time: 5 minutes | Cook time: 0 minutes | Serves 2

- ➢ 2 cups unsweetened strong-brewed coffee
- ➢ 1 cup unsweetened almond milk
- ➢ 1 cup unsweetened coconut milk
- ➢ 2 tablespoons chia seeds
- ➢ 2 tablespoons flaxseed meal
- ➢ 2 tablespoons coconut oil
- ➢ ⅛ teaspoon ground cinnamon
- ➢ Monk fruit sweetener, granulated, to taste

1. Make coffee ice cubes. Pour the coffee into an ice cube tray and freeze for 4 hours minimum. 2. Blend the smoothie. Put all of the coffee ice cubes (2 cups worth), almond milk, coconut milk, chia seeds, flaxseed meal, coconut oil, and cinnamon in a blender and blend until smooth and creamy. 3. Add a sweetener. Add in as much (or as little) sweetener as you like and blend again. 4. Serve. Pour into two tall glasses and serve immediately.

Per Serving:

calories: 444 | fat: 44g | protein: 6g | carbs: 6g | net carbs: 2g | fiber: 4g

Egg Omelet Roll with Cream Cheese & Salmon

Prep time: 15 minutes | Cook time: 5 minutes | Serves 1

- ➢ ½ avocado, sliced
- ➢ 2 tablespoons chopped chives
- ➢ ½ package smoked salmon, cut into strips
- ➢ 1 spring onions, sliced
- ➢ 3 eggs
- ➢ 2 tablespoons cream cheese
- ➢ 1 tablespoon butter
- ➢ Salt and black pepper, to taste

1. In a small bowl, combine the chives and cream cheese; set aside. Beat the eggs in a large bowl and season with salt and black pepper. 2. Melt the butter in a pan over medium heat. Add the eggs to the pan and cook for about 3 minutes. Flip the omelet over and continue cooking for another 2 minutes until golden. 3. Remove the omelet to a plate and spread the chive mixture over. Arrange the salmon, avocado, and onion slices. Wrap the omelet and serve immediately.

Per Serving:

calories: 646 | fat: 53g | protein: 28g | carbs: 12g | net carbs: 7g | fiber: 5g

CHAPTER 2 Poultry

Roast Chicken with Herb Stuffing

Prep time: 5 minutes | Cook time: 1 hour 35 minutes | Serves 8

- ➤ 5 pounds whole chicken
- ➤ 1 bunch oregano
- ➤ 1 bunch thyme
- ➤ 1 tablespoon marjoram
- ➤ 1 tablespoon parsley
- ➤ 1 tablespoon olive oil
- ➤ 2 pounds Brussels sprouts
- ➤ 1 lemon
- ➤ 4 tablespoons butter

1. Preheat your oven to 450ºF. 2. Stuff the chicken with oregano, thyme, and lemon. Roast for 15 minutes. Reduce the heat to 325ºF and cook for 40 minutes. Spread the butter over the chicken, and sprinkle parsley and marjoram. 3. Add the brussels sprouts. Return to the oven and bake for 40 more minutes. 4. Let sit for 10 minutes before carving.

Per Serving:

calories: 391 | fat: 21g | protein: 41g | carbs: 11g | net carbs: 7g | fiber: 4g

Crack Chicken Breasts

Prep time: 5 minutes | Cook time: 15 minutes | Serves 2

- ➤ ½ pound (227 g) boneless, skinless chicken breasts
- ➤ 2 ounces (57 g) cream cheese, softened
- ➤ ½ cup grass-fed bone broth
- ➤ ¼ cup tablespoons keto-friendly ranch dressing
- ➤ ½ cup shredded full-fat Cheddar cheese
- ➤ 3 slices bacon, cooked and chopped into small pieces

1. Combine all the ingredients except the Cheddar cheese and bacon in the Instant Pot. 2. Secure the lid. Select the Manual mode and set the cooking time for 15 minutes at High Pressure. 3. Once cooking is complete, do a quick pressure release. Carefully open the lid. 4. Add

the Cheddar cheese and bacon and stir well, then serve.

Per Serving:

calories: 549 | fat: 46g | protein: 32g | carbs: 2g | net carbs: 2g | fiber: 0g

Basil Turkey Meatballs

Prep time: 5 minutes | Cook time: 10 minutes | Serves 4

- ➤ 1 pound ground turkey
- ➤ 2 tablespoons chopped sun-dried tomatoes
- ➤ 2 tablespoons chopped basil
- ➤ ½ teaspoon garlic powder
- ➤ 1 egg
- ➤ ½ teaspoon salt
- ➤ ¼ cup almond flour
- ➤ 2 tablespoons olive oil
- ➤ ½ cup shredded mozzarella cheese
- ➤ ¼ teaspoon pepper

1. Place everything, except the oil in a bowl. Mix with your hands until combined. Form into 16 balls. Heat the olive oil in a skillet over medium heat. Cook the meatballs for 4-5 minutes per each side. Serve.

Per Serving:

calories: 343 | fat: 22g | protein: 28g | carbs: 7g | net carbs: 5g | fiber: 2g

Turkey & Leek Soup

Prep time: 10 minutes | Cook time: 30 minutes | Serves 4

- ➤ 3 celery stalks, chopped
- ➤ 2 leeks, chopped
- ➤ 1 tbsp butter
- ➤ 6 cups chicken stock
- ➤ Salt and ground black pepper, to taste
- ➤ ¼ cup fresh parsley, chopped
- ➤ 3 cups zoodles
- ➤ 3 cups turkey meat, cooked and chopped
- ➤ 1Set a pot over medium heat, stir in leeks and

celery and cook for 5 minutes. Place in the parsley, turkey meat, black pepper, salt, and stock, and cook for 20 minutes. Stir in the zoodles, and cook turkey soup for 5 minutes. Serve in bowls and enjoy.

Per Serving:

calories: 288 | fat: 11g | protein: 36g | carbs: 15g | net carbs: 12g | fiber: 3g

Jerk Chicken Kebabs

Prep time: 10 minutes | Cook time: 14 minutes | Serves 4

- 8 ounces (227 g) boneless, skinless chicken thighs, cut into 1-inch cubes
- 2 tablespoons jerk seasoning
- 2 tablespoons coconut oil
- ½ medium red bell pepper, seeded and cut into 1-inch pieces
- ¼ medium red onion, peeled and cut into 1-inch pieces
- ½ teaspoon salt

1. Place chicken in a medium bowl and sprinkle with jerk seasoning and coconut oil. Toss to coat on all sides. 2. Using eight (6-inch) skewers, build skewers by alternating chicken, pepper, and onion pieces, about three repetitions per skewer. 3. Sprinkle salt over skewers and place into ungreased air fryer basket. Adjust the temperature to 370ºF (188ºC) and air fry for 14 minutes, turning skewers halfway through cooking. Chicken will be golden and have an internal temperature of at least 165ºF (74ºC) when done. Serve warm.

Per Serving:

calories: 238 | fat: 15g | protein: 18g | carbs: 7g | net carbs: 5g | fiber: 2g

Cajun Chicken

Prep time: 15 minutes | Cook time: 25 minutes | Serves 4

- 1 teaspoon Cajun seasoning
- ¼ cup apple cider vinegar
- 1 pound (454 g) chicken fillet
- 1 tablespoon sesame oil
- ¼ cup water

1. Put all ingredients in the instant pot. Close and seal the lid. 2. Cook the chicken fillets on Manual mode (High Pressure) for 25 minutes. 3. Allow the natural pressure release for 10 minutes.

Per Serving:

calories: 249 | fat: 12g | protein: 33g | carbs: 0g | net carbs: 0g | fiber: 0g

Garlic Parmesan Drumsticks

Prep time: 5 minutes | Cook time: 25 minutes | Serves 4

- 8 (4-ounce / 113-g) chicken drumsticks
- ½ teaspoon salt
- ⅛ teaspoon ground black pepper
- ½ teaspoon garlic powder
- 2 tablespoons salted butter, melted
- ½ cup grated Parmesan cheese
- 1 tablespoon dried parsley

1. Sprinkle drumsticks with salt, pepper, and garlic powder. Place drumsticks into ungreased air fryer basket. 2. Adjust the temperature to 400ºF (204ºC) and air fry for 25 minutes, turning drumsticks halfway through cooking. Drumsticks will be golden and have an internal temperature of at least 165ºF (74ºC) when done. 3. Transfer drumsticks to a large serving dish. Pour butter over drumsticks, and sprinkle with Parmesan and parsley. Serve warm.

Per Serving:

calories: 452 | fat: 28g | protein: 45g | carbs: 2g | net carbs: 2g | fiber: 0g

Thyme Chicken Thighs

Prep time: 5 minutes | Cook time: 15 minutes | Serves 4

- ½ cup chicken stock
- 1 tablespoon olive oil
- ½ cup chopped onion
- 4 chicken thighs
- ¼ cup heavy cream
- 2 tablespoons Dijon mustard
- 1 teaspoon thyme
- 1 teaspoon garlic powder

1. Heat the olive oil in a pan. Cook the chicken for about 4 minutes per side. Set aside. Sauté the onion in the same pan for 3 minutes, add the stock, and simmer for 5 minutes. Stir in mustard and heavy cream,

along with thyme and garlic powder. Pour the sauce over the chicken and serve.

Per Serving:

calories: 321 | fat: 23g | protein: 19g | carbs: 5g | net carbs: 4g | fiber: 1g

Duck & Vegetable Casserole

Prep time: 15 minutes | Cook time: 20 minutes | Serves 2

- ➤ 2 duck breasts, skin on and sliced
- ➤ 2 zucchinis, sliced
- ➤ 1 tablespoon coconut oil
- ➤ 1 green onion bunch, chopped
- ➤ 1 carrot, chopped
- ➤ 2 green bell peppers, seeded and chopped
- ➤ Salt and ground black pepper, to taste

1. Set a pan over medium heat and warm oil, stir in the green onions, and cook for 2 minutes. Place in the zucchini, bell peppers, black pepper, salt, and carrot, and cook for 10 minutes. 2. Set another pan over medium heat, add in duck slices and cook each side for 3 minutes. 3. Pour the mixture into the vegetable pan. Cook for 3 minutes. Set in bowls and enjoy.

Per Serving:

calories: 630 | fat: 44g | protein: 44g | carbs: 11g | net carbs: 9g | fiber: 3g

Lemon-Dijon Boneless Chicken

Prep time: 30 minutes | Cook time: 13 to 16 minutes | Serves 6

- ➤ ½ cup sugar-free mayonnaise
- ➤ 1 tablespoon Dijon mustard
- ➤ 1 tablespoon freshly squeezed lemon juice (optional)
- ➤ 1 tablespoon coconut aminos
- ➤ 1 teaspoon Italian seasoning
- ➤ 1 teaspoon sea salt
- ➤ ½ teaspoon freshly ground black pepper
- ➤ ¼ teaspoon cayenne pepper
- ➤ 1½ pounds (680 g) boneless, skinless chicken breasts or thighs

1. In a small bowl, combine the mayonnaise, mustard, lemon juice (if using), coconut aminos, Italian seasoning, salt, black pepper, and

cayenne pepper. 2. Place the chicken in a shallow dish or large zip-top plastic bag. Add the marinade, making sure all the pieces are coated. Cover and refrigerate for at least 30 minutes or up to 4 hours. 3. Set the air fryer to 400°F (204°C). Arrange the chicken in a single layer in the air fryer basket, working in batches if necessary. Air fry for 7 minutes. Flip the chicken and continue cooking for 6 to 9 minutes more, until an instant-read thermometer reads 160°F (71°C).

Per Serving:

calories: 203 | fat: 7g | protein: 32g | carbs: 1g | net carbs: 1g | fiber: 0g

Chicken Pesto Pizzas

Prep time: 10 minutes | Cook time: 12 minutes | Serves 4

- ➤ 1 pound (454 g) ground chicken thighs
- ➤ ¼ teaspoon salt
- ➤ ⅛ teaspoon ground black pepper
- ➤ ¼ cup basil pesto
- ➤ 1 cup shredded Mozzarella cheese
- ➤ 4 grape tomatoes, sliced

1. Cut four squares of parchment paper to fit into your air fryer basket. 2. Place ground chicken in a large bowl and mix with salt and pepper. Divide mixture into four equal sections. 3. Wet your hands with water to prevent sticking, then press each section into a 6-inch circle onto a piece of ungreased parchment. Place each chicken crust into air fryer basket, working in batches if needed. 4. Adjust the temperature to 350°F (177°C) and air fry for 10 minutes, turning crusts halfway through cooking. 5. Spread 1 tablespoon pesto across the top of each crust, then sprinkle with ¼ cup Mozzarella and top with 1 sliced tomato. Continue cooking at 350°F (177°C) for 2 minutes. Cheese will be melted and brown when done. Serve warm.

Per Serving:

calories: 387 | fat: 29g | protein: 30g | carbs: 2g | net carbs: 2g | fiber: 0g

Chicken with Mushrooms and Shallots

Prep time: 15 minutes | Cook time: 6 to 8 hours | Serves 2

- ➤ 1 teaspoon unsalted butter, at room temperature, or extra-virgin olive oil
- ➤ 2 cups thinly sliced cremini mushrooms

- ➢ 1 teaspoon fresh thyme
- ➢ 2 garlic cloves, minced
- ➢ 1 shallot, minced
- ➢ 3 tablespoons dry sherry
- ➢ 2 bone-in, skinless chicken thighs, about 6 ounces (170 g) each
- ➢ ⅛ teaspoon sea salt
- ➢ Freshly ground black pepper

1. Grease the inside of the slow cooker with the butter. 2. Put the mushrooms, thyme, garlic, and shallot into the slow cooker, tossing them gently to combine. Pour in the sherry. 3. Season the chicken with the salt and pepper and place the thighs on top of the mushroom mixture. 4. Cover and cook on low for 6 to 8 hours.

Per Serving:

calories: 243 | fat: 9g | protein: 35g | carbs: 4g | net carbs: 3g | fiber: 1g

Lemon Thyme Roasted Chicken

Prep time: 10 minutes | Cook time: 60 minutes | Serves 6

1 (4-pound / 1.8-kg) chicken

- ➢ 2 teaspoons dried thyme
- ➢ 1 teaspoon garlic powder
- ➢ ½ teaspoon onion powder
- ➢ 2 teaspoons dried parsley
- ➢ 1 teaspoon baking powder
- ➢ 1 medium lemon
- ➢ 2 tablespoons salted butter, melted

1. Rub chicken with thyme, garlic powder, onion powder, parsley, and baking powder. 2. Slice lemon and place four slices on top of chicken, breast side up, and secure with toothpicks. Place remaining slices inside of the chicken. 3. Place entire chicken into the air fryer basket, breast side down. 4. Adjust the temperature to 350ºF (177ºC) and air fry for 60 minutes. 5. After 30 minutes, flip chicken so breast side is up. 6. When done, internal temperature should be 165ºF (74ºC) and the skin golden and crispy. To serve, pour melted butter over entire chicken.

Per Serving:

calories: 495 | fat: 32g | protein: 43g | carbs: 2g | net carbs: 2g | fiber: 1g

Easy Marinated Chicken Thighs

Prep time: 10 minutes | Cook time: 15 minutes | Serves 3

- ➢ ½ cup olive oil
- ➢ ¼ cup balsamic vinegar
- ➢ 1 teaspoon minced garlic (1 or 2 cloves)
- ➢ Juice of ½ lemon
- ➢ ½ teaspoon red pepper flakes
- ➢ 1 pound (454 g) boneless skinless chicken thighs
- ➢ Salt, to taste
- ➢ Freshly ground black pepper, to taste

1. In a large container (or in a plastic freezer bag), whisk together the olive oil, vinegar, garlic, lemon juice, and red pepper flakes. Add the chicken and toss well to combine. Season with salt and black pepper. Refrigerate to marinate for at least 30 minutes, and preferably a couple of hours. 2. Cook the chicken on a grill, in a grill pan, large pan, or cast-iron skillet over medium-high heat, for 5 to 7 minutes per side or until browned and cooked through. Serve hot. Refrigerate leftovers in an airtight container for up to 1 week.

Per Serving:

calories: 496 | fat: 40g | protein: 30g | carbs: 4g | net carbs: 4g | fiber: 0g

Chicken Skewers with Peanut Sauce

Prep time: 10 minutes | Cook time: 15 minutes | Serves 2

- ➢ 1 pound boneless skinless chicken breast, cut into chunks
- ➢ 3 tablespoons soy sauce (or coconut aminos), divided
- ➢ ½ teaspoon Sriracha sauce, plus ¼ teaspoon
- ➢ 3 teaspoons toasted sesame oil, divided
- ➢ Ghee, for oiling
- ➢ 2 tablespoons peanut butter
- ➢ Pink Himalayan salt
- ➢ Freshly ground black pepper

1. In a large zip-top bag, combine the chicken chunks with 2 tablespoons of soy sauce, ½ teaspoon of Sriracha sauce, and 2 teaspoons of sesame oil. Seal the bag, and let the chicken marinate for an hour or so in the refrigerator or up to overnight. 2. If you are using

wood 8-inch skewers, soak them in water for 30 minutes before using. 3. I like to use my grill pan for the skewers, because I don't have an outdoor grill. If you don't have a grill pan, you can use a large skillet. Preheat your grill pan or grill to low. Oil the grill pan with ghee. 4. Thread the chicken chunks onto the skewers. 5. Cook the skewers over low heat for 10 to 15 minutes, flipping halfway through. 6. Meanwhile, mix the peanut dipping sauce. Stir together the remaining 1 tablespoon of soy sauce, ¼ teaspoon of Sriracha sauce, 1 teaspoon of sesame oil, and the peanut butter. Season with pink Himalayan salt and pepper. 7. Serve the chicken skewers with a small dish of the peanut sauce.

Per Serving:

calories: 586 | fat: 29g | protein: 75g | carbs: 6g | net carbs: 5g | fiber: 1g

Coconut Curry Chicken

Prep time: 15 minutes | Cook time: 3 to 4 hours | Serves 6

- ➤ 1 tablespoon coconut oil
- ➤ 1 teaspoon cumin seeds
- ➤ 2 medium onions, grated
- ➤ 7 to 8 ounces (198 to 227 g) canned plum tomatoes
- ➤ 1 teaspoon salt
- ➤ 1 teaspoon turmeric
- ➤ ½ to 1 teaspoon Kashmiri chili powder (optional)
- ➤ 2 to 3 fresh green chiles, chopped
- ➤ 1 cup coconut cream
- ➤ 12 chicken thighs, skinned, trimmed, and cut into bite-size chunks
- ➤ 1 teaspoon garam masala
- ➤ Handful fresh coriander leaves, chopped

1. Heat the oil in a frying pan (or in the slow cooker if you have a sear setting). Add the cumin seeds. When sizzling and aromatic, add the onions and cook until they are browning, about 5 to 7 minutes. 2. In a blender, purée the tomatoes and add them to the pan with the salt, turmeric, chili powder (if using), and fresh green chiles. 3. Stir together and put everything in the slow cooker. Pour in the coconut cream. Add the meat and stir to coat with the sauce. 4. Cover and cook on low for 4 hours, or on high for 3 hours. 5. Taste the sauce and adjust the seasoning. If the sauce is very liquidy, turn the cooker to

high and cook for 30 minutes more with the lid off. 6. Add the garam masala and throw in the fresh coriander leaves to serve.

Per Serving:

calories: 648 | fat: 32g | protein: 78g | carbs: 9g | net carbs: 7g | fiber: 2g

Lemon Chicken

Prep time: 5 minutes | Cook time: 20 to 25 minutes | Serves 4

- ➤ 8 bone-in chicken thighs, skin on
- ➤ 1 tablespoon olive oil
- ➤ 1½ teaspoons lemon-pepper seasoning
- ➤ ½ teaspoon paprika
- ➤ ½ teaspoon garlic powder
- ➤ ¼ teaspoon freshly ground black pepper
- ➤ Juice of ½ lemon

1. Preheat the air fryer to 360°F (182°C). 2. Place the chicken in a large bowl and drizzle with the olive oil. Top with the lemon-pepper seasoning, paprika, garlic powder, and freshly ground black pepper. Toss until thoroughly coated. 3. Working in batches if necessary, arrange the chicken in a single layer in the basket of the air fryer. Pausing halfway through the cooking time to turn the chicken, air fry for 20 to 25 minutes, until a thermometer inserted into the thickest piece registers 165°F (74°C). 4. Transfer the chicken to a serving platter and squeeze the lemon juice over the top.

Per Serving:

calories: 430 | fat: 28g | protein: 35g | carbs: 2g | net carbs: 2g | fiber: 0g

Cheesy Chicken and Ham Roll-ups

Prep time: 5 minutes | Cook time: 40 minutes | Serves 4

4 boneless, skinless chicken breast halves (approximately 2½ pounds / 1.1 kg)

- ➤ 4 slices prosciutto
- ➤ 4 slices Swiss cheese
- ➤ 1 teaspoon salt, or more as needed
- ➤ 1 teaspoon black pepper, or more as needed
- ➤ 2 teaspoons dried thyme
- ➤ Avocado oil

- ➤ 1 cup shredded Gruyère cheese
- ➤ ½ cup chicken broth, preferably homemade
- ➤ 1 tablespoon Dijon mustard
- ➤ 2 tablespoons butter
- ➤ ½ cup heavy cream
- ➤ ½ cup grated Parmesan cheese

1. One at a time, place the chicken breasts between two slices of wax paper or parchment paper and use a flat meat hammer or rolling pin to pound the chicken until each piece is ½ inch (13 mm) thick. Try to pound so that the chicken ends up in a long rectangular shape instead of a circle. 2. Cut the sliced prosciutto in half lengthwise. Place ½ slice of prosciutto and 1 slice of Swiss cheese on each piece of chicken, then roll up. Secure with toothpicks. 3. Mix the salt, pepper, and thyme in a small bowl, then use the mixture to generously season the outside of each roll. 4. Heat the oil in a skillet large enough to fit the 4 rolls. Brown the rolls on all sides, starting with the side with the seam. 5. Once browned, place ½ slice of prosciutto on top of each roll and sprinkle with Gruyère. Pour in the broth, cover the pan with a tight-fitting lid, and cook over medium-low heat for 30 minutes, or until the chicken is cooked through. 6. Use tongs to remove the chicken rolls to a broiler pan or heavy rimmed baking sheet and let rest. Preheat the broiler (on low heat if adjustable). 7. Heat the liquid left over in the skillet over medium heat. Add the mustard, then the butter, then the cream, whisking constantly. Finally, add the Parmesan cheese and whisk until melted. Taste and adjust salt and pepper as needed. 8. Place the chicken under the broiler for a minute to give the cheese a nice golden-brown color. Pour the sauce over the chicken and serve immediately.

Per Serving:

calories: 507 | fat: 40g | protein: 33g | carbs: 4g | net carbs: 4g | fiber: 0g

Chicken Legs with Leeks

Prep time: 30 minutes | Cook time: 18 minutes | Serves 6

- ➤ 2 leeks, sliced
- ➤ 2 large-sized tomatoes, chopped
- ➤ 3 cloves garlic, minced
- ➤ ½ teaspoon dried oregano
- ➤ 6 chicken legs, boneless and skinless
- ➤ ½ teaspoon smoked cayenne pepper
- ➤ 2 tablespoons olive oil

- ➤ A freshly ground nutmeg

1. In a mixing dish, thoroughly combine all ingredients, minus the leeks. Place in the refrigerator and let it marinate overnight. 2. Lay the leeks onto the bottom of the air fryer basket. Top with the chicken legs. 3. Roast chicken legs at 375ºF (191ºC) for 18 minutes, turning halfway through. Serve with hoisin sauce.

Per Serving:

calories: 275 | fat: 15g | protein: 25g | carbs: 10g | net carbs: 8g | fiber: 2g

Chicken with Monterey Jack Cheese

Prep time: 15 minutes | Cook time: 35 minutes | Serves 3

- ➤ 2 tablespoons butter
- ➤ 1 teaspoon garlic, minced
- ➤ 1 pound chicken breasts
- ➤ 1 teaspoon creole seasoning
- ➤ ¼ cup scallions, chopped
- ➤ ½ cup tomatoes, chopped
- ➤ ½ cup chicken stock
- ➤ ¼ cup whipping cream
- ➤ ½ cup Monterey Jack cheese, grated
- ➤ ¼ cup fresh cilantro, chopped
- ➤ Salt and black pepper, to taste
- ➤ 4 ounces cream cheese
- ➤ 8 eggs
- ➤ A pinch of garlic powder

1. Set a pan over medium heat and warm 1 tablespoon butter. Add chicken, season with creole seasoning and cook each side for 2 minutes; remove to a plate. Melt the rest of the butter and stir in garlic and tomatoes; cook for 4 minutes. Return the chicken to the pan and pour in stock; cook for 15 minutes. Place in whipping cream, scallions, salt, Monterey Jack cheese, and pepper; cook for 2 minutes. 2. In a blender, combine the cream cheese with garlic powder, salt, eggs, and pepper, and pulse well. Place the mixture into a lined baking sheet, and then bake for 10 minutes in the oven at 325ºF. Allow the cheese sheet to cool down, place on a cutting board, roll, and slice into medium slices. Split the slices among bowls and top with chicken mixture. Sprinkle with chopped cilantro to serve.

Per Serving:

calories: 571 | fat: 39g | protein: 43g | carbs: 8g | net carbs: 6g | fiber:

1g

Hot Goan-Style Coconut Chicken

Prep time: 20 minutes | Cook time: 4 to 6 hours | Serves 6

- ➤ Spice Paste:
- ➤ 8 dried Kashmiri chiles, broken into pieces
- ➤ 2 tablespoons coriander seeds
- ➤ 2-inch piece cassia bark, broken into pieces
- ➤ 1 teaspoon black peppercorns
- ➤ 1 teaspoon cumin seeds
- ➤ 1 teaspoon fennel seeds
- ➤ 4 cloves
- ➤ 2 star anise
- ➤ 1 tablespoon poppy seeds
- ➤ 1 cup freshly grated coconut, or desiccated coconut shreds
- ➤ 6 garlic cloves
- ➤ ⅓ cup water
- ➤ Chicken:
- ➤ 12 chicken thigh and drumstick pieces, on the bone, skinless
- ➤ 1 teaspoon salt (or to taste)
- ➤ 1 teaspoon turmeric
- ➤ 2 tablespoons coconut oil
- ➤ 2 medium onions, finely sliced
- ➤ ⅓ cup water
- ➤ ½ teaspoon ground nutmeg
- ➤ 2 teaspoons tamarind paste
- ➤ Handful fresh coriander leaves, chopped for garnish
- ➤ 1 or 2 fresh red chiles, for garnish

Make the Spice Paste: 1. In a dry frying pan, roast the Kashmiri chiles, coriander seeds, cassia bark, peppercorns, cumin seeds, fennel seeds, cloves, and star anise until fragrant, about 1 minute. Add the poppy seeds and continue roasting for a few minutes. Then remove from the heat and leave to cool. 2. Once cooled, grind the toasted spices in your spice grinder and set aside. 3. In the same pan, add the dried coconut and toast it for 5 to 7 minutes, until it just starts to turn golden. 4. Transfer to a blender with the garlic, and add the water. Blend to make a thick, wet paste. 5. Add the ground spices and blend again to mix together. Make the Chicken: 6. In a large bowl, toss the chicken with the salt and turmeric. Marinate for 15 to 20 minutes. In the meantime, heat the slow cooker to high. 7. Heat the oil in a frying pan (or in the slow cooker if you have a sear setting). Cook the sliced onions for 10 minutes, and then add the spice and coconut paste. Cook until it becomes fragrant. 8. Transfer everything to the slow cooker. Add the chicken, then the water. Cover and cook on low for 6 hours, or on high for 4 hours. 9. Sprinkle in the nutmeg and stir in the tamarind paste. Cover and cook for another 5 minutes. 10. Garnish with fresh coriander leaves and whole red chiles to serve.

Per Serving:

calories: 583 | fat: 26g | protein: 77g | carbs: 7g | net carbs: 4g | fiber: 3g

Buttered Duck Breast

Prep time: 10 minutes | Cook time: 12 minutes | Serves 1

- ➤ 1 medium duck breast, skin scored
- ➤ 1 tablespoon heavy cream
- ➤ 2 tablespoons butter
- ➤ Salt and black pepper, to taste
- ➤ 1 cup kale
- ➤ ¼ teaspoon fresh sage

1. Set the pan over medium heat and warm half of the butter. Place in sage and heavy cream, and cook for 2 minutes. Set another pan over medium heat. Place in the remaining butter and duck breast as the skin side faces down, cook for 4 minutes, flip, and cook for 3 more minutes. 2. Place the kale to the pan containing the sauce, cook for 1 minute. Set the duck breast on a flat surface and slice. Arrange the duck slices on a platter and drizzle over the sauce.

Per Serving:

calories: 485 | fat: 37g | protein: 35g | carbs: 3g | net carbs: 2g | fiber: 1g

My Favorite Creamy Pesto Chicken

Prep time: 10 minutes | Cook time: 20 minutes | Serves 4

- ➤ Chicken:
- ➤ ¼ cup (60 ml) avocado oil
- ➤ 1 pound (455 g) boneless, skinless chicken breasts, thinly sliced
- ➤ 1 small white onion, thinly sliced
- ➤ ½ cup (105 g) sun-dried tomatoes, drained and

chopped

- ¾ teaspoon dried oregano leaves
- ½ teaspoon dried thyme leaves
- ⅛ teaspoon red pepper flakes
- Pesto Cream Sauce:
- 2 cloves garlic
- ¼ cup (37 g) pine nuts
- ¼ cup (17 g) nutritional yeast
- ½ cup (120 ml) chicken bone broth
- ½ cup (120 ml) full-fat coconut milk
- ½ teaspoon finely ground sea salt
- ½ teaspoon ground black pepper
- ½ ounce (14 g) fresh basil leaves and stems
- 2 medium zucchinis, spiral sliced, raw or cooked, for serving

1. Heat the oil in a large frying pan over medium heat. When hot, add the chicken, onion, sun-dried tomatoes, oregano, thyme, and red pepper flakes. Sauté for 5 minutes, or until fragrant. 2. Meanwhile, place all the ingredients for the pesto cream sauce, except the basil, in a food processor or blender. Blend on high until smooth, about 30 seconds. Add the basil and pulse to break it up slightly, but before the sauce turns a bright green color—don't pulverize the basil! 3. Pour the sauce into the pan and toss the chicken to coat. Reduce the heat to low, cover, and cook for 15 minutes, stirring every couple of minutes, until the chicken is cooked through. 4. Divide the spiral-sliced zucchini among 4 dinner plates and top with equal portions of the chicken and sauce. Dig in!

Per Serving:

calories: 455 | fat: 29g | protein: 32g | carbs: 16g | net carbs: 11g | fiber: 4g

Chicken Enchilada Bowl

Prep time: 10 minutes | Cook time: 35 minutes | Serves 4

- 2 (6-ounce / 170-g) boneless, skinless chicken breasts
- 2 teaspoons chili powder
- ½ teaspoon garlic powder
- ½ teaspoon salt
- ¼ teaspoon pepper
- 2 tablespoons coconut oil
- ¾ cup red enchilada sauce

- ¼ cup chicken broth
- 1 (4-ounce / 113-g) can green chilies
- ¼ cup diced onion
- 2 cups cooked cauliflower rice
- 1 avocado, diced
- ½ cup sour cream
- 1 cup shredded Cheddar cheese

1. Sprinkle the chili powder, garlic powder, salt, and pepper on chicken breasts. 2. Set your Instant Pot to Sauté and melt the coconut oil. Add the chicken breasts and sear each side for about 5 minutes until golden brown. 3. Pour the enchilada sauce and broth over the chicken. Using a wooden spoon or rubber spatula, scrape the bottom of pot to make sure nothing is sticking. Stir in the chilies and onion. 4. Secure the lid. Select the Manual mode and set the cooking time for 25 minutes at High Pressure. 5. Once cooking is complete, do a quick pressure release. Carefully open the lid. 6. Remove the chicken and shred with two forks. Serve the chicken over the cauliflower rice and place the avocado, sour cream, and Cheddar cheese on top.

Per Serving:

calories: 434 | fat: 26g | protein: 29g | carbs: 12g | net carbs: 7g | fiber: 5g

Simple Shredded Chicken

Prep time: 5 minutes | Cook time: 6 to 8 hours | Serves 8

4 pounds (1.8 kg) boneless, skinless chicken thighs

- Sea salt, to taste
- 2 cups chicken broth, homemade or store-bought
- 10 cloves garlic, peeled

Make This in a Slow Cooker: 1. Season the chicken with the salt on both sides. Place the meat, broth, and garlic in a slow cooker and cook on low for 6 to 8 hours. 2. Remove the chicken from the slow cooker, reserving any liquid. Allow it to cool slightly, then shred it with 2 forks. Taste the shredded meat and spoon some of the reserved liquid over it if needed for additional flavor. Make This in an Instant Pot: 1. Season the chicken with the salt on both sides. Place it in the multicooker and add the broth and garlic. Cook on high pressure for 12 minutes. When cooking is finished, allow the cooker to depressurize on its own; don't flip the valve to release it. 2. Store in an airtight container in the refrigerator for up to 5 days.

Per Serving:

calories: 547 | fat: 34g | protein: 54g | carbs: 3g | net carbs: 3g | fiber: 0g

Cheddar Chicken Tenders

Prep time: 5 minutes | Cook time: 37 minutes | Serves 4

- 2 eggs
- 3 tablespoons butter, melted
- 3 cups coarsely crushed cheddar cheese
- ½ cup pork rinds, crushed
- 1 pound chicken tenders
- Pink salt to taste

1. Preheat oven to 350ºF and line a baking sheet with parchment paper. Whisk the eggs with the butter in one bowl and mix the cheese and pork rinds in another bowl. 2. Season chicken with salt, dip in egg mixture, and coat generously in cheddar mixture. Place on the baking sheet, cover with aluminium foil and bake for 25 minutes. Remove foil and bake further for 12 minutes to golden brown. Serve chicken with mustard dip.

Per Serving:

calories: 562 | fat: 43g | protein: 36g | carbs: 3g | net carbs: 2g | fiber: 2g

Chicken and Bacon Rolls

Prep time: 10 minutes | Cook time: 35 minutes | Serves 4

- 1 tablespoon fresh chives, chopped
- 8 ounces blue cheese
- 2 pounds chicken breasts, skinless, boneless, halved
- 12 bacon slices
- 2 tomatoes, chopped
- Salt and ground black pepper, to taste

1. Set a pan over medium heat, place in the bacon, cook until halfway done, remove to a plate. 2. In a bowl, stir together blue cheese, chives, tomatoes, pepper and salt. 3. Use a meat tenderizer to flatten the chicken breasts, season and lay blue cheese mixture on top. 4 Roll them up, and wrap each in a bacon slice. 5 Place the wrapped chicken breasts in a greased baking dish, and roast in the oven at 370ºF for 30 minutes. 6 Serve on top of wilted kale.

Per Serving:

calories: 632 | fat: 38g | protein: 67g | carbs: 6g | net carbs: 5g | fiber: 1g

Simple Chicken Masala

Prep time: 10 minutes | Cook time: 17 minutes | Serves 3

- 12 ounces (340 g) chicken fillet
- 1 tablespoon masala spices
- 1 tablespoon avocado oil
- 3 tablespoons organic almond milk

1. Heat up avocado oil in the instant pot on Sauté mode for 2 minutes. 2. Meanwhile, chop the chicken fillet roughly and mix it up with masala spices. 3. Add almond milk and transfer the chicken in the instant pot. 4. Cook the chicken bites on Sauté mode for 15 minutes. Stir the meal occasionally.

Per Serving:

calories: 211 | fat: 9g | protein: 25g | carbs: 6g | net carbs: 6g | fiber: 0g

Greek Chicken with Gravy and Asparagus

Prep time: 15 minutes | Cook time: 1½ hours | Serves 6

1 (3½-pound/1.6-kg) whole chicken, giblets removed and reserved

- 3 tablespoons refined avocado oil or melted coconut oil
- 1½ tablespoons Greek seasoning
- 1 apple, roughly chopped
- Handful of fresh parsley
- 6 sprigs fresh oregano
- 6 sprigs fresh thyme
- 4 small cloves garlic
- GRAVY:
- Giblets (from above)
- 3 tablespoons melted duck fat
- 1 teaspoon tapioca starch

1. pound (455 g) asparagus, tough ends removed, for serving 1. Preheat the oven to 350°F (177°C). Set the chicken in a roasting pan or large cast-iron frying pan. Coat all sides of the bird with the oil, then top with the Greek seasoning. Stuff the bird with the apple, parsley, oregano, thyme, and garlic. Roast for 1 hour 15 minutes, or until the internal temperature in the thigh reaches 165°F (74°C) and the juices run clear. 2. While the bird is cooking, cook the giblets:

Place the giblets in a small saucepan and cover with about 1½ cups (350 ml) of water, then cover the pan with a lid and bring to a boil. Reduce the heat to low and simmer for 30 minutes. Strain the giblet pieces, reserving the flavorful cooking liquid. Discard the giblets. 3. About 10 minutes before the bird is done, steam the asparagus. 4. When the chicken is done, remove it from the oven and transfer the bird to a serving platter. Remove the stuffing and surround the chicken with the steamed asparagus. 5. Place the roasting pan on the stovetop over medium heat. Add ½ cup (120 ml) of the giblet cooking liquid and the melted duck fat to the pan and whisk to combine. Add the tapioca starch and continue to whisk until the gravy has thickened. 6. Drizzle the gravy over the bird or serve on the side.

Per Serving:

calories: 580 | fat: 41g | protein: 50g | carbs: 4g | net carbs: 2g | fiber: 2g

Cheesy Bacon and Broccoli Chicken

Prep time: 10 minutes | Cook time: 1 hour | Serves 2

- ➤ 2 tablespoons ghee
- ➤ 2 boneless skinless chicken breasts
- ➤ Pink Himalayan salt
- ➤ Freshly ground black pepper
- ➤ 4 bacon slices
- ➤ 6 ounces cream cheese, at room temperature
- ➤ 2 cups frozen broccoli florets, thawed
- ➤ ½ cup shredded Cheddar cheese

1. Preheat the oven to 375°F. 2. Choose a baking dish that is large enough to hold both chicken breasts and coat it with the ghee. 3. Pat dry the chicken breasts with a paper towel, and season with pink Himalayan salt and pepper. 4. Place the chicken breasts and the bacon slices in the baking dish, and bake for 25 minutes. 5. Transfer the chicken to a cutting board and use two forks to shred it. Season it again with pink Himalayan salt and pepper. 6. Place the bacon on a paper towel−lined plate to crisp up, and then crumble it. 7. In a medium bowl, mix to combine the cream cheese, shredded chicken,

broccoli, and half of the bacon crumbles. Transfer the chicken mixture to the baking dish, and top with the Cheddar and the remaining half of the bacon crumbles. 8. Bake until the cheese is bubbling and browned, about 35 minutes, and serve.

Per Serving:

calories: 935 | fat: 66g | protein: 75g | carbs: 10g | net carbs: 8g | fiber: 3g

Chicken Fajitas with Bell Peppers

Prep time: 10 minutes | Cook time: 5 minutes | Serves 4

- ➤ 1½ pounds (680 g) boneless, skinless chicken breasts
- ➤ ¼ cup avocado oil
- ➤ 2 tablespoons water
- ➤ 1 tablespoon Mexican hot sauce
- ➤ 2 cloves garlic, minced
- ➤ 1 teaspoon lime juice
- ➤ 1 teaspoon ground cumin
- ➤ 1 teaspoon salt
- ➤ 1 teaspoon erythritol
- ➤ ¼ teaspoon chili powder
- ➤ ¼ teaspoon smoked paprika
- ➤ 5 ounces (142 g) sliced yellow bell pepper strips
- ➤ 5 ounces (142 g) sliced red bell pepper strips
- ➤ 5 ounces (142 g) sliced green bell pepper strips

1. Slice the chicken into very thin strips lengthwise. Cut each strip in half again. Imagine the thickness of restaurant fajitas when cutting. 2. In a measuring cup, whisk together the avocado oil, water, hot sauce, garlic, lime juice, cumin, salt, erythritol, chili powder, and paprika to form a marinade. Add to the pot, along with the chicken and peppers. 3. Close the lid and seal the vent. Cook on High Pressure for 5 minutes. Quick release the steam.

Per Serving:

calories: 319 | fat: 18g | protein: 34g | carbs: 6g | net carbs: 4g | fiber: 2g

CHAPTER 3 Beef, Pork, and Lamb

Pork Chops with Pecan Crust

Prep time: 10 minutes | Cook time: 25 minutes | Serves 4

- ➤ 2 eggs, lightly beaten
- ➤ 2 tablespoons coconut milk
- ➤ 1½ cups finely chopped pecans
- ➤ ¼ cup Parmesan cheese
- ➤ 4 (4-ounce) pork loin chops, about ½ inch thick
- ➤ Sea salt, for seasoning
- ➤ Freshly ground black pepper, for seasoning
- ➤ 2 tablespoons good-quality olive oil

1. Prepare the pork chops. Stir together the eggs and coconut milk in a small bowl. On a small plate, mix the pecans and Parmesan together and set the plate beside the egg mixture. Pat the pork chops dry and season them lightly with salt and pepper. Dip the pork chops first in the egg mixture, letting the excess run off, then roll them through the pecan mixture so they're coated. Set them aside on a plate. 2. Fry the pork. In a large skillet over medium heat, warm the olive oil. Fry the pork chops in a single layer, turning them several times, until they're cooked through and golden, 10 to 12 minutes per side. 3. Serve. Divide the pork chops between four plates and serve them immediately.

Per Serving:

calories: 567 | fat: 48g | protein: 33g | carbs: 6g | net carbs: 2g | fiber: 4g

Beef Stuffed Kale Rolls

Prep time: 15 minutes | Cook time: 30 minutes | Serves 4

- ➤ 8 ounces (227 g) ground beef
- ➤ 1 teaspoon chives
- ➤ ¼ teaspoon cayenne pepper
- ➤ 4 kale leaves
- ➤ 1 tablespoon cream cheese
- ➤ ¼ cup heavy cream
- ➤ ½ cup chicken broth

1. In the mixing bowl, combine the ground beef, chives, and cayenne pepper. 2. Then fill and roll the kale leaves with ground beef mixture. 3. Place the kale rolls in the Instant Pot. 4. Add cream cheese, heavy cream, and chicken broth. Close the lid. 5. Select Manual mode mode and set cooking time for 30 minutes on High Pressure 6. When timer beeps, make a quick pressure release. Open the lid. Serve warm.

Per Serving:

calories: 153 | fat: 7g | protein: 19g | carbs: 2g | net carbs: 2g | fiber: 0g

Chipotle-Spiced Meatball Subs

Prep time: 15 minutes | Cook time: 35 minutes | Serves 15

- ➤ Meatballs:
- ➤ 1⅔ pounds (750 g) ground pork
- ➤ 1 pound (455 g) ground chicken
- ➤ ½ cup (160 g) grated white onions
- ➤ 1½ teaspoons dried oregano leaves
- ➤ 1¼ teaspoons ground cumin
- ➤ 1 teaspoon finely ground gray sea salt
- ➤ Sauce:
- ➤ 2½ cups (600 ml) crushed tomatoes
- ➤ ½ cup (120 ml) refined avocado oil or melted chicken fat
- ➤ ⅔ cup (80 ml) chicken bone broth
- ➤ 1 tablespoon dried oregano leaves
- ➤ 1¼ teaspoons chipotle powder
- ➤ 1 teaspoon garlic powder
- ➤ ½ teaspoon onion powder
- ➤ ½ teaspoon smoked paprika
- ➤ ½ teaspoon finely ground gray sea salt
- ➤ ¼ teaspoon ground black pepper
- ➤ For Serving:
- ➤ 1 large head green cabbage
- ➤ Finely chopped fresh cilantro (optional)

1. Preheat the oven to 350°F (177°C) and line a rimmed baking sheet with parchment paper or a silicone baking mat. 2. Place the ingredients for the meatballs in a large bowl. Mix with your hands until combined. 3. Wet your hands and pinch a 1½-tablespoon piece from the bowl, then roll it between your palms to form a ball. Place

on the prepared baking sheet and repeat with the remaining meat mixture, making a total of 30 meatballs. Keeping your palms wet will help you shape the meatballs quicker. 4. Bake the meatballs for 25 to 30 minutes, until the internal temperature reaches 165°F (74°C). 5. Meanwhile, place the ingredients for the sauce in a large saucepan. Stir to combine, then cover, placing the lid slightly askew to allow steam to escape. Bring to a boil over medium-high heat, then reduce the heat to low and simmer for 20 minutes. 6. While the meatballs and sauce are cooking, remove 30 medium-sized leaves from the head of cabbage and lightly steam for 1 to 2 minutes. 7. Remove the meatballs from the oven and transfer to the saucepan with the sauce. Turn them to coat, cover, and cook on low for 5 minutes. 8. To serve, stack 2 cabbage leaves on top of one another, top with 2 meatballs, a dollop of extra sauce, and a sprinkle of cilantro, if using.

Per Serving:

calories: 253 | fat: 17g | protein: 18g | carbs: 8g | net carbs: 5g | fiber: 3g

Chile Verde Pulled Pork with Tomatillos

Prep time: 15 minutes | Cook time: 1 hour 3 minutes | Serves 6

- ➤ 2 pounds (907 g) pork shoulder, cut into 6 equal-sized pieces
- ➤ 1 teaspoon sea salt
- ➤ ½ teaspoon ground black pepper
- ➤ 2 jalapeño peppers, deseeded and stemmed
- ➤ 1 pound (454 g) tomatillos, husks removed and quartered
- ➤ 3 garlic cloves
- ➤ 1 tablespoon lime juice
- ➤ 3 tablespoons fresh cilantro, chopped
- ➤ 1 medium white onion, chopped
- ➤ 1 teaspoon ground cumin
- ➤ ½ teaspoon dried oregano
- ➤ 1⅔ cups chicken broth
- ➤ 1½ tablespoons olive oil

1. Season the pork pieces with the salt and pepper. Gently rub the seasonings into the pork cuts. Set aside. 2. Combine the jalapeños, tomatillos, garlic cloves, lime juice, cilantro, onions, cumin, oregano, and chicken broth in the blender. Pulse until well combined. Set aside. 3. Select Sauté mode and add the olive oil to the pot. Once the oil is hot, add the pork cuts and sear for 4 minutes per side or until browned. 4. Pour the jalapeño sauce over the pork and lightly stir to coat well. 5. Lock the lid. Select Manual mode and set cooking time for 55 minutes on High Pressure. 6. When cooking is complete, allow the pressure to release naturally for 10 minutes and then release the remaining pressure. 7. Open the lid. Transfer the pork pieces to a cutting board and use two forks to shred the pork. 8. Transfer the shredded pork back to the pot and stir to combine the pork with the sauce. Transfer to a serving platter. Serve warm.

Per Serving:

calories: 381 | fat: 25g | protein: 29g | carbs: 11g | net carbs: 8g | fiber: 3g

Italian Sausage and Cheese Meatballs

Prep time: 10 minutes | Cook time: 20 minutes | Serves 4

- ➤ ½ pound (227 g) bulk Italian sausage
- ➤ ½ pound (227 g) 85% lean ground beef
- ➤ ½ cup shredded sharp Cheddar cheese
- ➤ ½ teaspoon onion powder
- ➤ ½ teaspoon garlic powder
- ➤ ½ teaspoon black pepper

1. In a large bowl, gently mix the sausage, ground beef, cheese, onion powder, garlic powder, and pepper until well combined. 2. Form the mixture into 16 meatballs. Place the meatballs in a single layer in the air fryer basket. Set the air fryer to 350ºF (177ºC) for 20 minutes, turning the meatballs halfway through the cooking time. Use a meat thermometer to ensure the meatballs have reached an internal temperature of 160ºF / 71ºC (medium).

Per Serving:

calories: 379 | fat: 31g | protein: 22g | carbs: 1g | net carbs: 1g | fiber: 0g

Steak with Tallow Herb Butter

Prep time: 10 minutes | Cook time: 6 minutes | Serves 4

- ➤ 13 ounces (370 g) boneless sirloin steak (aka strip steak or beef strip loin steak), about 1 inch (2.5 cm) thick
- ➤ ¾ teaspoon ground black pepper
- ➤ ¼ teaspoon garlic powder

- ➢ ¼ teaspoon finely ground gray sea salt
- ➢ Tallow Herb Butter:
- ➢ ¼ cup (52 g) tallow
- ➢ 1 sprig fresh thyme
- ➢ 1 sprig fresh rosemary
- ➢ 1 sprig fresh parsley
- ➢ 1 sprig fresh sage

1. Remove the steak from the fridge and place on a clean plate. Sprinkle the pepper, garlic powder, and salt over both sides of the steak. Wet your hands and rub the spices into the steak, on both sides, until a paste forms. If you require abit more water, wet your hands again. Allow the coated steak to sit for 30 minutes. 2. Meanwhile, make the tallow herb butter: Melt the tallow in a small saucepan on medium heat. Add the remaining ingredients, cover, and reduce the heat to low. Simmer for 10 minutes. Once complete, strain the herbs and transfer the tallow herb butter back to the saucepan. Place the saucepan at the back of the stovetop, just to keep warm. 3. Ten minutes before the steak is ready, place an oven rack in the top position, place a large cast-iron frying pan on the rack, and turn the broiler on to high. (If your oven doesn't have a high/low setting for broil, simply set it to broil.) 4. Allow the cast-iron pan to heat up in the oven for 10 minutes. Wearing an oven mitt, remove the pan from the oven, leaving the broiler on. Place the pan on the stovetop and set the element to high. 5. Place the steak in the pan and sear for 30 seconds without moving it, then flip the steak over and sear the other side for 30 seconds. (Remember to use an oven mitt when touching the pan handle.) 6. Once seared, transfer the pan with the steak to the oven. Broil for 2 to 4 minutes, take the pan out of the oven and flip it, then return it to the oven to broil for another 2 to 4 minutes, depending on your desired doneness. (For medium-rare, cook for a total of 4 minutes; for medium, 5 minutes; for medium-well, 6 minutes; and for well-done, 8 minutes.) 7. Remove the pan from the oven and allow the steak to cool for 5 minutes. 8. Transfer to a cutting board to slice, divide among 4 plates, and drizzle with the tallow herb butter.

Per Serving:

calories: 385 | fat: 31g | protein: 17g | carbs: 10g | net carbs: 3g | fiber: 7g

Classic Italian Bolognese Sauce

Prep time: 10 minutes | Cook time: 22 minutes | Serves 5

- ➢ 1 pound (454 g) ground beef
- ➢ 2 garlic cloves
- ➢ 1 onion, chopped
- ➢ 1 teaspoon oregano
- ➢ 1 teaspoon sage
- ➢ 1 teaspoon rosemary
- ➢ 7 ounces (198 g) canned chopped tomatoes
- ➢ 1 tablespoon olive oil

1. Heat olive oil in a saucepan. Add onion and garlic and cook for 3 minutes. Add beef and cook until browned, about 4-5 minutes. Stir in the herbs and tomatoes. Cook for 15 minutes. Serve with zoodles.

Per Serving:

calories: 216 | fat: 14g | protein: 18g | carbs: 4g | net carbs: 3g | fiber: 1g

Pan-Fried Pork Chops with Peppers and Onions

Prep time: 5 minutes | Cook time: 25 minutes | Serves 4

- ➢ 4 (4-ounce / 113-g) pork chops, untrimmed
- ➢ 1½ teaspoons salt, divided
- ➢ 1 teaspoon freshly ground black pepper, divided
- ➢ ½ cup extra-virgin olive oil, divided
- ➢ 1 red or orange bell pepper, thinly sliced
- ➢ 1 green bell pepper, thinly sliced
- ➢ 1 small yellow onion, thinly sliced
- ➢ 2 teaspoons dried Italian herbs (such as oregano, parsley, or rosemary)
- ➢ 2 garlic cloves, minced
- ➢ 1 tablespoon balsamic vinegar

1. Season the pork chops with 1 teaspoon salt and ½ teaspoon pepper. 2. In a large skillet, heat ¼ cup olive oil over medium-high heat. Fry the pork chops in the oil until browned and almost cooked through but not fully cooked, 4 to 5 minutes per side, depending on the thickness of chops. Remove from the skillet and cover to keep warm. 3. Pour the remaining ¼ cup olive oil in the skillet and sauté the sliced peppers, onions, and herbs over medium-high heat until tender, 6 to 8 minutes. Add the garlic, stirring to combine, and return the pork to skillet. Cover, reduce the heat to low, and cook for another 2 to 3 minutes, or until the pork is cooked through. 4. Turn off the heat. Using a slotted spoon, transfer the pork, peppers, and onions to a serving platter. Add the vinegar to the oil in the skillet and whisk to

combine well. Drizzle the vinaigrette over the pork and serve warm.

Per Serving:

calories: 522 | fat: 47g | protein: 19g | carbs: 8g | net carbs: 6g | fiber: 2g

Turmeric Pork Loin

Prep time: 10 minutes | Cook time: 22 minutes | Serves 4

➢ 1 pound (454 g) pork loin
➢ 1 teaspoon ground turmeric
➢ 1 teaspoon coconut oil
➢ ½ teaspoon salt
➢ ½ cup organic almond milk

1. Cut the pork loin into the strips and sprinkle with salt and ground turmeric. 2. Heat up the coconut oil on Sauté mode for 1 minute and add pork strips. 3. Sauté them for 6 minutes. Stir the meat from time to time. 4. After this, add almond milk and close the lid. 5. Sauté the pork for 15 minutes.

Per Serving:

calories: 226 | fat: 11g | protein: 30g | carbs: 2g | net carbs: 2g | fiber: 0g

Rib Eye with Chimichurri Sauce

Prep time: 15 minutes | Cook time: 15 minutes | Serves 4

➢ For The Chimichurri:
➢ ½ cup good-quality olive oil
➢ ½ cup finely chopped fresh parsley
➢ 2 tablespoons red wine vinegar
➢ 2 tablespoons finely chopped fresh cilantro
➢ 1½ tablespoons minced garlic
➢ 1 tablespoon finely chopped chile pepper
➢ ½ teaspoon sea salt
➢ ¼ teaspoon freshly ground black pepper
➢ For The Steak:
➢ 4 (5-ounce) rib eye steaks
➢ 1 tablespoon good-quality olive oil
➢ Sea salt, for seasoning
➢ Freshly ground black pepper, for seasoning

Make The Chimichurri: 1. In a medium bowl, stir together the olive oil, parsley, vinegar, cilantro, garlic, chile, salt, and pepper. Let it stand for 15 minutes to mellow the flavors. Make The Steak: 1.

Prepare the steaks. Let the steaks come to room temperature and lightly oil them with the olive oil and season them with salt and pepper. 2. Grill the steaks. Preheat the grill to high heat. Grill the steaks for 6 to 7 minutes per side for medium (140°F internal temperature) or until they're done the way you like them. 3. Rest and serve. Let the steaks rest for 10 minutes and then serve them topped with generous spoonfuls of the chimichurri sauce.

Per Serving:

calories: 503 | fat: 42g | protein: 29g | carbs: 1g | net carbs: 1g | fiber: 0g

Beef Satay Skewers

Prep time: 30 minutes | Cook time: 15 minutes | Serves 6

➢ Marinade:
➢ ½ cup full-fat coconut milk
➢ 3 tablespoons coconut aminos
➢ 2 to 3 dashes of fish sauce
➢ ½ small yellow onion, finely chopped
➢ 2 cloves garlic, grated or minced
➢ 1 teaspoon ground cumin
➢ ¼ teaspoon ground ginger
➢ Pinch of red pepper flakes
➢ Pinch of sea salt
➢ Pinch of ground black pepper
➢ 2 pounds (907 g) sirloin steak, sliced
➢ 1 medium red onion, cut into 1½-inch chunks
➢ Satay Sauce:
➢ ½ cup coconut aminos
➢ ½ cup unsweetened peanut, almond, or sunflower seed butter
➢ ¼ cup rice vinegar
➢ 2 to 3 dashes of fish sauce
➢ ½ teaspoon toasted sesame seeds
➢ ¼ teaspoon ground black pepper
➢ ¼ teaspoon sea salt
➢ ¼ teaspoon red pepper flakes
➢ For Garnish:
➢ ¼ cup chopped fresh cilantro leaves
➢ 1 lime, cut into wedges

1. Whisk together all the ingredients for the marinade in a large mixing bowl. 2. Place the steak in the bowl with the marinade and

massage the marinade into it. Cover and place in the refrigerator to marinate overnight. 3. When you're ready to grill the steak, soak 12 to 16 (depending on how many slices of meat you have) bamboo or wooden skewers for 10 minutes and preheat a grill or grill pan to medium-high heat. Thread the marinated steak pieces on the skewers, alternating them with the onion pieces. 4. Grill the skewers for 4 to 6 minutes on each side, or to your desired level of doneness, so the steak is seared but not burned. Remove from the heat, cover with foil, and let rest for 5 minutes. 5. While the skewers are resting, make the satay sauce: Whisk together all the ingredients for the sauce in a small mixing bowl. 6. Garnish the skewers with cilantro, squeeze lime juice over the meat, and serve with the satay sauce on the side.

Per Serving:

calories: 605 | fat: 30g | protein: 57g | carbs: 19g | net carbs: 16g | fiber: 3g

Winter Veal and Sauerkraut

Prep time: 10 minutes | Cook time: 1 hour | Serves 4

- ➤ 1 pound veal, cut into cubes
- ➤ 18 ounces sauerkraut, rinsed and drained
- ➤ Salt and black pepper, to taste
- ➤ ½ cup ham, chopped
- ➤ 1 onion, chopped
- ➤ 2 garlic cloves, minced
- ➤ 1 tablespoon butter
- ➤ ½ cup Parmesan cheese, grated
- ➤ ½ cup sour cream

1. Heat a pot with the butter over medium heat, add in the onion, and cook for 3 minutes. Stir in garlic, and cook for 1 minute. Place in the veal and ham, and cook until slightly browned. Place in the sauerkraut, and cook until the meat becomes tender, about 30 minutes. Stir in sour cream, pepper, and salt. Top with Parmesan cheese and bake for 20 minutes at 350°F.

Per Serving:

calories: 410 | fat: 25g | protein: 32g | carbs: 10g | net carbs: 6g | fiber: 4g

Ground Beef Stroganoff

Prep time: 10 minutes | Cook time: 20 minutes | serves 6

- ➤ 1½ pounds ground beef
- ➤ ½ cup finely chopped onions
- ➤ 2 cloves garlic, minced
- ➤ 4 ounces white mushrooms, sliced
- ➤ 4 ounces cream cheese (½ cup), softened
- ➤ 1 cup beef broth
- ➤ ¼ cup heavy whipping cream
- ➤ ¼ cup water
- ➤ 1 tablespoon Worcestershire sauce
- ➤ Salt and ground black pepper
- ➤ ½ cup sour cream

1. In a large skillet over medium heat, cook the ground beef with the onions, garlic, and mushrooms, crumbling the meat with a large spoon it as cooks, until the meat is browned and the onions are softened and translucent, about 10 minutes. Drain the fat, if necessary. 2. Stir in the cream cheese and cook until melted. Add the broth, cream, water, and Worcestershire sauce and stir to combine. Continue to simmer for 5 minutes. 3. Season to taste with salt and pepper. Stir in the sour cream and serve. Leftovers can be stored in an airtight container in the refrigerator for up to 5 days.

Per Serving:

calories: 396 | fat: 32g | protein: 22g | carbs: 23g | net carbs: 2g | fiber: 0g

Garlic Beef Roast

Prep time: 2 minutes | Cook time: 70 minutes | Serves 6

- ➤ 2 pounds (907 g) top round roast
- ➤ ½ cup beef broth
- ➤ 2 teaspoons salt
- ➤ 1 teaspoon black pepper
- ➤ 3 whole cloves garlic
- ➤ 1 bay leaf

1. Add the roast, broth, salt, pepper, garlic, and bay leaf to the pot. 2. Close the lid and seal the vent. Cook on High Pressure for 15 minutes. Let the steam naturally release for 15 minutes before Manually releasing. 3. Remove the beef from the pot and slice or shred it. Store it in an airtight container in the fridge or freezer.

Per Serving:

calories: 178 | fat: 4g | protein: 32g | carbs: 1g | net carbs: 1g | fiber: 0g

Pork Larb Lettuce Wraps

Prep time: 8 minutes | Cook time: 20 minutes | Serves 2

- ➤ 1 pound (454 g) ground pork
- ➤ ¼ medium onion, finely chopped
- ➤ 1 fresh long red chile, thinly sliced
- ➤ 2 garlic cloves, minced
- ➤ Juice of 1 lime
- ➤ 2 tablespoons chopped fresh basil
- ➤ 1 tablespoon chopped fresh cilantro or dried coriander
- ➤ 1 tablespoon fish sauce
- ➤ 1 teaspoon granulated erythritol
- ➤ 1 teaspoon dried mint
- ➤ 1 tablespoon extra-virgin olive oil
- ➤ Pink Himalayan sea salt
- ➤ Freshly ground black pepper
- ➤ 4 large, firm leaves of iceberg or butterhead lettuce
- ➤ 4 lime wedges, for garnish

1. In a large bowl, combine the pork, onion, chile, and garlic. 2. In a small bowl, combine the lime juice, basil, cilantro, fish sauce, erythritol, and mint. 3. In a large sauté pan or skillet, heat the olive oil over medium-high heat. Add the pork mixture and cook for 8 to 10 minutes, until no pink remains. 4. Add the sauce and cook for 5 to 8 minutes more, until most of the sauce is reduced. Season with salt and pepper. 5. Divide the meat mixture among the 4 lettuce leaves, fold into wraps, and serve with a wedge of lime.

Per Serving:

calories: 675 | fat: 55g | protein: 39g | carbs: 5g | net carbs: 5g | fiber: 0g

Barbacoa Beef Roast

Prep time: 10 minutes | Cook time: 8 hours | Serves 2

- ➤ 1 pound beef chuck roast
- ➤ Pink Himalayan salt
- ➤ Freshly ground black pepper
- ➤ 4 chipotle peppers in adobo sauce (I use La Costeña 12-ounce can)
- ➤ 1 (6-ounce) can green jalapeño chiles
- ➤ 2 tablespoons apple cider vinegar
- ➤ ½ cup beef broth

1. With the crock insert in place, preheat the slow cooker to low. 2. Season the beef chuck roast on both sides with pink Himalayan salt and pepper. Put the roast in the slow cooker. 3. In a food processor (or blender), combine the chipotle peppers and their adobo sauce, jalapeños, and apple cider vinegar, and pulse until smooth. Add the beef broth, and pulse a few more times. Pour the chile mixture over the top of the roast. 4. Cover and cook on low for 8 hours. 5. Transfer the beef to a cutting board, and use two forks to shred the meat. 6. Serve hot.

Per Serving:

calories: 723 | fat: 46g | protein: 66g | carbs: 7g | net carbs: 2g | fiber: 5g

Stuffed Pork Loin with Sun-Dried Tomato and Goat Cheese

Prep time: 15 minutes | Cook time: 30 to 40 minutes | Serves 6

- ➤ 1 to 1½ pounds (454 to 680 g) pork tenderloin
- ➤ 1 cup crumbled goat cheese
- ➤ 4 ounces (113 g) frozen spinach, thawed and well drained
- ➤ 2 tablespoons chopped sun-dried tomatoes
- ➤ 2 tablespoons extra-virgin olive oil (or seasoned oil marinade from sun-dried tomatoes), plus ¼ cup, divided
- ➤ ½ teaspoon salt
- ➤ ½ teaspoon freshly ground black pepper
- ➤ Zucchini noodles or sautéed greens, for serving

1. Preheat the oven to 350°F(180°C). Cut cooking twine into eight (6-inch) pieces. 2. Cut the pork tenderloin in half lengthwise, leaving about an inch border, being careful to not cut all the way through to the other side. Open the tenderloin like a book to form a large rectangle. Place it between two pieces of parchment paper or plastic wrap and pound to about ¼-inch thickness with a meat mallet, rolling pin, or the back of a heavy spoon. 3. In a small bowl, combine the goat cheese, spinach, sun-dried tomatoes, 2 tablespoons olive oil, salt, and pepper and mix to incorporate well. 4. Spread the filling over the surface of the pork, leaving a 1-inch border from one long edge and both short edges. To roll, start from the long edge with filling and roll towards the opposite edge. Tie cooking twine around the pork to secure it closed, evenly spacing each of the eight pieces of twine

along the length of the roll. 5. In a Dutch oven or large oven-safe skillet, heat ¼ cup olive oil over medium-high heat. Add the pork and brown on all sides. Remove from the heat, cover, and bake until the pork is cooked through, 45 to 75 minutes, depending on the thickness of the pork. Remove from the oven and let rest for 10 minutes at room temperature. 6. To serve, remove the twine and discard. Slice the pork into medallions and serve over zucchini noodles or sautéed greens, spooning the cooking oil and any bits of filling that fell out during cooking over top.

Per Serving:

calories: 308 | fat: 17g | protein: 31g | carbs: 3g | net carbs: 2g | fiber: 1g

Blue Pork

Prep time: 5 minutes | Cook time: 20 minutes | Serves 2

- ➢ 1 teaspoon coconut oil
- ➢ 2 pork chops
- ➢ 2 ounces (57 g) blue cheese, crumbled
- ➢ 1 teaspoon lemon juice
- ➢ ¼ cup heavy cream

1. Heat the coconut oil in the Instant Pot on Sauté mode. 2. Put the pork chops in the Instant Pot and cook on Sauté mode for 5 minutes on each side. 3. Add the lemon juice and crumbled cheese. Stir to mix well. 4. Add heavy cream and close the lid. 5. Select Manual mode and set cooking time for 10 minutes on High Pressure. 6. When timer beeps, perform a natural pressure release for 5 minutes, then release any remaining pressure. Open the lid. 7. Serve immediately.

Per Serving:

calories: 300 | fat: 26g | protein: 15g | carbs: 1g | net carbs: 1g | fiber: 0g

Easy Smoked Ham Hocks with Smoky Whole-Grain Mustard

Prep time: 5 minutes | Cook time: 10 minutes | Serves 4

- ➢ Smoky Whole-Grain Mustard:
- ➢ ¼ cup prepared yellow mustard
- ➢ ¼ cup brown mustard seeds
- ➢ 2 tablespoons Swerve confectioners'-style sweetener or equivalent amount of liquid or powdered sweetener

- ➢ ¼ cup coconut vinegar or apple cider vinegar
- ➢ 2 teaspoons chili powder
- ➢ ½ teaspoon freshly ground black pepper
- ➢ 2 tablespoons coconut oil, melted
- ➢ ½ teaspoon liquid smoke
- ➢ 4 (3 ounces / 85 g) smoked ham hock steaks
- ➢ 2 cups sauerkraut, warmed, for serving
- ➢ Cornichons or other pickles of choice, for serving

1. To make the mustard: In a small bowl, stir together the prepared mustard, mustard seeds, sweetener, vinegar, chili powder, and pepper. Stir in the melted coconut oil and liquid smoke; mix well to combine. Refrigerate overnight to allow the flavors to blend before using. 2. Preheat the oven to 425°F (220°C). Place the smoked ham hocks on a rimmed baking sheet and bake for 10 minutes, or until the skin gets crispy. 3. Place each ham hock on a plate with ½ cup sauerkraut and 2 to 4 tablespoons of the smoky mustard. 4. Store extras in an airtight container in the fridge for up to 3 days. To reheat, place in a skillet over medium heat and sauté for 3 minutes per side, or until warmed to your liking.

Per Serving:

calories: 195 | fat: 15g | protein: 9g | carbs: 6g | net carbs: 4g | fiber: 2g

Beef with Grilled Vegetables

Prep time: 15 minutes | Cook time: 15 minutes | Serves 4

- ➢ 4 sirloin steaks
- ➢ Salt and black pepper to taste
- ➢ 4 tbsp olive oil
- ➢ 3 tbsp balsamic vinegar
- ➢ Vegetables
- ➢ ½ lb asparagus, trimmed
- ➢ 1 cup green beans
- ➢ 1 cup snow peas
- ➢ 1 red bell peppers, seeded, cut into strips
- ➢ 1 orange bell peppers, seeded, cut into strips
- ➢ 1 medium red onion, quartered

1. Set the grill pan over high heat. 2. Grab 2 separate bowls; put the beef in one and the vegetables in another. Mix salt, pepper, olive oil, and balsamic vinegar in a small bowl, and pour half of the mixture over the beef and the other half over the vegetables. Coat the

ingredients in both bowls with the sauce and cook the beef first. 3. Place the steaks in the grill pan and sear both sides for 2 minutes each, then continue cooking for 6 minutes on each side. When done, remove the beef onto a plate; set aside. 4. Pour the vegetables and marinade in the pan; and cook for 5 minutes, turning once. Share the vegetables into plates. Top with each piece of beef, the sauce from the pan, and serve with a rutabaga mash.

Per Serving:

calories: 554 | fat: 39g | protein: 38g | carbs: 15g | net carbs: 10g | fiber: 5g

Italian Beef Burgers

Prep time: 10 minutes | Cook time: 12 minutes | Serves 4

- ➢ 1 pound 75% lean ground beef
- ➢ ¼ cup ground almonds
- ➢ 2 tablespoons chopped fresh basil
- ➢ 1 teaspoon minced garlic
- ➢ ¼ teaspoon sea salt
- ➢ 1 tablespoon olive oil
- ➢ 1 tomato, cut into 4 thick slices
- ➢ ¼ sweet onion, sliced thinly

1. In a medium bowl, mix together the ground beef, ground almonds, basil, garlic, and salt until well mixed. 2. Form the beef mixture into four equal patties and flatten them to about ½ inch thick. 3. Place a large skillet on medium-high heat and add the olive oil. 4. Panfry the burgers until cooked through, flipping them once, about 12 minutes in total. 5. Pat away any excess grease with paper towels and serve the burgers with a slice of tomato and onion.

Per Serving:

calories: 441 | fat: 37g | protein: 22g | carbs: 4g | net carbs: 3g | fiber: 1g

Philly Cheesesteak-Stuffed Peppers

Prep time: 10 minutes | Cook time: 25 minutes | Serves 2

- ➢ 2 tablespoons butter
- ➢ 1 onion, thinly sliced
- ➢ 2 garlic cloves, minced
- ➢ 1 pound (454 g) steak, such as skirt, flank, or rib eye, thinly sliced

- ➢ Salt, to taste
- ➢ Freshly ground black pepper, to taste
- ➢ 2 green bell peppers, tops removed, peppers seeded and ribbed
- ➢ 2 slices provolone cheese

1. Preheat the oven to 350ºF (180ºC). 2. In a large skillet over medium heat, melt the butter. 3. Add the onion. Sauté for 5 to 7 minutes until the onion is softened and translucent. 4. Add the garlic and give everything a stir. 5. Add the steak and cook for 3 to 5 minutes until browned (the meat doesn't have to be totally cooked—you're going to put it in the oven). Season everything with salt and pepper. Remove from the heat. 6. Put the peppers in a baking dish just large enough to hold them. If necessary, slice a very thin piece from the bottom of each pepper to ensure it stands up straight. Fill each pepper with the steak and onion mixture and top with 1 slice of cheese. Bake for 15 to 20 minutes or until the peppers are fork-tender and the cheese has melted. Serve immediately.

Per Serving:

calories: 686 | fat: 44g | protein: 56g | carbs: 14g | net carbs: 10g | fiber: 4g

Pork Kebab with Yogurt Sauce

Prep time: 25 minutes | Cook time: 12 minutes | Serves 4

- ➢ 2 teaspoons olive oil
- ➢ ½ pound (227 g) ground pork
- ➢ ½ pound (227 g) ground beef
- ➢ 1 egg, whisked
- ➢ Sea salt and ground black pepper, to taste
- ➢ 1 teaspoon paprika
- ➢ 2 garlic cloves, minced
- ➢ 1 teaspoon dried marjoram
- ➢ 1 teaspoon mustard seeds
- ➢ ½ teaspoon celery seeds
- ➢ Yogurt Sauce:
- ➢ 2 tablespoons olive oil
- ➢ 2 tablespoons fresh lemon juice
- ➢ Sea salt, to taste
- ➢ ¼ teaspoon red pepper flakes, crushed
- ➢ ½ cup full-fat yogurt
- ➢ 1 teaspoon dried dill weed

1. Spritz the sides and bottom of the air fryer basket with 2 teaspoons

of olive oil. 2. In a mixing dish, thoroughly combine the ground pork, beef, egg, salt, black pepper, paprika, garlic, marjoram, mustard seeds, and celery seeds. 3. Form the mixture into kebabs and transfer them to the greased basket. Cook at 365ºF (185ºC) for 11 to 12 minutes, turning them over once or twice. 4. In the meantime, mix all the sauce ingredients and place in the refrigerator until ready to serve. Serve the pork kebabs with the yogurt sauce on the side. Enjoy!

Per Serving:

calories: 464 | fat: 38g | protein: 22g | carbs: 6g | net carbs: 5g | fiber: 1g

Crispy Baked Pork Chops with Mushroom Gravy

Prep time: 10 minutes | Cook time: 25 minutes | Serves 4

- ➢ 4 tablespoons extra-virgin olive oil, divided
- ➢ ½ cup almond flour
- ➢ 2 teaspoons dried sage, divided
- ➢ 1½ teaspoons salt, divided
- ➢ ½ teaspoon freshly ground black pepper, divided
- ➢ 1 large egg
- ➢ ¼ cup flax meal
- ➢ ¼ cup walnuts, very finely chopped
- ➢ 4 (4-ounce / 113-g) boneless pork chops
- ➢ 1 tablespoon unsalted butter
- ➢ 4 ounces (113 g) chopped mushrooms
- ➢ 2 cloves garlic, minced
- ➢ 1 teaspoon dried thyme
- ➢ 8 ounces (227 g) cream cheese, room temperature
- ➢ ½ cup heavy cream
- ➢ ¼ cup chicken stock

1. Preheat the oven to 400ºF (205ºC). Line a baking sheet with aluminum foil and coat with 1 tablespoon of olive oil. 2. In a small, shallow bowl, combine the almond flour, 1 teaspoon of sage, ½ teaspoon of salt, and ¼ teaspoon of pepper. In a second small bowl, whisk the egg. In a third small bowl, stir together the flax meal and walnuts. 3. One at a time, dredge each pork chop first in the flour mixture, then in the egg, then in the flax-and-walnut mixture to fully coat all sides. Place on the prepared baking sheet and drizzle the pork chops evenly with 1 tablespoon of olive oil. 4. Bake until cooked

through and golden brown, 18 to 25 minutes, depending on the thickness of the pork. 5. While the pork is baking, prepare the gravy. Heat the remaining 2 tablespoons of olive oil and the butter in a medium saucepan over medium heat. Add the mushrooms and sauté until very tender, 4 to 6 minutes. Add the garlic, remaining 1 teaspoon of sage and 1 teaspoon of salt, thyme, and remaining ¼ teaspoon of pepper, and sauté for an additional 30 seconds. 6. Add the cream cheese to the mushrooms, reduce heat to low, and stir until melted and creamy, 2 to 3 minutes. Whisk in the cream and stock until smooth. Cook over low heat, whisking frequently, until the mixture is thick and creamy, another 3 to 4 minutes. 7. Serve each pork chop covered with a quarter of the mushroom gravy.

Per Serving:

calories: 799 | fat: 69g | protein: 36g | carbs: 11g | net carbs: 7g | fiber: 4g

Creamy Pork Liver

Prep time: 5 minutes | Cook time: 7 minutes | Serves 3

- ➢ 14 ounces (397 g) pork liver, chopped
- ➢ 1 teaspoon salt
- ➢ 1 teaspoon butter
- ➢ ½ cup heavy cream
- ➢ 3 tablespoons scallions, chopped

1. Rub the liver with the salt on a clean work surface. 2. Put the butter in the Instant Pot and melt on the Sauté mode. 3. Add the heavy cream, scallions, and liver. 4. Stir and close the lid. Select Manual mode and set cooking time for 12 minutes on High Pressure. 5. When timer beeps, perform a natural pressure release for 5 minutes, then release any remaining pressure. Open the lid. 6. Serve immediately.

Per Serving:

calories: 300 | fat: 15g | protein: 35g | carbs: 6g | net carbs: 6g | fiber: 0g

Spinach and Provolone Steak Rolls

Prep time: 10 minutes | Cook time: 12 minutes | Makes 8 rolls

- ➢ 1 (1 pound / 454 g) flank steak, butterflied
- ➢ 8 (1 ounce / 28 g, ¼-inch-thick) deli slices provolone cheese
- ➢ 1 cup fresh spinach leaves

- ½ teaspoon salt
- ¼ teaspoon ground black pepper

1. Place steak on a large plate. Place provolone slices to cover steak, leaving 1-inch at the edges. Lay spinach leaves over cheese. Gently roll steak and tie with kitchen twine or secure with toothpicks. Carefully slice into eight pieces. Sprinkle each with salt and pepper. 2. Place rolls into ungreased air fryer basket, cut side up. Adjust the temperature to 400°F (204°C) and air fry for 12 minutes. Steak rolls will be browned and cheese will be melted when done and have an internal temperature of at least 150°F (66°C) for medium steak and 180°F (82°C) for well-done steak. Serve warm.

Per Serving:

calories: 199 | fat: 12g | protein: 23g | carbs: 1g | net carbs: 0g | fiber: 1g

Ginger Beef Flank Steak

Prep time: 8 minutes | Cook time: 13 minutes | Serves 2

- 14 ounces (397 g) beef flank steak, sliced
- 1 tablespoon almond flour
- ½ teaspoon minced ginger
- 1 ounce (28 g) scallions, sliced
- 1 tablespoon coconut oil
- ¾ cup water

1. Toss the beef strips in the almond flour and shake well. 2. Toss the coconut oil in the instant pot bowl and set the Sauté mode. 3. When the coconut oil is melted, add the beef flank steak slices and cook them for 3 minutes. Stir them from time to time. 4. Add minced ginger. 5. Pour the water over the meat and lock the instant pot lid. 6. Press the Manual mode (High Pressure) and set the timer for 10 minutes. 7. Make a quick pressure release. 8. Top the cooked beef with sliced scallions.

Per Serving:

calories: 513 | fat: 26g | protein: 63g | carbs: 4g | net carbs: 2g | fiber: 2g

Lamb Kebabs with Mint and Pistachio Pesto

Prep time: 15 minutes | Cook time: 15 minutes | Serves 4

- 1½ cups fresh mint leaves
- ¼ cup shelled pistachios

- 2 cloves garlic, chopped
- Zest and juice of 1 orange
- ¼ cup sesame oil
- 1 teaspoon salt
- ¼ teaspoon freshly ground black pepper
- ¼ cup extra-virgin olive oil
- ½ cup apple cider vinegar
- 1 pound (454 g) boneless leg of lamb, cut into 1-inch cubes

1. Combine the mint, pistachios, and garlic in the bowl of a food processor or blender and process until very finely chopped. Add the orange zest and juice, sesame oil, salt, and pepper, and pulse until smooth. With the processor running, stream in the olive oil until smooth. 2. Place ¼ cup of the mint pesto in a small bowl, add the vinegar, and whisk to form a marinade. Place the lamb cubes in the marinade and toss to coat. Cover and refrigerate for at least 1 hour, up to 24 hours. 3. While the lamb is marinating, soak four wooden skewers in water for 30 to 60 minutes. Preheat the oven to 450°F (235°C). 4. Thread the lamb cubes onto the soaked skewers, dividing evenly among the four. Place the skewers on a broiler pan or rimmed baking sheet lined with foil. 5. Cook until browned and cooked through, 12 to 15 minutes, flipping halfway through cooking time. Serve the skewers drizzled with the remaining mint pesto.

Per Serving:

calories: 592 | fat: 52g | protein: 22g | carbs: 5g | net carbs: 4g | fiber: 1g

Slow Cooker Herb-and-Garlic Short Rib Stew

Prep time: 10 minutes | Cook time: 4 to 6 hours | Serves 4

- 1 pound (454 g) boneless beef short ribs
- 1 teaspoon salt
- ½ teaspoon garlic powder
- ¼ teaspoon freshly ground black pepper
- 4 tablespoons extra-virgin olive oil, divided
- ½ small yellow onion, diced
- 1 carrot, peeled and diced
- 2 ribs celery, diced
- 4 ounces (113 g) sliced mushrooms
- 6 cloves garlic, minced
- 2 teaspoons dried thyme

- ➢ 2 teaspoons dried rosemary (or 2 tablespoons fresh)
- ➢ 1 teaspoon dried oregano
- ➢ 3 cups beef stock
- ➢ 1 (14½-ounce / 411-g) can diced tomatoes, with juices
- ➢ ½ cup dry red wine

1. Season the short ribs with the salt, garlic powder, and pepper. 2. Heat 2 tablespoons of olive oil in a large skillet over high heat. Add the short ribs and brown until dark in color, 2 to 3 minutes per side. Transfer to the bowl of a slow cooker. 3. Add the remaining 2 tablespoons of olive oil to the skillet and reduce heat to medium. Add the onion, carrot, celery, and mushrooms and sauté until just tender but not fully cooked, 3 to 4 minutes. Add the garlic and sauté, stirring, for an additional 30 seconds. Transfer the contents of the skillet to the slow cooker with the ribs. 4. Add the thyme, rosemary, oregano, stock, tomatoes with their juices, and wine, and cook on low for 4 to 6 hours, or until meat is very tender. 5. Remove the ribs from the stew and shred using two forks. Return the shredded meat to the stew and stir to combine well. Serve warm.

Per Serving:

calories: 549 | fat: 43g | protein: 24g | carbs: 14g | net carbs: 9g | fiber: 5g

Beef Sausage Casserole

Prep time: 10 minutes | Cook time: 25 minutes | Serves 8

- ➢ ⅓ cup almond flour
- ➢ 2 eggs
- ➢ 2 pounds beef sausage, chopped
- ➢ Salt and black pepper, to taste
- ➢ 1 tablespoon dried parsley
- ➢ ¼ teaspoon red pepper flakes
- ➢ ¼ cup Parmesan cheese, grated
- ➢ ¼ teaspoon onion powder
- ➢ ½ teaspoon garlic powder
- ➢ ¼ teaspoon dried oregano
- ➢ 1 cup ricotta cheese
- ➢ 1 cup sugar-free marinara sauce
- ➢ 1½ cups cheddar cheese, shredded

1. In a bowl, combine the sausage, black pepper, pepper flakes, oregano, eggs, Parmesan cheese, onion powder, almond flour, salt, parsley, and garlic powder. Form balls, lay them on a greased baking sheet, place in the oven at 370ºF, and bake for 15 minutes. 2. Remove the balls from the oven and cover with half of the marinara sauce. Pour ricotta cheese all over followed by the rest of the marinara sauce. Scatter the cheddar cheese and bake in the oven for 10 minutes. Allow the meatballs casserole to cool before serving.

Per Serving:

calories: 519 | fat: 39g | protein: 36g | carbs: 6g | net carbs: 4g | fiber: 2g

Kung Pao Beef

Prep time: 15 minutes | Cook time: 20 minutes | Serves 4

- ➢ Sauce/Marinade:
- ➢ ¼ cup coconut aminos
- ➢ 1½ tablespoons white wine vinegar
- ➢ 1½ tablespoons sherry wine
- ➢ 1 tablespoon avocado oil
- ➢ 1 teaspoon chili paste
- ➢ Stir-Fry:
- ➢ 1 pound (454 g) flank steak, thinly sliced against the grain and cut into bite-size pieces
- ➢ 2 tablespoons avocado oil, divided into 1 tablespoon and 1 tablespoon
- ➢ 2 medium bell peppers (6 ounces / 170 g each), red and green, chopped into bite-size pieces
- ➢ 2 cloves garlic, minced
- ➢ ¼ cup roasted peanuts

1. Make the sauce/marinade: In a small bowl, whisk together the coconut aminos, white wine vinegar, sherry wine, avocado oil, and chili paste. 2. Make the stir-fry: Place the sliced steak into a medium bowl. Pour half of the sauce/marinade (about ¼ cup) over it and stir to coat. Cover and chill for at least 30 minutes, up to 2 hours. 3. About 10 minutes before marinating time is up or when you are ready to cook, in a large wok or sauté pan, heat 1 tablespoon of the oil over medium-high heat. Add the bell peppers and sauté for 7 to 8 minutes, until soft and browned. 4. Add the garlic and sauté for about 1 minute, until fragrant. 5. Remove the peppers and garlic, and cover to keep warm. 6. Add the remaining 1 tablespoon oil to the pan and heat over very high heat. Add the steak, arrange in a single layer, and cook undisturbed for 2 to 4 minutes per side, until browned on each side. If it's not cooked through yet, you can stir-fry for longer. Remove the

meat from the pan and cover to keep warm. 7. Add the reserved marinade to the pan. Bring to a vigorous simmer and continue to simmer for a few minutes, until thickened. 8. Add the cooked meat, cooked peppers, and roasted peanuts to the pan and toss in the sauce.

Per Serving:

calories: 341 | fat: 20g | protein: 27g | carbs: 9g | net carbs: 7g | fiber: 2g

London Broil with Herb Butter

Prep time: 30 minutes | Cook time: 20 to 25 minutes | Serves 4

- ➢ 1½ pounds (680 g) London broil top round steak
- ➢ ¼ cup olive oil
- ➢ 2 tablespoons balsamic vinegar
- ➢ 1 tablespoon Worcestershire sauce
- ➢ 4 cloves garlic, minced
- ➢ Herb Butter:
- ➢ 6 tablespoons unsalted butter, softened
- ➢ 1 tablespoon chopped fresh parsley
- ➢ ¼ teaspoon salt
- ➢ ¼ teaspoon dried ground rosemary or thyme
- ➢ ¼ teaspoon garlic powder
- ➢ Pinch of red pepper flakes

1. Place the beef in a gallon-size resealable bag. In a small bowl, whisk together the olive oil, balsamic vinegar, Worcestershire sauce, and garlic. Pour the marinade over the beef, massaging gently to coat, and seal the bag. Let sit at room temperature for an hour or refrigerate overnight. 2. To make the herb butter: In a small bowl, mix the butter with the parsley, salt, rosemary, garlic powder, and red pepper flakes until smooth. Cover and refrigerate until ready to use. 3. Preheat the air fryer to 400ºF (204ºC). 4. Remove the beef from the marinade (discard the marinade) and place the beef in the air fryer basket. Pausing halfway through the cooking time to turn the meat, air fry for 20 to 25 minutes, until a thermometer inserted into the thickest part indicates the desired doneness, 125ºF / 52ºC (rare) to 150ºF / 66ºC (medium). Let the beef rest for 10 minutes before slicing. Serve topped with the herb butter.

Per Serving:

calories: 519 | fat: 38g | protein: 39g | carbs: 3g | net carbs: 3g | fiber: 0g

Pork Nachos

Prep time: 10 minutes | Cook time: 10 minutes | Serves 4

- ➢ 1bag low carb tortilla chips
- ➢ 2 cups leftover pulled pork
- ➢ 1 red bell pepper, seeded and chopped
- ➢ 1 red onion, diced
- ➢ 2 cups shredded Monterey Jack cheese

1. Preheat oven to 350ºF. Arrange the chips in a medium cast iron pan, scatter pork over, followed by red bell pepper, and onion, and sprinkle with cheese. Place the pan in the oven and cook for 10 minutes until the cheese has melted. Allow cooling for 3 minutes and serve.

Per Serving:

calories: 345 | fat: 25g | protein: 22g | carbs: 8g | net carbs: 7g | fiber: 1g

Pork Steaks with Pico de Gallo

Prep time: 15 minutes | Cook time: 12 minutes | Serves 6

- ➢ 1 tablespoon butter
- ➢ 2 pounds (907 g) pork steaks
- ➢ 1 bell pepper, deseeded and sliced
- ➢ ½ cup shallots, chopped
- ➢ 2 garlic cloves, minced
- ➢ ¼ cup dry red wine
- ➢ 1 cup chicken bone broth
- ➢ ¼ cup water
- ➢ Salt, to taste
- ➢ ¼ teaspoon freshly ground black pepper, or more to taste
- ➢ Pico de Gallo:
- ➢ 1 tomato, chopped
- ➢ 1 chili pepper, seeded and minced
- ➢ ½ cup red onion, chopped
- ➢ 2 garlic cloves, minced
- ➢ 1 tablespoon fresh cilantro, finely chopped
- ➢ Sea salt, to taste

1. Press the Sauté button to heat up the Instant Pot. Melt the butter and sear the pork steaks about 4 minutes or until browned on both sides. 2. Add bell pepper, shallot, garlic, wine, chicken bone broth, water, salt, and black pepper to the Instant Pot. 3. Secure the lid. Choose the Manual mode and set cooking time for 8 minutes at High

pressure. 4. Meanwhile, combine the ingredients for the Pico de Gallo in a small bowl. Refrigerate until ready to serve. 5. Once cooking is complete, use a quick pressure release. Carefully remove the lid. 6. Serve warm pork steaks with the chilled Pico de Gallo on the side.

Per Serving:

calories: 448 | fat: 29g | protein: 39g | carbs: 4g | net carbs: 2g | fiber: 2g

Grilled Soy Lime Flank Steak

Prep time: 30 minutes | Cook time: 15 minutes | Serves 2

➢   ½ cup olive oil

➢   ¼ cup gluten-free soy sauce

➢   Juice of ½ lime

➢   1 garlic clove, minced

➢   Salt, to taste

➢   Freshly ground black pepper, to taste

➢   1 pound (454 g) flank steak

1. In a large container with a lid or in a plastic freezer bag, combine the olive oil, soy sauce, lime juice, garlic, and some salt and pepper. Add the steak and turn it a few times, or cover and shake, to make sure all the meat is covered with marinade. Refrigerate for at least 20 minutes (30 minutes to 1 hour would be best). 2. Remove the steak from the marinade. In a large skillet or on a grill over medium-high heat, cook the steak for 5 to 7 minutes per side. Remove from the heat and let it rest for 5 to 10 minutes before slicing and serving.

Per Serving:

calories: 466 | fat: 40g | protein: 25g | carbs: 2g | net carbs: 2g | fiber: 0g

CHAPTER 4 Fish and Seafood

Flounder Meuniere

Prep time: 15 minutes | Cook time: 10 minutes | Serves 4

- ➢ 16 ounces (454 g) flounder fillet
- ➢ ½ teaspoon ground black pepper
- ➢ ½ teaspoon salt
- ➢ ½ cup almond flour
- ➢ 2 tablespoons olive oil
- ➢ 1 tablespoon lemon juice
- ➢ 1 teaspoon chopped fresh parsley

1. Cut the fish fillets into 4 servings and sprinkle with salt, ground black pepper, and lemon juice. 2. Heat up the instant pot on Sauté mode for 2 minutes and add olive oil. 3. Coat the flounder fillets in the almond flour and put them in the hot olive oil. 4. Sauté the fish fillets for 4 minutes and then flip on another side. 5. Cook the meal for 3 minutes more or until it is golden brown. 6. Sprinkle the cooked flounder with the fresh parsley.

Per Serving:

calories: 214 | fat: 10g | protein: 28g | carbs: 1g | net carbs: 1g | fiber: 0g

Simple Lemon-Herb Whitefish

Prep time: 5 minutes | Cook time: 14 minutes | Serves 6

- ➢ 6 white fish fillets (5 ounces / 142 g each), preferably lake whitefish, grouper, or halibut
- ➢ 1 teaspoon sea salt
- ➢ ½ teaspoon black pepper
- ➢ 3 tablespoons olive oil
- ➢ 2 teaspoons lemon zest
- ➢ 2 teaspoons lemon juice
- ➢ 2 cloves garlic, minced
- ➢ 1 teaspoon minced capers (optional)
- ➢ 3 tablespoons minced fresh parsley
- ➢ 3 tablespoons minced fresh dill

1. Preheat the oven to 400ºF (205ºC). Line a sheet pan with foil or parchment paper and grease lightly. 2. Place the fish fillets in a single layer on the pan. Season the fish on both sides with the sea salt and black pepper. 3. In a small bowl, whisk together the oil, lemon zest, lemon juice, garlic, capers (if using), parsley, and dill. Spoon about 1 tablespoon of the lemon-herb oil over each piece of fish, then use a brush to spread it. 4. Bake for 10 to 14 minutes, depending on the thickness of the fish, until the fish flakes easily with a fork.

Per Serving:

calories: 325 | fat: 17g | protein: 37g | carbs: 0g | net carbs: 0g | fiber: 0g

Salmon Fillets and Bok Choy

Prep time: 5 minutes | Cook time: 8 minutes | Serves 4

- ➢ 1½ cups water
- ➢ 2 tablespoons unsalted butter
- ➢ 4 (1-inch thick) salmon fillets
- ➢ ½ teaspoon cayenne pepper
- ➢ Sea salt and freshly ground pepper, to taste
- ➢ 2 cups Bok choy, sliced
- ➢ 1 cup chicken broth
- ➢ 3 cloves garlic, minced
- ➢ 1 teaspoon grated lemon zest
- ➢ ½ teaspoon dried dill weed

1. Pour the water into your Instant Pot and insert a trivet. 2. Brush the salmon with the melted butter and season with the cayenne pepper, salt, and black pepper on all sides. 3. Lock the lid. Select the Manual mode and set the cooking time for 3 minutes at Low Pressure. 4. When the timer beeps, perform a quick pressure release. Carefully remove the lid. 5. Add the remaining ingredients. 6. Lock the lid. Select the Manual mode and set the cooking time for 5 minutes at High Pressure. 7. When the timer beeps, perform a quick pressure release. Carefully remove the lid. 8. Serve the poached salmon with the veggies on the side.

Per Serving:

calories: 209 | fat: 11g | protein: 24g | carbs: 2g | net carbs: 2g | fiber: 1g

Sardine Fritter Wraps

Prep time: 5 minutes | Cook time: 8 minutes |

Serves 4

- ⅓ cup (80 ml) refined avocado oil, for frying
- Fritters:
- 2 (4.375 ounces/125 g) cans sardines, drained
- ½ cup (55 g) blanched almond flour
- 2 large eggs
- 2 tablespoons finely chopped fresh parsley
- 2 tablespoons finely diced red bell pepper
- 2 cloves garlic, minced
- ½ teaspoon finely ground gray sea salt
- ¼ teaspoon ground black pepper
- For Serving:
- 8 romaine lettuce leaves
- 1 small English cucumber, sliced thin
- 8 tablespoons (105 g) mayonnaise
- Thinly sliced green onions

1. Pour the avocado oil into a large frying pan. Heat on medium for a couple of minutes. 2. Meanwhile, prepare the fritters: Place the fritter ingredients in a medium-sized bowl and stir to combine, being careful not to mash the heck out of the sardines. Spoon about 1 tablespoon of the mixture into the palm of your hand and roll it into a ball, then flatten it like a burger patty. Repeat with the remaining fritter mixture, making a total of 16 small patties. 3. Fry the fritters in the hot oil for 2 minutes per side, then transfer to a cooling rack. You may have to fry the fritters in batches if your pan isn't large enough to fit them all without overcrowding. 4. Meanwhile, divide the lettuce leaves among 4 dinner plates. Top with the sliced cucumber. When the fritters are done, place 2 fritters on each leaf. Top with a dollop of mayonnaise, sprinkle with sliced green onions, and serve!

Per Serving:

calories: 612 | fat: 56g | protein: 23g | carbs: 6g | net carbs: 4g | fiber: 2g

Spicy Tuna Hand Rolls

Prep time: 10 minutes | Cook time: 0 minutes | Serves 6

- Tuna:
- 12 ounces sushi-grade ahi tuna, finely chopped
- 2 tablespoons Sriracha sauce
- 1 tablespoon mayonnaise, homemade or store-bought
- 1 teaspoon toasted sesame oil

- Hand Rolls:
- 3 sheets nori
- 1 medium-sized avocado, thinly sliced
- ½ cucumber, julienned
- Black and white sesame seeds, for garnish (optional)
- Soy sauce, for serving

1. Put the tuna, Sriracha, mayonnaise, and sesame oil in a small bowl and mix with a spoon. 2. Cut the nori sheets in half lengthwise to create 6 rectangular wrappers. 3. Place a wrapper on the palm of one of your hands. Put 2 ounces of tuna and 3 or 4 slices each of avocado and cucumber on the left end of the wrapper, on a diagonal to make rolling easier. Starting from the bottom-left corner, tightly roll into a cone shape, moistening the edge of the nori to create a seal. Garnish the top of the roll with sesame seeds, if desired. Repeat with the remaining ingredients. 4. Serve the rolls with soy sauce. These are best eaten immediately, as they don't store well.

Per Serving:

calories: 133 | fat: 6g | protein: 15g | carbs: 4g | net carbs: 2g | fiber: 2g

Scallops & Mozza Broccoli Mash

Prep time: 5 minutes | Cook time: 35 minutes | Serves 4

- Mozza Broccoli Mash:
- ¼ cup (55 g) coconut oil or ghee, or ¼ cup (60 ml) avocado oil
- 6 cups (570 g) broccoli florets
- 4 cloves garlic, minced
- 1 (2-in/5-cm) piece fresh ginger root, grated
- ⅔ cup (160 ml) chicken bone broth
- ½ cup (70 g) shredded mozzarella cheese (dairy-free or regular)
- Scallops:
- 1 pound (455 g) sea scallops
- ¼ teaspoon finely ground sea salt
- ¼ teaspoon ground black pepper
- 2 tablespoons coconut oil, avocado oil, or ghee
- Lemon wedges, for serving

1. Prepare the mash: Heat the oil in a large frying pan over low heat. Add the broccoli, garlic, and ginger and cook, uncovered, for 5 minutes, or until the garlic is fragrant. 2. Pour in the broth, then cover

and cook on low for 25 minutes, or until the broccoli is easily mashed. 3. About 5 minutes before the broccoli is ready, prepare the scallops: Pat the scallops dry and season them on both sides with the salt and pepper. Heat the oil in a medium-sized frying pan over medium heat. When the oil is hot, add the scallops. Cook for 2 minutes per side, or until lightly golden. 4. When the broccoli is done, add the cheese and mash with a fork. Divide the mash among 4 dinner plates and top with the scallops. Serve with lemon wedges and enjoy!

Per Serving:

calories: 353 | fat: 25g | protein: 19g | carbs: 12g | net carbs: 5g | fiber: 7g

Paprika Shrimp

Prep time: 5 minutes | Cook time: 6 minutes | Serves 2

➢ 8 ounces (227 g) medium shelled and deveined shrimp
➢ 2 tablespoons salted butter, melted
➢ 1 teaspoon paprika
➢ ½ teaspoon garlic powder
➢ ¼ teaspoon onion powder
➢ ½ teaspoon Old Bay seasoning

1. Toss all ingredients together in a large bowl. Place shrimp into the air fryer basket. 2. Adjust the temperature to 400ºF (204ºC) and set the timer for 6 minutes. 3. Turn the shrimp halfway through the cooking time to ensure even cooking. Serve immediately.

Per Serving:

calories: 155 | fat: 9g | protein: 16g | carbs: 3g | net carbs: 2g | fiber: 1g

Crab-Stuffed Avocado Boats

Prep time: 5 minutes | Cook time: 7 minutes | Serves 4

➢ 2 medium avocados, halved and pitted
➢ 8 ounces (227 g) cooked crab meat
➢ ¼ teaspoon Old Bay seasoning
➢ 2 tablespoons peeled and diced yellow onion
➢ 2 tablespoons mayonnaise

1. Scoop out avocado flesh in each avocado half, leaving ½ inch around edges to form a shell. Chop scooped-out avocado. 2. In a medium bowl, combine crab meat, Old Bay seasoning, onion, mayonnaise, and chopped avocado. Place ¼ mixture into each

avocado shell. 3. Place avocado boats into ungreased air fryer basket. Adjust the temperature to 350ºF (177ºC) and air fry for 7 minutes. Avocado will be browned on the top and mixture will be bubbling when done. Serve warm.

Per Serving:

calories: 272 | fat: 21g | protein: 11g | carbs: 9g | net carbs: 6g | fiber: 3g

Lemon Pepper Shrimp

Prep time: 15 minutes | Cook time: 8 minutes | Serves 2

➢ Oil, for spraying
➢ 12 ounces (340 g) medium raw shrimp, peeled and deveined
➢ 3 tablespoons lemon juice
➢ 1 tablespoon olive oil
➢ 1 teaspoon lemon pepper
➢ ¼ teaspoon paprika
➢ ¼ teaspoon granulated garlic

1. Preheat the air fryer to 400ºF (204ºC). Line the air fryer basket with parchment and spray lightly with oil. 2. In a medium bowl, toss together the shrimp, lemon juice, olive oil, lemon pepper, paprika, and garlic until evenly coated. 3. Place the shrimp in the prepared basket. 4. Cook for 6 to 8 minutes, or until pink and firm. Serve immediately.

Per Serving:

calories: 186 | fat: 6g | protein: 27g | carbs: 4g | net carbs: 3g | fiber: 1g

Clam Chowder

Prep time: 5 minutes | Cook time: 15 minutes | Serves 4

➢ 4 slices bacon, chopped into ½-inch squares
➢ 2 tablespoons unsalted butter
➢ ½ small yellow onion, chopped
➢ 4 ribs celery, cut into ¼-inch-thick half-moons
➢ 1 cup chopped cauliflower florets, cut to about ½ inch thick
➢ 4 ounces (113 g) chopped mushrooms
➢ 4 cloves garlic, minced
➢ 1 teaspoon dried tarragon
➢ 1 teaspoon salt
➢ ¼ teaspoon freshly ground black pepper

- 8 ounces (227 g) bottled clam juice
- 1 cup vegetable stock or broth
- ½ cup heavy cream
- 8 ounces (227 g) cream cheese, room temperature
- 3 (6½-ounce / 184-g) cans chopped clams, with juice
- ¼ cup freshly chopped Italian parsley

1. Place the bacon in a medium saucepan over medium heat. Fry until just browned and most of the fat has been rendered, 3 to 4 minutes. Remove the bacon with a slotted spoon, reserving the rendered fat. 2. Add the butter to the pan with the fat and melt over medium heat. Add the onion, celery, cauliflower, and mushrooms and sauté until vegetables are just tender, 4 to 5 minutes. Add the garlic, tarragon, salt, and pepper and sauté for another 30 seconds or until fragrant. 3. Add the clam juice, stock, cream, and cream cheese and whisk until the cheese is melted and creamy, 2 to 3 minutes. Add the clams and their juice, bring to a simmer, and cook for 1 to 2 minutes so the flavors meld. Stir in the parsley and serve warm.

Per Serving:

calories: 671 | fat: 54g | protein: 34g | carbs: 15g | net carbs: 13g | fiber: 2g

Parmesan Salmon Loaf

Prep time: 15 minutes | Cook time: 25 minutes | Serves 6

- 12 ounces (340 g) salmon, boiled and shredded
- 3 eggs, beaten
- ½ cup almond flour
- 1 teaspoon garlic powder
- ¼ cup grated Parmesan
- 1 teaspoon butter, softened
- 1 cup water, for cooking

1. Pour water in the instant pot. 2. Mix up the rest of the ingredients in the mixing bowl and stir until smooth. 3. After this, transfer the salmon mixture in the loaf pan and flatten; insert the pan in the instant pot. Close and seal the lid. 4. Cook the meal on Manual mode (High Pressure) for 25 minutes. 5. When the cooking time is finished, make a quick pressure release and cool the loaf well before serving.

Per Serving:

calories: 172 | fat: 10g | protein: 19g | carbs: 2g | net carbs: 2g | fiber: 0g

Fish Gratin

Prep time: 30 minutes | Cook time: 17 minutes | Serves 4

- 1 tablespoon avocado oil
- 1 pound (454 g) hake fillets
- 1 teaspoon garlic powder
- Sea salt and ground white pepper, to taste
- 2 tablespoons shallots, chopped
- 1 bell pepper, seeded and chopped
- ½ cup Cottage cheese
- ½ cup sour cream
- 1 egg, well whisked
- 1 teaspoon yellow mustard
- 1 tablespoon lime juice
- ½ cup Swiss cheese, shredded

1. Brush the bottom and sides of a casserole dish with avocado oil. Add the hake fillets to the casserole dish and sprinkle with garlic powder, salt, and pepper. 2. Add the chopped shallots and bell peppers. 3. In a mixing bowl, thoroughly combine the Cottage cheese, sour cream, egg, mustard, and lime juice. Pour the mixture over fish and spread evenly. 4. Cook in the preheated air fryer at 370ºF (188ºC) for 10 minutes. 5. Top with the Swiss cheese and cook an additional 7 minutes. Let it rest for 10 minutes before slicing and serving. Bon appétit!

Per Serving:

calories: 390 | fat: 26g | protein: 34g | carbs: 6g | net carbs: 5g | fiber: 1g

Cod with Creamy Mustard Sauce

Prep time: 10 minutes | Cook time: 10 minutes | Serves 4

- Fish:
- Oil, for spraying
- 1 pound (454 g) cod fillets
- 2 tablespoons olive oil
- 1 tablespoon lemon juice
- 1 teaspoon salt
- ½ teaspoon freshly ground black pepper
- Mustard Sauce:
- ½ cup heavy cream
- 3 tablespoons Dijon mustard
- 1 tablespoon unsalted butter

➢ 1 teaspoon salt

Make the Fish: 1. Line the air fryer basket with parchment and spray lightly with oil. 2. Rub the cod with the olive oil and lemon juice. Season with the salt and black pepper. 3. Place the cod in the prepared basket. You may need to work in batches, depending on the size of your air fryer. 4. Roast at 350°F (177°C) for 5 minutes. Increase the temperature to 400°F (204°C) and cook for another 5 minutes, until flaky and the internal temperature reaches 145°F (63°C). Make the Mustard Sauce: 5. In a small saucepan, mix together the heavy cream, mustard, butter, and salt and bring to a simmer over low heat. Cook for 3 to 4 minutes, or until the sauce starts to thicken. 6. Transfer the cod to a serving plate and drizzle with the mustard sauce. Serve immediately.

Per Serving:

calories: 246 | fat: 18g | protein: 17g | carbs: 2g | net carbs: 2g | fiber: 0g

Dill Lemon Salmon

Prep time: 10 minutes | Cook time: 4 minutes | Serves 4

➢ 1 pound (454 g) salmon fillet
➢ 1 tablespoon butter, melted
➢ 2 tablespoons lemon juice
➢ 1 teaspoon dried dill
➢ 1 cup water

1. Cut the salmon fillet on 4 servings. 2. Line the instant pot baking pan with foil and put the salmon fillets inside in one layer. 3. Then sprinkle the fish with dried dill, lemon juice, and butter. 4. Pour water in the instant pot and insert the rack. 5. Place the baking pan with salmon on the rack and close the lid. 6. Cook the meal on Manual mode (High Pressure) for 4 minutes. Allow the natural pressure release for 5 minutes and remove the fish from the instant pot.

Per Serving:

calories: 178 | fat: 10g | protein: 22g | carbs: 0g | net carbs: 0g | fiber: 0g

Zoodles in Clam Sauce

Prep time: 5 minutes | Cook time: 7 minutes | Serves 2

➢ ¼ cup MCT oil, duck fat, or bacon fat
➢ 2 tablespoons minced onions
➢ 2 cloves garlic, minced

➢ 1 (6½-ounce / 184-g) can whole clams, drained and chopped
➢ ¼ teaspoon fine sea salt
➢ ⅛ teaspoon freshly ground black pepper
➢ 2 cups zoodles
➢ Fresh basil leaves, for garnish (optional)

1. Heat the oil in a cast-iron skillet over medium heat. Add the onions and garlic and cook until the onions are translucent, about 4 minutes. Add the chopped clams and heat for 3 minutes. Season with the salt and pepper. 2. Serve over zoodles, garnished with basil, if desired. 3. Store extra sauce and zoodles separately in airtight containers in the fridge for up to 3 days. Reheat in a skillet over medium heat until warmed.

Per Serving:

calories: 355 | fat: 29g | protein: 16g | carbs: 8g | net carbs: 7g | fiber: 1g

Almond Milk Curried Fish

Prep time: 10 minutes | Cook time: 3 minutes | Serves 2

➢ 8 ounces (227 g) cod fillet, chopped
➢ 1 teaspoon curry paste
➢ 1 cup organic almond milk

1. Mix up curry paste and almond milk and pour the liquid in the instant pot. 2. Add chopped cod fillet and close the lid. 3. Cook the fish curry on Manual mode (High Pressure) for 3 minutes. 4. Then make the quick pressure release for 5 minutes.

Per Serving:

calories: 138 | fat: 4g | protein: 21g | carbs: 5g | net carbs: 5g | fiber: 0g

Chili Tilapia

Prep time: 5 minutes | Cook time: 20 minutes | Serves 4

➢ 4 tilapia fillets, boneless
➢ 1 teaspoon chili flakes
➢ 1 teaspoon dried oregano
➢ 1 tablespoon avocado oil
➢ 1 teaspoon mustard

1. Rub the tilapia fillets with chili flakes, dried oregano, avocado oil, and mustard and put in the air fryer. 2. Cook it for 10 minutes per side at 360°F (182°C).

Per Serving:

calories: 155 | fat: 7g | protein: 23g | carbs: 1g | net carbs: 1g | fiber: 0g

Baked Lemon-Butter Fish

Prep time: 10 minutes | Cook time: 20 minutes | Serves 2

- 4 tablespoons butter, plus more for coating
- 2 (5-ounce) tilapia fillets
- Pink Himalayan salt
- Freshly ground black pepper
- ·2 garlic cloves, minced
- 1 lemon, zested and juiced
- 2 tablespoons capers, rinsed and chopped

1. Preheat the oven to 400°F. Coat an 8-inch baking dish with butter. 2. Pat dry the tilapia with paper towels, and season on both sides with pink Himalayan salt and pepper. Place in the prepared baking dish. 3. In a medium skillet over medium heat, melt the butter. Add the garlic and cook for 3 to 5 minutes, until slightly browned but not burned. 4. Remove the garlic butter from the heat, and mix in the lemon zest and 2 tablespoons of lemon juice. 5. Pour the lemon-butter sauce over the fish, and sprinkle the capers around the baking pan. 6. Bake for 12 to 15 minutes, until the fish is just cooked through, and serve.

Per Serving:

calories: 299 | fat: 26g | protein: 16g | carbs: 5g | net carbs: 3g | fiber: 1g

Red Cabbage Tilapia Taco Bowl

Prep time: 15 minutes | Cook time: 10 minutes | Serves 4

- 2 cups cauli rice
- 2 teaspoons ghee
- 4 tilapia fillets, cut into cubes
- ¼ teaspoon taco seasoning
- Salt and chili pepper to taste
- ¼ head red cabbage, shredded
- 1 ripe avocado, pitted and chopped

1. Sprinkle cauli rice in a bowl with a little water and microwave for 3 minutes. Fluff after with a fork and set aside. Melt ghee in a skillet over medium heat, rub the tilapia with the taco seasoning, salt, and chili pepper, and fry until brown on all sides, for about 8 minutes in total. 2. Transfer to a plate and set aside. In 4 serving bowls, share the

cauli rice, cabbage, fish, and avocado. Serve with chipotle lime sour cream dressing.

Per Serving:

calories: 315 | fat: 23g | protein: 21g | carbs: 6g | net carbs: 3g | fiber: 3g

Sheet-Pan Cajun Crab Legs and Veggies

Prep time: 15 minutes | Cook time: 30 minutes | Serves 6

- Coconut oil, for greasing
- 2 zucchini, halved lengthwise and sliced
- 3 cups roughly chopped cauliflower
- 10 tablespoons butter or ghee, melted, divided
- 2 tablespoons Cajun seasoning
- 1 tablespoon minced garlic
- 6 ounces (170 g) Polish sausages or bratwurst, cut into rounds ½-inch thick
- 2 pounds (907 g) frozen snow crab legs (about two clusters), thawed in the refrigerator overnight or for a few minutes under cold running water
- ½ lemon
- Chopped fresh parsley, for garnish

1. Preheat the oven to 450°F (235°C). Line a large baking sheet with aluminum foil and grease the foil with oil. 2. Arrange the zucchini halves cut-side up on the prepared baking sheet. Add the cauliflower and spread it out in an even layer. 3. In a small bowl, stir together 5 tablespoons of melted butter, Cajun seasoning, and garlic until well mixed. Pour half of the butter mixture over the veggies, making sure to cover the cauliflower. 4. Bake for 15 to 20 minutes until the veggies are tender. 5. Place the sausage slices among the vegetables. Break up the crab legs and add them to the pan. Drizzle with the remaining butter mixture. Bake for an additional 10 minutes. 6. Squeeze the lemon half over the top, garnish with parsley, and serve immediately with the remaining 5 tablespoons of butter for dipping.

Per Serving:

calories: 415 | fat: 29g | protein: 33g | carbs: 5g | net carbs: 3g | fiber: 2g

Cucumber and Salmon Salad

Prep time: 10 minutes | Cook time: 8 to 10

minutes | Serves 2

- 1 pound (454 g) salmon fillet
- 1½ tablespoons olive oil, divided
- 1 tablespoon sherry vinegar
- 1 tablespoon capers, rinsed and drained
- 1 seedless cucumber, thinly sliced
- ¼ Vidalia onion, thinly sliced
- 2 tablespoons chopped fresh parsley
- Salt and freshly ground black pepper, to taste

1. Preheat the air fryer to 400ºF (204ºC). 2. Lightly coat the salmon with ½ tablespoon of the olive oil. Place skin-side down in the air fryer basket and air fry for 8 to 10 minutes until the fish is opaque and flakes easily with a fork. Transfer the salmon to a plate and let cool to room temperature. Remove the skin and carefully flake the fish into bite-size chunks. 3. In a small bowl, whisk the remaining 1 tablespoon olive oil and the vinegar until thoroughly combined. Add the flaked fish, capers, cucumber, onion, and parsley. Season to taste with salt and freshly ground black pepper. Toss gently to coat. Serve immediately or cover and refrigerate for up to 4 hours.

Per Serving:

calories: 470 | fat: 35g | protein: 30g | carbs: 6g | net carbs: 5g | fiber: 1g

Apple Cider Mussels

Prep time: 10 minutes | Cook time: 2 minutes | Serves 5

- 2 pounds (907 g) mussels, cleaned, peeled
- 1 teaspoon onion powder
- 1 teaspoon ground cumin
- 1 tablespoon avocado oil
- ¼ cup apple cider vinegar

1. Mix mussels with onion powder, ground cumin, avocado oil, and apple cider vinegar. 2. Put the mussels in the air fryer and cook at 395ºF (202ºC) for 2 minutes.

Per Serving:

calories: 210 | fat: 9g | protein: 23g | carbs: 7g | net carbs: 6g | fiber: 1g

Scallops in Lemon-Butter Sauce

Prep time: 10 minutes | Cook time: 6 minutes | Serves 2

- 8 large dry sea scallops (about ¾ pound / 340 g)
- Salt and freshly ground black pepper, to taste
- 2 tablespoons olive oil
- 2 tablespoons unsalted butter, melted
- 2 tablespoons chopped flat-leaf parsley
- 1 tablespoon fresh lemon juice
- 2 teaspoons capers, drained and chopped
- 1 teaspoon grated lemon zest
- 1 clove garlic, minced

1. Preheat the air fryer to 400ºF (204ºC). 2. Use a paper towel to pat the scallops dry. Sprinkle lightly with salt and pepper. Brush with the olive oil. Arrange the scallops in a single layer in the air fryer basket. Pausing halfway through the cooking time to turn the scallops, air fry for about 6 minutes until firm and opaque. 3. Meanwhile, in a small bowl, combine the oil, butter, parsley, lemon juice, capers, lemon zest, and garlic. Drizzle over the scallops just before serving.

Per Serving:

calories: 304 | fat: 22g | protein: 21g | carbs: 5g | net carbs: 4g | fiber: 1g

Quick Shrimp Skewers

Prep time: 10 minutes | Cook time: 5 minutes | Serves 5

4 pounds (1.8 kg) shrimp, peeled

- 1 tablespoon dried rosemary
- 1 tablespoon avocado oil
- 1 teaspoon apple cider vinegar

1. Mix the shrimps with dried rosemary, avocado oil, and apple cider vinegar. 2. Then sting the shrimps into skewers and put in the air fryer. 3. Cook the shrimps at 400ºF (204ºC) for 5 minutes.

Per Serving:

calories: 240 | fat: 4g | protein: 47g | carbs: 1g | net carbs: 1g | fiber: 0g

Sole Asiago

Prep time: 10 minutes | Cook time: 8 minutes | Serves 4

- 4 (4 ounces) sole fillets
- ¾ cup ground almonds
- ¼ cup Asiago cheese

> 2 eggs, beaten

> 2½ tablespoons melted coconut oil

1. Preheat the oven to 350°F. Line a baking sheet with parchment paper and set aside. 2. Pat the fish dry with paper towels. 3. Stir together the ground almonds and cheese in a small bowl. 4. Place the bowl with the beaten eggs in it next to the almond mixture. 5. Dredge a sole fillet in the beaten egg and then press the fish into the almond mixture so it is completely coated. Place on the baking sheet and repeat until all the fillets are breaded. 6. Brush both sides of each piece of fish with the coconut oil. 7. Bake the sole until it is cooked through, about 8 minutes in total. 8. Serve immediately.

Per Serving:

calories: 406 | fat: 31g | protein: 29g | carbs: 6g | net carbs: 3g | fiber: 3g

Lemony Fish and Asparagus

Prep time: 5 minutes | Cook time: 3 minutes | Serves 4

> 2 lemons

> 2 cups cold water

> 2 tablespoons extra-virgin olive oil

> 4 (4-ounce / 113-g) white fish fillets, such as cod or haddock

> 1 teaspoon fine sea salt

> 1 teaspoon ground black pepper

> 1 bundle asparagus, ends trimmed

> 2 tablespoons lemon juice

> Fresh dill, for garnish

1. Grate the zest off the lemons until you have about 1 tablespoon and set the zest aside. Slice the lemons into ⅛-inch slices. 2. Pour the water into the Instant Pot. Add 1 tablespoon of the olive oil to each of two stackable steamer pans. 3. Sprinkle the fish on all sides with the lemon zest, salt, and pepper. 4. Arrange two fillets in each steamer pan and top each with the lemon slices and then the asparagus. Sprinkle the asparagus with the salt and drizzle the lemon juice over the top. 5. Stack the steamer pans in the Instant Pot. Cover the top steamer pan with its lid. 6. Lock the lid. Select the Manual mode and set the cooking time for 3 minutes at High Pressure. 7. Once cooking is complete, do a natural pressure release for 7 minutes, then release any remaining pressure. Carefully open the lid. 8. Lift the steamer pans out of the Instant Pot. 9. Transfer the fish and asparagus to a serving plate. Garnish with the lemon slices and dill. 10. Serve

immediately.

Per Serving:

calories: 163 | fat: 6g | protein: 24g | carbs: 7g | net carbs: 4g | fiber: 3g

Tuna Salad Wrap

Prep time: 5 minutes | Cook time: 0 minutes | Serves 2

> 2 (5 ounce / 142 g) cans tuna packed in olive oil, drained

> 3 tablespoons mayonnaise

> 1 tablespoon chopped red onion

> 2 teaspoons dill relish

> ¼ teaspoon pink Himalayan sea salt

> ¼ teaspoon freshly ground black pepper

> Pinch of dried or fresh dill

> 2 low-carb tortillas

> 2 romaine lettuce leaves

> ¼ cup grated Cheddar cheese

1. In a medium bowl, combine the tuna, mayonnaise, onion, relish, salt, pepper, and dill. 2. Place a lettuce leaf on each tortilla, then split the tuna mixture evenly between the wraps, spreading it evenly over the lettuce. 3. Sprinkle the Cheddar on top of each, then fold the tortillas and serve.

Per Serving:

calories: 549 | fat: 33g | protein: 42g | carbs: 21g | net carbs: 5g | fiber: 16g

Stuffed Trout

Prep time: 5 minutes | Cook time: 20 minutes | Serves 4

> 2 (7-ounce/200-g) head-off, gutted trout

> 2 tablespoons refined avocado oil or melted coconut oil

> 2 teaspoons dried dill weed

> 1 teaspoon dried thyme leaves

> ½ teaspoon ground black pepper

> ¼ teaspoon finely ground gray sea salt

> ½ lemon, sliced

> 1 green onion, green part only, sliced in half lengthwise

1. Preheat the oven to 400°F (205°C). 2. Place the fish in a large

cast-iron frying pan or on an unlined rimmed baking sheet and coat with the oil. In a small bowl, mix together the dried herbs, pepper, and salt. Sprinkle the fish—top, bottom, and inside—with the herb mixture. 3. Open up the fish and place the lemon and green onion slices inside. Lay it flat on the pan or baking sheet and transfer to the oven. Bake for up to 20 minutes, until the desired doneness is reached. 4. Cut the fish in half before transferring to a serving platter.

Per Serving:

calories: 219 | fat: 12g | protein: 27g | carbs: 1g | net carbs: 1g | fiber: 0g

Friday Night Fish Fry

Prep time: 10 minutes | Cook time: 10 minutes | Serves 4

- ➢ 1 large egg
- ➢ ½ cup powdered Parmesan cheese (about 1½ ounces / 43 g)
- ➢ 1 teaspoon smoked paprika
- ➢ ¼ teaspoon celery salt
- ➢ ¼ teaspoon ground black pepper
- ➢ 4 (4-ounce / 113-g) cod fillets
- ➢ Chopped fresh oregano or parsley, for garnish (optional)
- ➢ Lemon slices, for serving (optional)

1. Spray the air fryer basket with avocado oil. Preheat the air fryer to 400°F (204°C). 2. Crack the egg in a shallow bowl and beat it lightly with a fork. Combine the Parmesan cheese, paprika, celery salt, and pepper in a separate shallow bowl. 3. One at a time, dip the fillets into the egg, then dredge them in the Parmesan mixture. Using your hands, press the Parmesan onto the fillets to form a nice crust. As you finish, place the fish in the air fryer basket. 4. Air fry the fish in the air fryer for 10 minutes, or until it is cooked through and flakes easily with a fork. Garnish with fresh oregano or parsley and serve with lemon slices, if desired. 5. Store leftovers in an airtight container in the refrigerator for up to 3 days. Reheat in a preheated 400°F (204°C) air fryer for 5 minutes, or until warmed through.

`

Per Serving:

calories: 290 | fat: 13g | protein: 39g | carbs: 3g | net carbs: 3g | fiber: 0g

Salmon with Tarragon-Dijon Sauce

Prep time: 5 minutes | Cook time: 15 minutes | Serves 4

- ➢ 1¼ pounds (567 g) salmon fillet (skin on or removed), cut into 4 equal pieces
- ➢ ¼ cup avocado oil mayonnaise
- ➢ ¼ cup Dijon or stone-ground mustard
- ➢ Zest and juice of ½ lemon
- ➢ 2 tablespoons chopped fresh tarragon or 1 to 2 teaspoons dried tarragon
- ➢ ½ teaspoon salt
- ➢ ¼ teaspoon freshly ground black pepper
- ➢ 4 tablespoons extra-virgin olive oil, for serving

1. Preheat the oven to 425°F(220°C). Line a baking sheet with parchment paper. 2. Place the salmon pieces, skin-side down, on a baking sheet. 3. In a small bowl, whisk together the mayonnaise, mustard, lemon zest and juice, tarragon, salt, and pepper. Top the salmon evenly with the sauce mixture. 4. Bake until slightly browned on top and slightly translucent in the center, 10 to 12 minutes, depending on the thickness of the salmon. Remove from the oven and leave on the baking sheet for 10 minutes. Drizzle each fillet with 1 tablespoon olive oil before serving.

Per Serving:

calories: 490 | fat: 39g | protein: 27g | carbs: 3g | net carbs: 2g | fiber: 1g

Sushi Shrimp Rolls

Prep time: 5 minutes | Cook time: 0 minutes | Serves 5

- ➢ 2 cups cooked and chopped shrimp
- ➢ 1 tablespoon sriracha sauce
- ➢ ¼ cucumber, julienned
- ➢ 5 hand roll nori sheets
- ➢ ¼ cup mayonnaise

1. Combine shrimp, mayonnaise, cucumber and sriracha sauce in a bowl. Lay out a single nori sheet on a flat surface and spread about 1/5 of the shrimp mixture. Roll the nori sheet as desired. Repeat with the other ingredients. Serve with sugar-free soy sauce.

Per Serving:

calories: 180 | fat: 12g | protein: 16g | carbs: 2g | net carbs: 1g | fiber:

1g

Shrimp Scampi with Zucchini Noodles

Prep time: 5 minutes | Cook time: 10 minutes | Serves 4

- ½ cup extra-virgin olive oil, divided
- 1 pound (454 g) shrimp, peeled and deveined
- 1 teaspoon salt
- ¼ teaspoon freshly ground black pepper
- 2 tablespoons unsalted butter
- 6 garlic cloves, minced
- 2 tablespoons dry white wine or chicken broth
- ½ teaspoon red pepper flakes
- Zest and juice of 1 lemon
- ¼ cup chopped fresh Italian parsley
- 4 cups spiralized zucchini noodles (about 2 medium zucchini)

1. In a large skillet, heat ¼ cup of olive oil over medium-high heat. Add the shrimp, sprinkle with salt and pepper, and sauté for 2 to 3 minutes, or until the shrimp is just pink. Using a slotted spoon, transfer the shrimp to a bowl and cover to keep warm. 2. Reduce heat to low and add the remaining ¼ cup of olive oil, butter, and garlic. Cook the garlic, stirring frequently, until very fragrant, 3 to 4 minutes. 3. Whisk in the wine, red pepper flakes, and lemon zest and juice. Increase the heat to medium-high and bring to a simmer. Remove the skillet from the heat as soon as the liquid simmers. Return the shrimp to the skillet, add the parsley, and toss. 4. To serve, place the raw zucchini noodles in a large bowl. Add the shrimp and sauce and toss to coat.

Per Serving:

calories: 414 | fat: 34g | protein: 25g | carbs: 5g | net carbs: 3g | fiber: 2g

Coconut Cream Mackerel

Prep time: 10 minutes | Cook time: 6 minutes | Serves 4

- 2 pounds (907 g) mackerel fillet
- 1 cup coconut cream
- 1 teaspoon ground coriander
- 1 teaspoon cumin seeds
- 1 garlic clove, peeled, chopped

1. Chop the mackerel roughly and sprinkle it with coconut cream, ground coriander, cumin seeds, and garlic. 2. Then put the fish in the air fryer and cook at 400ºF (204ºC) for 6 minutes.

Per Serving:

calories: 430 | fat: 31g | protein: 29g | carbs: 6g | net carbs: 5g | fiber: 1g

Blackened Red Snapper

Prep time: 13 minutes | Cook time: 8 to 10 minutes | Serves 4

- 1½ teaspoons black pepper
- ¼ teaspoon thyme
- ¼ teaspoon garlic powder
- ⅛ teaspoon cayenne pepper
- 1 teaspoon olive oil
- 4 (4 ounces / 113 g) red snapper fillet portions, skin on
- 4 thin slices lemon
- Cooking spray

1. Mix the spices and oil together to make a paste. Rub into both sides of the fish. 2. Spray the air fryer basket with nonstick cooking spray and lay snapper steaks in basket, skin-side down. 3. Place a lemon slice on each piece of fish. 4. Roast at 390ºF (199ºC) for 8 to 10 minutes. The fish will not flake when done, but it should be white through the center.

Per Serving:

calories: 134 | fat: 3g | protein: 22g | carbs: 2g | net carbs: 1g | fiber: 1g

One-Pot Shrimp Alfredo and Zoodles

Prep time: 10 minutes | Cook time: 25 minutes | Serves 5

- Zoodles:
- 3 medium zucchini (about 21 ounces / 595 g)
- 1 teaspoon sea salt
- Shrimp and Sauce:
- 2 tablespoons butter or ghee
- 3 garlic cloves, minced
- 1 pound (454 g) shrimp, peeled and deveined
- 4 ounces (113 g) cream cheese, at room temperature

- ½ cup heavy (whipping) cream
- ½ teaspoon sea salt
- ¼ teaspoon freshly ground black pepper
- 1 cup freshly grated Parmesan cheese
- ¼ teaspoon cayenne pepper (optional)

Make the Zoodles 1. Trim off the ends of the zucchini. Using a vegetable spiral slicer, swirl the zucchini into noodle shapes (zoodles). 2. Lay the zoodles on a kitchen towel and sprinkle with the salt. Let sit while you prepare the Alfredo sauce. 3. While the sauce is simmering, fold the zoodles up in the towel and squeeze out as much water as you can. Make the Shrimp and Sauce 4. In a large pot, melt the butter over medium heat. Add the garlic and cook for 3 minutes until fragrant. Add the shrimp and cook for 4 to 6 minutes, just until the shrimp start to turn pink. Remove the shrimp to a plate. 5. Add the cream cheese to the pot and whisk until melted. Pour in the cream slowly, whisking constantly. Add the salt and pepper. Let the sauce simmer for 5 to 10 minutes, whisking often, until thickened. 6. Remove the pot from the heat and stir in the Parmesan and cayenne (if using). Taste and adjust the salt and pepper to your liking. 7. Add the zoodles, cover, and cook for 5 minutes. The zoodles will release a bit of water, which will thin out the thick sauce a bit. 8. Add the shrimp and toss before serving.

Per Serving:

calories: 329 | fat: 25g | protein: 20g | carbs: 6g | net carbs: 5g | fiber: 1g

Trout Casserole

Prep time: 5 minutes | Cook time: 10 minutes | Serves 3

- 1½ cups water
- 1½ tablespoons olive oil
- 3 plum tomatoes, sliced
- ½ teaspoon dried oregano
- 1 teaspoon dried basil
- 3 trout fillets
- ½ teaspoon cayenne pepper, or more to taste
- ⅓ teaspoon black pepper
- Salt, to taste
- 1 bay leaf
- 1 cup shredded Pepper Jack cheese

1. Pour the water into your Instant Pot and insert a trivet. 2. Grease a baking dish with the olive oil. Add the tomatoes slices to the baking dish and sprinkle with the oregano and basil. 3. Add the fish fillets and season with the cayenne pepper, black pepper, and salt. Add the bay leaf. Lower the baking dish onto the trivet. 4. Lock the lid. Select the Manual mode and set the cooking time for 10 minutes at High Pressure. 5. When the timer beeps, perform a quick pressure release. Carefully remove the lid. 6. Scatter the Pepper Jack cheese on top, lock the lid, and allow the cheese to melt. 7. Serve warm.

Per Serving:

calories: 361 | fat: 24g | protein: 25g | carbs: 12g | net carbs: 11g | fiber: 1g

CHAPTER 5 Snacks and Appetizers

Cream Cheese and Berries

Prep time: 5 minutes | Cook time: 0 minutes | Serves 1

- 2 ounces (57 g) cream cheese
- 2 large strawberries, cut into thin slices or chunks
- 5 blueberries
- ⅛ cup chopped pecans

1. Place the cream cheese on a small plate or in a bowl. 2. Pour the berries and chopped pecans on top. Enjoy!

Per Serving:

calories: 330 | fat: 31g | protein: 6g | carbs: 7g | net carbs: 5g | fiber: 2g

Hangover Bacon-Wrapped Pickles

Prep time: 5 minutes | Cook time: 20 minutes | Serves 4

- 3 large pickles
- 6 strips uncooked no-sugar-added bacon, cut in half lengthwise
- ¼ cup ranch dressing

1. Preheat oven to 425°F. Line a baking sheet with foil. 2. Quarter each pickle lengthwise (yielding twelve spears). 3. Wrap each spear with a half strip bacon. Place on baking sheet. 4. Bake 20 minutes or until crispy, flipping at the midpoint. 5. Serve your crispy bacon-wrapped pickles while still hot with a side of the ranch dipping sauce.

Per Serving:

calories: 96| fat: 6g | protein: 6g | carbs: 3g | net carbs: 2g | fiber: 1g

Pecan Ranch Cheese Ball

Prep time: 15 minutes | Cook time: 0 minutes | serves 8

- 2 (8 ounces) packages cream cheese, softened
- 1 cup shredded sharp cheddar cheese
- 2 tablespoons ranch seasoning
- 1 cup chopped raw pecans
- Serving Suggestions:
- Celery sticks
- Mini sweet peppers
- Pork rinds

1. Put the cream cheese, cheddar cheese, and ranch seasoning in a medium-sized bowl. Using a spoon, mix the ingredients together until well blended. 2. Shape the mixture into a ball or disc shape and roll it in the pecans. Wrap and refrigerate overnight before serving. 3. Serve with the scoopers of your choice. Leftovers can be stored in an airtight container in the refrigerator for up to 5 days.

Per Serving:

calories: 303 | fat: 27g | protein: 9g | carbs: 11g | net carbs: 5g | fiber: 2g

Parmesan Chicken Balls with Chives

Prep time: 10 minutes | Cook time: 15 minutes | Serves 4

- 1 teaspoon coconut oil, softened
- 1 cup ground chicken
- ¼ cup chicken broth
- 1 tablespoon chopped chives
- 1 teaspoon cayenne pepper
- 3 ounces (85 g) Parmesan cheese, grated

1. Set your Instant Pot to Sauté and heat the coconut oil. 2. Add the remaining ingredients except the cheese to the Instant Pot and stir to mix well. 3. Secure the lid. Select the Manual mode and set the cooking time for 15 minutes at High Pressure. 4. Once cooking is complete, do a quick pressure release. Carefully open the lid. 5. Add the grated cheese and stir until combined. Form the balls from the cooked chicken mixture and allow to cool for 10 minutes, then serve.

Per Serving:

calories: 154 | fat: 9g | protein: 18g | carbs: 1g | net carbs: 1g | fiber: 0g

Crispy Grilled Kale Leaves

Prep time: 10 minutes | Cook time: 5 minutes

| Serves 4

- ½ cup good-quality olive oil
- 2 teaspoons freshly squeezed lemon juice
- ½ teaspoon garlic powder
- 7 cups large kale leaves, thoroughly washed and patted dry
- Sea salt, for seasoning
- Freshly ground black pepper, for seasoning

1. Preheat the grill. Set the grill to medium-high heat. 2. Mix the dressing. In a large bowl, whisk together the olive oil, lemon juice, and garlic powder until it thickens. 3. Prepare the kale. Add the kale leaves to the bowl and use your fingers to massage the dressing thoroughly all over the leaves. Season the leaves lightly with salt and pepper. 4. Grill and serve. Place the kale leaves in a single layer on the preheated grill. Grill for 1 to 2 minutes, turn the leaves over, and grill the other side for 1 minute, until they're crispy. Put the leaves on a platter and serve.

Per Serving:

calories: 282 | fat: 28g | protein: 3g | carbs: 9g | net carbs: 6g | fiber: 3g

Devilish Eggs

Prep time: 10 minutes | Cook time: 9 minutes | Serves 6

- 6 large eggs
- 3 tablespoons full-fat mayonnaise
- 1 teaspoon plain white vinegar
- 1 teaspoon spicy mustard
- ⅛ teaspoon salt
- ⅛ teaspoon black pepper
- ⅛ teaspoon ground cayenne
- ⅛ teaspoon paprika

1. Preferred Method: Hard-boil eggs using a steamer basket in the Instant Pot® on high pressure for 9 minutes. Release pressure and remove eggs. 2. Alternate Method: Place eggs in a large pot. Cover with water by 1". Cover with a lid and place the pot over high heat until it reaches a boil. Turn off heat, leave covered, and let it sit for 13 minutes. Then, remove the eggs from the pan, place them in an ice water bath, and let them cool 5 minutes. 3. When cooled, peel eggs and slice in half lengthwise. Place yolks in a medium bowl. 4. Mash and mix yolks with mayonnaise, vinegar, mustard, salt, and black pepper. 5. Scrape mixture into a sandwich-sized plastic bag and snip

off one corner, making a hole about the width of a pencil. Use makeshift pastry bag to fill egg white halves with yolk mixture. 6. Garnish Devilish Eggs with cayenne and paprika (mostly for color) and serve.

Per Serving:

calories: 125| fat: 9g | protein: 6g | carbs: 1g | net carbs: 1g | fiber: 0g

Snappy Bacon Asparagus

Prep time: 20 minutes | Cook time: 25 minutes | Serves 6

- 24 asparagus spears
- 6 strips no-sugar-added bacon, uncooked
- 2 tablespoons olive oil
- ⅛ teaspoon salt

1. My favorite part of preparing asparagus is the SNAP. Grab the "nonpointed" end of stalk and bend until it breaks. This usually happens about an inch from the end with the cut. Now, line up asparagus and cut entire bunch at "snapping" point, making all of your stalks uniform in length. Fancy, right? 2. On a microwave-safe plate, microwave asparagus 2 minutes to soften. Let cool 5 minutes. 3. Lay strip of bacon on a cutting board at 45-degree angle. Lay four asparagus spears centered on bacon in an "up and down" position. 4. Pick up bacon and asparagus where they meet and wrap two ends of bacon around asparagus in opposite directions. 5. Wrap bacon tightly and secure, pinning bacon to asparagus at ends with toothpicks. Don't worry if bacon doesn't cover entire spears. 6. Brush asparagus with olive oil and sprinkle with salt. 7. Heat a medium nonstick skillet over medium heat. Cook asparagus/bacon 3–5 minutes per side while turning to cook thoroughly. Continue flipping until bacon is brown and crispy.

Per Serving:

calories: 90 | fat: 7g | protein: 5g | carbs: 3g | net carbs: 3g | fiber: 1g

Sautéed Asparagus with Lemon-Tahini Sauce

Prep time: 5 minutes | Cook time: 10 minutes | Serves 4

- 16 asparagus spears, woody ends snapped off
- 2 tablespoons avocado oil
- Lemon-Tahini Sauce:
- 2 tablespoons tahini
- 1 tablespoon avocado oil

- ➤ 2½ teaspoons lemon juice
- ➤ 1 small clove garlic, minced
- ➤ 1/16 teaspoon finely ground sea salt
- ➤ Pinch of ground black pepper
- ➤ 1 to 1½ tablespoons water

1. Place the asparagus and oil in a large frying pan over medium heat. Cook, tossing the spears in the oil every once in a while, until the spears begin to brown slightly, about 10 minutes. 2. Meanwhile, make the sauce: Place the tahini, oil, lemon juice, garlic, salt, pepper, and 1 tablespoon of water in a medium-sized bowl. Whisk until incorporated. If the dressing is too thick, add the additional ½ tablespoon of water and whisk again. 3. Place the cooked asparagus on a serving plate and drizzle with the lemon tahini sauce.

Per Serving:

calories: 106 | fat: 8g | protein: 4g | carbs: 6g | net carbs: 3g | fiber: 3g

Buffalo Chicken Meatballs

Prep time: 5 minutes | Cook time: 10 minutes | Serves 4

- ➤ 1 pound (454 g) ground chicken
- ➤ ½ cup almond flour
- ➤ 2 tablespoons cream cheese
- ➤ 1 packet dry ranch dressing mix
- ➤ ½ teaspoon salt
- ➤ ¼ teaspoon pepper
- ➤ ¼ teaspoon garlic powder
- ➤ 1 cup water
- ➤ 2 tablespoons butter, melted
- ➤ ⅓ cup hot sauce
- ➤ ¼ cup crumbled feta cheese
- ➤ ¼ cup sliced green onion

1. In large bowl, mix ground chicken, almond flour, cream cheese, ranch, salt, pepper, and garlic powder. Roll mixture into 16 balls. 2. Place meatballs on steam rack and add 1 cup water to Instant Pot. Click lid closed. Press the Meat/Stew button and set time for 10 minutes. 3. Combine butter and hot sauce. When timer beeps, remove meatballs and place in clean large bowl. Toss in hot sauce mixture. Top with sprinkled feta and green onions to serve.

Per Serving:

calories: 367 | fat: 25g | protein: 25g | carbs: 9g | net carbs: 7g | fiber: 2g

Curried Broccoli Skewers

Prep time: 15 minutes | Cook time: 1 minute | Serves 2

- ➤ 1 cup broccoli florets
- ➤ ½ teaspoon curry paste
- ➤ 2 tablespoons coconut cream
- ➤ 1 cup water, for cooking

1. In the shallow bowl mix up curry paste and coconut cream. 2. Then sprinkle the broccoli florets with curry paste mixture and string on the skewers. 3. Pour water and insert the steamer rack in the instant pot. 4. Place the broccoli skewers on the rack. Close and seal the lid. 5. Cook the meal on Manual mode (High Pressure) for 1 minute. 6. Make a quick pressure release.

Per Serving:

calories: 58 | fat: 4g | protein: 2g | carbs: 4g | net carbs: 2g | fiber: 2g

Parmesan Crisps

Prep time: 5 minutes | Cook time: 5 minutes | Makes about 25 crisps

- ➤ 2 cups grated Parmesan cheese

1. Heat the oven to 400ºF (205ºC). Line a baking sheet with a silicone mat or parchment paper. Scoop a generous tablespoon of the cheese onto the sheet and flatten it slightly. Repeat with the rest of the cheese, leaving about 1 inch (2.5 cm) space in between them. 2. Bake for 3 to 5 minutes, until crisp.

Per Serving:

calories: 169 | fat: 11g | protein: 11g | carbs: 6g | net carbs: 6g | fiber: 0g

Broccoli with Garlic-Herb Cheese Sauce

Prep time: 5 minutes | Cook time: 3 minutes | Serves 4

- ➤ ½ cup water
- ➤ 1 pound (454 g) broccoli (frozen or fresh)
- ➤ ½ cup heavy cream
- ➤ 1 tablespoon butter
- ➤ ½ cup shredded Cheddar cheese
- ➤ 3 tablespoons garlic and herb cheese spread
- ➤ Pinch of salt
- ➤ Pinch of black pepper

1. Add the water to the pot and place the trivet inside. 2. Put the steamer basket on top of the trivet. Place the broccoli in the basket. 3. Close the lid and seal the vent. Cook on Low Pressure for 1 minute. Quick release the steam. Press Cancel. 4. Carefully remove the steamer basket from the pot and drain the water. If you steamed a full bunch of broccoli, pull the florets off the stem. (Chop the stem into bite-size pieces, it's surprisingly creamy.) 5. Turn the pot to Sauté mode. Add the cream and butter. Stir continuously while the butter melts and the cream warms up. 6. When the cream begins to bubble on the edges, add the Cheddar cheese, cheese spread, salt, and pepper. Whisk continuously until the cheeses are melted and a sauce consistency is reached, 1 to 2 minutes. 7. Top one-fourth of the broccoli with 2 tablespoons cheese sauce.

Per Serving:

calories: 134 | fat: 12g | protein:4 g | carbs: 5g | net carbs: 3g | fiber: 2g

Salami, Pepperoncini, and Cream Cheese Pinwheels

Prep time: 20 minutes | Cook time: 0 minutes | Serves 2

➢ 8 ounces cream cheese, at room temperature
➢ ¼ pound salami, thinly sliced
➢ 2 tablespoons sliced pepperoncini (I use Mezzetta)

1. Lay out a sheet of plastic wrap on a large cutting board or counter. 2. Place the cream cheese in the center of the plastic wrap, and then add another layer of plastic wrap on top. Using a rolling pin, roll the cream cheese until it is even and about ¼ inch thick. Try to make the shape somewhat resemble a rectangle. 3. Pull off the top layer of plastic wrap. 4. Place the salami slices so they overlap to completely cover the cream-cheese layer. 5. Place a new piece of plastic wrap on top of the salami layer so that you can flip over your cream cheese–salami rectangle. Flip the layer so the cream cheese side is up. 6. Remove the plastic wrap and add the sliced pepperoncini in a layer on top. 7. Roll the layered ingredients into a tight log, pressing the meat and cream cheese together. (You want it as tight as possible.) Then wrap the roll with plastic wrap and refrigerate for at least 6 hours so it will set. 8. Use a sharp knife to cut the log into slices and serve.

Per Serving:

calories: 583 | fat: 54g | protein: 19g | carbs: 7g | net carbs: 7g | fiber:

0g

Keto Asian Dumplings

Prep time: 20 minutes | Cook time: 20 minutes | Serves 4

➢ Dipping Sauce:
➢ ¼ cup gluten-free soy sauce
➢ 2 tablespoons sesame oil
➢ 1 tablespoon rice vinegar
➢ 1 teaspoon chili garlic sauce
➢ Filling:
➢ 1 tablespoon sesame oil
➢ 2 garlic cloves
➢ 1 teaspoon grated fresh ginger
➢ 1 celery stalk, minced
➢ ½ onion, minced
➢ 1 carrot, minced
➢ 8 ounces (227 g) ground pork
➢ 8 ounces (227 g) shrimp, peeled, deveined, and finely chopped
➢ 2 tablespoons gluten-free soy sauce
➢ ½ teaspoon fish sauce
➢ Salt and freshly ground black pepper, to taste
➢ 3 scallions, green parts only, chopped
➢ 1 head napa cabbage, rinsed, leaves separated (about 12 leaves)

Make the Dipping Sauce 1. In a small bowl, whisk together the soy sauce, sesame oil, vinegar, and chili garlic sauce. Set aside. Make the Filling 2. In a large skillet over medium heat, heat the sesame oil. 3. Add the garlic, ginger, celery, onion, and carrot. Sauté for 5 to 7 minutes until softened. 4. Add the pork. Cook for 5 to 6 minutes, breaking it up with a spoon, until it starts to brown. 5. Add the shrimp and stir everything together well. 6. Stir in the soy sauce and fish sauce. Season with a little salt and pepper. Give it a stir and add the scallions. Keep it warm over low heat until ready to fill the dumplings. 7. Steam the cabbage leaves: Place the leaves in a large saucepan with just 1 to 2 inches of boiling water. Cook for about 5 minutes or until the leaves become tender. Remove from the water and set aside to drain. 8. Lay each leaf out flat. Put about 2 tablespoons of filling in the center of one leaf. Wrap the leaf over itself, tucking the sides in so the whole thing is tightly wrapped. Secure with a toothpick. Continue with the remaining leaves and filling. Serve with the dipping sauce. Refrigerate leftovers in an airtight container for up to 3 days.

3 dumplings: calories: 305 | fat: 17g | protein: 27g | carbs: 11g | net carbs: 8g | fiber: 3g

Rosemary Chicken Wings

Prep time: 10 minutes | Cook time: 16 minutes | Serves 4

➤ 4 boneless chicken wings
➤ 1 tablespoon olive oil
➤ 1 teaspoon dried rosemary
➤ ½ teaspoon garlic powder
➤ ¼ teaspoon salt

1. In the mixing bowl, mix up olive oil, dried rosemary, garlic powder, and salt. 2. Then rub the chicken wings with the rosemary mixture and leave for 10 minutes to marinate. 3. After this, put the chicken wings in the instant pot, add the remaining rosemary marinade and cook them on Sauté mode for 8 minutes from each side.

Per Serving:

calories: 222 | fat: 11g | protein: 27g | carbs: 2g | net carbs: 2g | fiber: 0g

Gourmet "Cheese" Balls

Prep time: 1 hour 20 minutes | Cook time: 0 minutes | serves 6

➤ 1 cup raw hazelnuts, soaked overnight
➤ ¼ cup water
➤ 2 tablespoons nutritional yeast
➤ 1 teaspoon apple cider vinegar
➤ 1 teaspoon miso paste
➤ 1 teaspoon mustard
➤ ½ cup almond flour
➤ 1 cup slivered almonds
➤ 1 teaspoon dried oregano

1. In a high-powered blender, combine the hazelnuts, water, nutritional yeast, vinegar, miso paste, and mustard, and blend until well combined, thick, and creamy. 2. Transfer the mixture to a medium bowl. 3. Slowly stir in the almond flour until the mixture forms a dough-like consistency. Set aside. 4. In a separate, small bowl, toss the almonds and oregano together and set aside. 5. Using a soup spoon or tablespoon, scoop some mixture into your hand and shape it into a bite-size ball. Place the ball on a baking sheet. Repeat until you have used all the mixture (about 2 dozen balls). 6. One by one, roll the hazelnut balls in the almond and oregano mixture until thoroughly coated, placing each coated ball back on the baking sheet. 7. Place the sheet in the refrigerator for 1 hour to allow the balls to set.

Per Serving:

calories: 308 | fat: 27g | protein: 10g | carbs: 11g | net carbs: 5g | fiber: 6g

Asiago Shishito Peppers

Prep time: 5 minutes | Cook time: 10 minutes | Serves 4

➤ Oil, for spraying
➤ 6 ounces (170 g) shishito peppers
➤ 1 tablespoon olive oil
➤ ½ teaspoon salt
➤ ½ teaspoon lemon pepper
➤ ⅓ cup grated Asiago cheese, divided

1. Line the air fryer basket with parchment and spray lightly with oil. 2. Rinse the shishitos and pat dry with paper towels. 3. In a large bowl, mix together the shishitos, olive oil, salt, and lemon pepper. Place the shishitos in the prepared basket. 4. Roast at 350ºF (177ºC) for 10 minutes, or until blistered but not burned. 5. Sprinkle with half of the cheese and cook for 1 more minute. 6. Transfer to a serving plate. Immediately sprinkle with the remaining cheese and serve.

Per Serving:

calories: 90 | fat: 6g | protein: 3g | carbs: 7g | net carbs: 6g | fiber: 1g

Bone Broth Fat Bombs

Prep time: 5 minutes | Cook time: 0 minutes | Makes 12 fat bombs

➤ 1 tablespoon grass-fed powdered gelatin
➤ 2 cups homemade bone broth, any type, warmed
➤ Special Equipment:
➤ Silicone mold with 12 (1⅞ ounces / 53 g) cavities

1. Sprinkle the gelatin over the broth and whisk to combine. 2. Place the silicone mold on a rimmed sheet pan (for easy transport). Pour the broth into the mold. Place in the fridge or freezer until the gelatin is fully set, about 2 hours. To release the fat bombs from the mold, gently push on the mold to pop them out. 3. Store in an airtight container in the fridge for up to 5 days or in the freezer for several months.

Per Serving:

calories: 27 | fat: 5g | protein: 2g | carbs: 2g | net carbs: 2g | fiber: 0g

Cauliflower Cheesy Garlic Bread

Prep time: 10 minutes | Cook time: 30 minutes | Serves 6

- Butter, or olive oil, for the baking sheet
- 1 head cauliflower, roughly chopped into florets
- 3 cups shredded Mozzarella cheese, divided
- ½ cup grated Parmesan cheese
- ¼ cup cream cheese, at room temperature
- 3 teaspoons garlic powder, plus more for sprinkling
- 1 teaspoon onion powder
- ½ teaspoon red pepper flakes
- 1 tablespoon salt, plus more for seasoning
- Freshly ground black pepper, to taste
- 2 eggs, whisked
- Sugar-free marinara sauce, warmed, for dipping

1. Preheat the oven to 400ºF (205ºC). 2. Grease a baking sheet with butter. Set aside. Alternatively, use a pizza stone. 3. In a food processor, pulse the cauliflower until fine. Transfer to a microwave-safe bowl and microwave on high power, uncovered, for 2 minutes. Cool slightly. Place the cauliflower in a thin cloth or piece of cheesecloth and twist to remove any water (not a lot will come out but the little that's there needs to be removed). Transfer to a large bowl. 4. Add 2 cups of Mozzarella, the Parmesan, cream cheese, garlic powder, onion powder, red pepper flakes, and salt. Season generously with black pepper. Stir well to combine. 5. Add the eggs and use your hands to mix, ensuring everything is coated with egg. Transfer to the prepared baking sheet. Spread the mixture out into a large rectangle, about 1 inch thick. Sprinkle with more salt, pepper, and garlic powder. Bake for 20 minutes or until the bread starts to turn golden brown. 6. Remove from the oven, top with the remaining 1 cup of Mozzarella, and bake for about 10 minutes more or until the cheese melts. Cool slightly and cut into breadsticks. Serve with the marinara sauce for dipping. Refrigerate leftovers in an airtight container for up to 4 days.

Per Serving:

calories: 296 | fat: 20g | protein: 21g | carbs: 10g | net carbs: 7g | fiber: 3g

Zucchini and Cheese Tots

Prep time: 15 minutes | Cook time: 10 minutes | Serves 6

- 4 ounces (113 g) Parmesan, grated
- 4 ounces (113 g) Cheddar cheese, grated
- 1 zucchini, grated
- 1 egg, beaten
- 1 teaspoon dried oregano
- 1 tablespoon coconut oil

1. In the mixing bowl, mix up Parmesan, Cheddar cheese, zucchini, egg, and dried oregano. 2. Make the small tots with the help of the fingertips. 3. Then melt the coconut oil in the instant pot on Sauté mode. 4. Put the prepared zucchini tots in the hot coconut oil and cook them for 3 minutes from each side or until they are light brown. Cool the zucchini tots for 5 minutes.

Per Serving:

calories: 173 | fat: 13g | protein: 12g | carbs: 2g | net carbs: 2g | fiber: 0g

Brussels Sprouts with Aioli Sauce

Prep time: 5 minutes | Cook time: 7 minutes | Serves 4

- 1 tablespoon butter
- ½ cup chopped scallions
- ¾ pound (340 g) Brussels sprouts
- Aioli Sauce:
- ¼ cup mayonnaise
- 1 tablespoon fresh lemon juice
- 1 garlic clove, minced
- ½ teaspoon Dijon mustard

1. Set your Instant Pot to Sauté and melt the butter. 2. Add the scallions and sauté for 2 minutes until softened. Add the Brussels sprouts and cook for another 1 minute. 3. Lock the lid. Select the Manual mode and set the cooking time for 4 minutes at High Pressure. 4. Meanwhile, whisk together all the ingredients for the Aioli sauce in a small bowl until well incorporated. 5. When the timer beeps, perform a quick pressure release. Carefully remove the lid. 6. Serve the Brussels sprouts with the Aioli sauce on the side.

Per Serving:

calories: 167 | fat: 14g | protein: 3g | carbs: 9g | net carbs: 5g | fiber: 3g

Mac Fatties

Prep time: 10 minutes | Cook time: 0 minutes | Makes 20 fat cups

- 1¾ cups (280 g) roasted and salted macadamia nuts
- ⅓ cup (70 g) coconut oil
- Rosemary Lemon Flavor:
- 1 teaspoon finely chopped fresh rosemary
- ¼ teaspoon lemon juice
- Spicy Cumin Flavor:
- ½ teaspoon ground cumin
- ¼ teaspoon cayenne pepper
- Turmeric Flavor:
- ½ teaspoon turmeric powder
- ¼ teaspoon ginger powder
- Garlic Herb Flavor:
- 1¼ teaspoons dried oregano leaves
- ½ teaspoon paprika
- ½ teaspoon garlic powder

1. Place the macadamia nuts and oil in a blender or food processor. Blend until smooth, or as close to smooth as you can get it with the equipment you're using. 2. Divide the mixture among 4 small bowls, placing ¼ cup (87 g) in each bowl. 3. To the first bowl, add the rosemary and lemon juice and stir to combine. 4. To the second bowl, add the cumin and cayenne and stir to combine. 5. To the third bowl, add the turmeric and ginger and stir to combine. 6. To the fourth bowl, add the oregano, paprika, and garlic powder and stir to combine. 7. Set a 24-well silicone or metal mini muffin pan on the counter. If using a metal pan, line 20 of the wells with mini foil liners. (Do not use paper; it would soak up all the fat.) Spoon the mixtures into the wells, using about 1 tablespoon per well. 8. Place in the freezer for 1 hour, or until firm. Enjoy directly from the freezer.

Per Serving:

calories: 139 | fat: 14g | protein: 1g | carbs: 2g | net carbs: 1g | fiber: 1g

Greens Chips with Curried Yogurt Sauce

Prep time: 10 minutes | Cook time: 5 to 6 minutes | Serves 4

- 1 cup low-fat Greek yogurt
- 1 tablespoon freshly squeezed lemon juice
- 1 tablespoon curry powder
- ½ bunch curly kale, stemmed, ribs removed and discarded, leaves cut into 2- to 3-inch pieces
- ½ bunch chard, stemmed, ribs removed and discarded, leaves cut into 2- to 3-inch pieces
- 1½ teaspoons olive oil

1. In a small bowl, stir together the yogurt, lemon juice, and curry powder. Set aside. 2. In a large bowl, toss the kale and chard with the olive oil, working the oil into the leaves with your hands. This helps break up the fibers in the leaves so the chips are tender. 3. Air fry the greens in batches at 390ºF (199ºC) for 5 to 6 minutes, until crisp, shaking the basket once during cooking. Serve with the yogurt sauce.

Per Serving:

calories: 76 | fat: 2g | protein: 6g | carbs: 11g | net carbs: 10g | fiber: 2g

Finger Tacos

Prep time: 15 minutes | Cook time: 0 minutes | serves 4

- 2 avocados, peeled and pitted
- 1 lime
- 1 tablespoon tamari
- 1 teaspoon sesame oil
- 1 teaspoon ginger powder
- 1 teaspoon togarashi (optional)
- ½ cup kale chiffonade
- ½ cup cabbage chiffonade
- 10 fresh mint leaves chiffonade
- ⅓ cup cauliflower rice
- 1 (0.18-ounce) package nori squares or seaweed snack sheets

1. Put the avocados into a large mixing bowl, and squeeze the lime over them. 2. Roughly mash the avocados with a fork, leaving the mixture fairly chunky. 3. Gently stir in the tamari, sesame oil, ginger powder, and togarashi (if using). 4. Gently fold in the kale, cabbage, mint, and cauliflower rice. 5. Arrange some nori squares on a plate. 6. Use a nori or seaweed sheet to pick up a portion of the avocado mixture and pop it into your mouth.

Per Serving:

calories: 180 | fat: 15g | protein: 4g | carbs: 13g | net carbs: 5g | fiber: 8g

Taste of the Mediterranean Fat Bombs

Prep time: 15 minutes | Cook time: 0 minutes | Makes 6 fat bombs

➤ 1 cup crumbled goat cheese
➤ 4 tablespoons jarred pesto
➤ 12 pitted Kalamata olives, finely chopped
➤ ½ cup finely chopped walnuts
➤ 1 tablespoon chopped fresh rosemary

1. In a medium bowl, combine the goat cheese, pesto, and olives and mix well using a fork. Place in the refrigerator for at least 4 hours to harden. 2. Using your hands, form the mixture into 6 balls, about ¾-inch diameter. The mixture will be sticky. 3. In a small bowl, place the walnuts and rosemary and roll the goat cheese balls in the nut mixture to coat. 4. Store the fat bombs in the refrigerator for up to 1 week or in the freezer for up to 1 month.

Per Serving:

1 fat bomb: calories: 220 | fat: 20g | protein: 7g | carbs: 4g | net carbs: 3g | fiber: 1g

Lemon Pepper Wings

Prep time: 5 minutes | Cook time: 16 minutes | Serves 6

➤ 1 to 2 cups coconut oil or other Paleo fat, for frying
➤ 1 pound (454 g) chicken wings (about 12 wings)
➤ ½ teaspoon fine sea salt, divided
➤ 1 teaspoon freshly ground black pepper, divided
➤ Sauce:
➤ ¼ cup MCT oil or extra-virgin olive oil
➤ Grated zest of 1 lemon
➤ Juice of 1 lemon

1. Preheat the oil to 350°F (180°C) in a deep-fryer or in a 4-inch-deep (or deeper) cast-iron skillet over medium heat. The oil should be at least 3 inches deep; add more oil if needed. 2. While the oil is heating, make the sauce: Place the MCT oil in a small dish. Add the lemon zest and juice and whisk to combine. 3. Fry the wings in the hot oil, about six at a time, until golden brown on all sides and cooked through, about 8 minutes. Remove the wings from the oil and sprinkle with half of the salt and pepper. Repeat with the remaining wings, salt, and pepper. 4. Place the wings on a serving platter and serve with the sauce. They are best served fresh. Store extra wings and sauce

separately in airtight containers in the fridge for up to 3 days. To reheat, place the wings on a rimmed baking sheet and heat in a preheated 400°F (205°C) oven for 4 minutes, or until the chicken is warm.

Per Serving:

calories: 286 | fat: 24g | protein: 16g | carbs: 1g | net carbs: 1g | fiber: 0g

Asparagus with Creamy Dip

Prep time: 5 minutes | Cook time: 1 minute | Serves 6

➤ 1 cup water
➤ 1½ pounds (680 g) asparagus spears, trimmed
➤ Dipping Sauce:
➤ ½ cup mayonnaise
➤ ½ cup sour cream
➤ 2 tablespoons chopped scallions
➤ 2 tablespoons fresh chervil
➤ 1 teaspoon minced garlic
➤ Salt, to taste

1. Pour the water into the Instant Pot and insert a steamer basket. Place the asparagus in the basket. 2. Lock the lid. Select the Manual mode and set the cooking time for 1 minute at High Pressure. 3. When the timer beeps, perform a quick pressure release. Carefully remove the lid. Transfer the asparagus to a plate. 4. Whisk together the remaining ingredients to make your dipping sauce. Serve the asparagus with the dipping sauce on the side.

Per Serving:

calories: 119 | fat: 9g | protein: 5g | carbs: 7g | net carbs: 4g | fiber: 3g

3-Ingredient Almond Flour Crackers

Prep time: 5 minutes | Cook time: 12 minutes | Serves 6

➤ 2 cups (8 ounces / 227 g) blanched almond flour
➤ ½ teaspoon sea salt
➤ 1 large egg, beaten

1. Preheat the oven to 350°F (180°C). Line a large baking sheet with parchment paper. 2. In a large bowl, mix together the almond flour and sea salt. Add the egg and mix well, until a dense, crumbly dough forms. (You can also mix in a food processor if you prefer.) 3. Place

the dough between two large pieces of parchment paper. Use a rolling pin to roll out to a very thin rectangle, about 1/16 inch thick. (It will tend to roll into an oval shape, so just rip off pieces of dough and re-attach to form a more rectangular shape.) 4. Cut the cracker dough into rectangles. Place on the lined baking sheet. Prick with a fork a few times. Bake for 8 to 12 minutes, until golden.

Per Serving:

calories: 226 | fat: 19g | protein: 9g | carbs: 8g | net carbs: 4g | fiber: 4g

Herbed Zucchini Slices

Prep time: 5 minutes | Cook time: 5 minutes | Serves 4

- ➢ 2 tablespoons olive oil
- ➢ 2 garlic cloves, chopped
- ➢ 1 pound (454 g) zucchini, sliced
- ➢ ½ cup water
- ➢ ½ cup sugar-free tomato purée
- ➢ 1 teaspoon dried thyme
- ➢ ½ teaspoon dried rosemary
- ➢ ½ teaspoon dried oregano

1. Set your Instant Pot to Sauté and heat the olive oil. 2. Add the garlic and sauté for 2 minutes until fragrant. 3. Add the remaining ingredients to the Instant Pot and stir well. 4. Lock the lid. Select the Manual mode and set the cooking time for 3 minutes at Low Pressure. 5. When the timer beeps, perform a quick pressure release. Carefully remove the lid. 6. Serve warm.

Per Serving:

calories: 87 | fat: 8g | protein: 2g | carbs: 5g | net carbs: 3g | fiber: 2g

Sarah's Expert Crackers

Prep time: 15 minutes | Cook time: 40 minutes | Serves 10

- ➢ 1 cup blanched almond flour
- ➢ 2 tablespoons hemp hearts
- ➢ 2 tablespoons flaxseed meal
- ➢ 2 tablespoons psyllium husk powder
- ➢ 2 tablespoons chia seeds
- ➢ 2 tablespoons shelled pumpkin seeds
- ➢ 2 tablespoons Everything and More seasoning
- ➢ ½ tablespoon salt
- ➢ 1½ cups water

- ➢ 1 squirt liquid stevia

1. Preheat oven to 350°F. 2. In a medium mixing bowl, combine dry ingredients. 3. Add water and liquid stevia and mix together until a thick dough is formed. 4. Place dough between two pieces of parchment paper and roll out to desired cracker thickness. 5. Remove top piece of parchment paper and use a pizza cutter to cut dough into desired cracker shapes. 6. While cracker shapes are still on bottom piece of parchment paper, put on a baking sheet and into oven. 7. Bake 30–40 minutes until centers of crackers are hard. 8. Let cool 5 minutes, then serve.

Per Serving:

calories: 111| fat: 6g | protein: 5g | carbs: 7g | net carbs: 5g | fiber: 2g

Cheddar Chips

Prep time: 10 minutes | Cook time: 5 minutes | Serves 4

- ➢ 1 cup shredded Cheddar cheese
- ➢ 1 tablespoon almond flour

1. Mix up Cheddar cheese and almond flour. 2. Then preheat the instant pot on Sauté mode. 3. Line the instant pot bowl with baking paper. 4. After this, make the small rounds from the cheese in the instant pot (on the baking paper) and close the lid. 5. Cook them for 5 minutes on Sauté mode or until the cheese is melted. 6. Then switch off the instant pot and remove the baking paper with cheese rounds from it. 7. Cool the chips well and remove them from the baking paper.

Per Serving:

calories: 154 | fat: 13g | protein: 9g | carbs: 2g | net carbs: 1g | fiber: 1g

Everything Bagel Cream Cheese Dip

Prep time: 10 minutes | Cook time: 0 minutes | Serves 4

- ➢ 1 (8-ounce / 227-g) package cream cheese, at room temperature
- ➢ ½ cup sour cream
- ➢ 1 tablespoon garlic powder
- ➢ 1 tablespoon dried onion, or onion powder
- ➢ 1 tablespoon sesame seeds
- ➢ 1 tablespoon kosher salt

1. In a small bowl, combine the cream cheese, sour cream, garlic

powder, dried onion, sesame seeds, and salt. Stir well to incorporate everything together. Serve immediately or cover and refrigerate for up to 6 days.

Per Serving:

calories: 291 | fat: 27g | protein: 6g | carbs: 6g | net carbs: 5g | fiber: 1g

Bok Choy Salad Boats with Shrimp

Prep time: 8 minutes | Cook time: 2 minutes | Serves 8

- ➢ 26 shrimp, cleaned and deveined
- ➢ 2 tablespoons fresh lemon juice
- ➢ 1 cup water
- ➢ Sea salt and ground black pepper, to taste
- ➢ 4 ounces (113 g) feta cheese, crumbled
- ➢ 2 tomatoes, diced
- ➢ ⅓ cup olives, pitted and sliced
- ➢ 4 tablespoons olive oil
- ➢ 2 tablespoons apple cider vinegar
- ➢ 8 Bok choy leaves
- ➢ 2 tablespoons fresh basil leaves, snipped
- ➢ 2 tablespoons chopped fresh mint leaves

1. Toss the shrimp and lemon juice in the Instant Pot until well coated. Pour in the water. 2. Lock the lid. Select the Manual mode and set the cooking time for 2 minutes at Low Pressure. 3. When the timer beeps, perform a quick pressure release. Carefully remove the lid. 4. Season the shrimp with salt and pepper to taste, then let them cool completely. 5. Toss the shrimp with the feta cheese, tomatoes, olives, olive oil, and vinegar until well incorporated. 6. Divide the salad evenly onto each Bok choy leaf and place them on a serving plate. Scatter the basil and mint leaves on top and serve immediately.

Per Serving:

calories: 129 | fat: 11g | protein: 5g | carbs: 3g | net carbs: 2g | fiber: 1g

Garlic Herb Butter

Prep time: 10 minutes | Cook time: 8 minutes | Serves 4

- ➢ ⅓ cup butter
- ➢ 1 teaspoon dried parsley
- ➢ 1 tablespoon dried dill

- ➢ ½ teaspoon minced garlic
- ➢ ¼ teaspoon dried thyme

1. Preheat the instant pot on Sauté mode. 2. Then add butter and melt it. 3. Add dried parsley, dill, minced garlic, and thyme. Stir the butter mixture well. 4. Transfer it in the butter mold and refrigerate until it is solid.

Per Serving:

calories: 138 | fat: 15g | protein: 0g | carbs: 1g | net carbs: 1g | fiber: 0g

Creamy Scallion Dip

Prep time: 10 minutes | Cook time: 11 minutes | Serves 4

- ➢ 5 ounces (142 g) scallions, diced
- ➢ 4 tablespoons cream cheese
- ➢ 1 tablespoon chopped fresh parsley
- ➢ 1 teaspoon garlic powder
- ➢ 2 tablespoons coconut cream
- ➢ ½ teaspoon salt
- ➢ 1 teaspoon coconut oil

1. Heat up the instant pot on Sauté mode. 2. Then add coconut oil and melt it. 3. Add diced scallions and sauté it for 6 to 7 minutes or until it is light brown. 4. Add cream cheese, parsley, garlic powder, salt, and coconut cream. 5. Close the instant pot lid and cook the scallions dip for 5 minutes on Manual mode (High Pressure). 6. Make a quick pressure release. Blend the dip will it is smooth if desired.

Per Serving:

calories: 76 | fat: 6g | protein: 2g | carbs: 4g | net carbs: 3g | fiber: 1g

Taco Beef Bites

Prep time: 10 minutes | Cook time: 15 minutes | Serves 6

- ➢ 10 ounces (283 g) ground beef
- ➢ 3 eggs, beaten
- ➢ ⅓ cup shredded Mozzarella cheese
- ➢ 1 teaspoon taco seasoning
- ➢ 1 teaspoon sesame oil

1. In the mixing bowl mix up ground beef, eggs, Mozzarella, and taco seasoning. 2. Then make the small meat bites from the mixture. 3. Heat up sesame oil in the instant pot. 4. Put the meat bites in the hot oil and cook them for 5 minutes from each side on Sauté mode.

calories: 132 | fat: 6g | protein: 17g | carbs: 1g | net carbs: 1g | fiber: 0g

Sweet Pepper Nacho Bites

Prep time: 5 minutes | Cook time: 5 minutes | Makes 24 bites

- ➢ 12 mini sweet peppers (approximately 8 ounces / 227 g)
- ➢ ½ cup shredded Monterey Jack cheese
- ➢ ½ cup guacamole
- ➢ Juice of 1 lime

1. Preheat the oven to 400ºF (205ºC). 2. Carefully cut each pepper in half lengthwise and remove the seeds. Place them cut side up on a rimmed baking sheet so they aren't touching. Place 1 teaspoon of shredded cheese inside each. Bake 3 to 5 minutes, until the cheese starts to melt. 3. Remove from the oven and top each with 1 teaspoon of guacamole. Squeeze the lime juice over top. Serve immediately.

Per Serving:

calories: 137 | fat: 12g | protein: 4g | carbs: 5g | net carbs: 3g | fiber: 2g

Granola Clusters

Prep time: 5 minutes | Cook time: 15 minutes | Serves 2

- ➢ ¼ cup almonds
- ➢ ¼ cup pecans
- ➢ ¼ cup macadamia nuts
- ➢ 1 large egg white
- ➢ 2 tablespoons ground flaxseed
- ➢ 1 tablespoon coconut oil, melted
- ➢ 1 tablespoon pumpkin seeds
- ➢ 1 tablespoon chia seeds
- ➢ 1 tablespoon unsweetened coconut flakes
- ➢ 1 tablespoon granulated erythritol
- ➢ ¼ teaspoon vanilla extract
- ➢ ⅛ teaspoon pink Himalayan sea salt

1. Preheat the oven to 325ºF (163ºC). Line a baking sheet with parchment paper. 2. In a food processor, combine the almonds, pecans, macadamia nuts, egg white, flaxseed, coconut oil, pumpkin seeds, chia seeds, coconut flakes, erythritol, vanilla, and salt. Pulse until the largest chunks of nuts are about the size of a pea. 3. Spread the

mixture evenly on the baking sheet. Bake for 15 to 18 minutes, until the granola is lightly browned. 4. Let cool for about 20 minutes, then break into clusters.

Per Serving:

calories: 482 | fat: 45g | protein: 12g | carbs: 15g | net carbs: 5g | fiber: 10g

Crispy Bacon Wrapped Onion Rings

Prep time: 15 minutes | Cook time: 40 minutes | Serves 6

- ➢ 1 extra-large (1 pound / 454 g) onion, sliced into ½-inch-thick rings
- ➢ 12 slices bacon, halved lengthwise
- ➢ Avocado oil cooking spray
- ➢ ½ cup (2 ounces / 57 g) grated Parmesan cheese

1. Preheat the oven to 400ºF (205ºC). Line a sheet pan with foil. If you have an ovenproof nonstick cooling rack, place it over the pan. (This is optional, but recommended for the crispiest bacon.) Grease the sheet pan or rack. 2. Wrap each onion ring tightly in a thin strip of bacon, trying to cover the whole ring without overlapping. As you finish each ring, place it on a large cutting board in a single layer. (You can also just use the baking sheet without the rack for this step and the next, then use the rack starting at step 5.) 3. Spray the onion rings with avocado oil spray, then sprinkle lightly with half of the grated Parmesan. Flip and repeat on the other side. 4. Place the onion rings on the prepared baking sheet. Bake for 30 to 35 minutes, flipping halfway through, until the bacon is cooked through and starting to get a little crispy on the edges. Drain the bacon grease from the pan occasionally if not using a rack. 5. Switch the oven to broil. Broil the onion rings for 3 to 5 minutes, until crispy. To crisp up more, let the onion rings cool from hot to warm.

Per Serving:

calories: 141 | fat: 8g | protein: 9g | carbs: 7g | net carbs: 6g | fiber: 1g

Cayenne Beef Bites

Prep time: 5 minutes | Cook time: 23 minutes | Serves 6

- ➢ 2 tablespoons olive oil
- ➢ 1 pound (454 g) beef steak, cut into cubes
- ➢ 1 cup beef bone broth

- ¼ cup dry white wine
- 1 teaspoon cayenne pepper
- ½ teaspoon dried marjoram
- Sea salt and ground black pepper, to taste

1. Set your Instant Pot to Sauté and heat the olive oil. 2. Add the beef and sauté for 2 to 3 minutes, stirring occasionally. 3. Add the remaining ingredients to the Instant Pot and combine well. 4. Lock the lid. Select the Manual mode and set the cooking time for 20 minutes at High Pressure. 5. When the timer beeps, perform a natural pressure release for 10 minutes, then release any remaining pressure. Carefully remove the lid. 6. Remove the beef from the Instant Pot to a platter and serve warm.

Per Serving:

calories: 173 | fat: 10g | protein: 19g | carbs: 1g | net carbs: 1g | fiber: 0g

Easy Peasy Peanut Butter Cookies

Prep time: 15 minutes | Cook time: 7 to 12 minutes | Makes 15 cookies

- ½ cup coconut flour
- ¼ cup sugar-free sweetener
- ½ teaspoon baking soda
- 4 tablespoons (low-carb or handmade) peanut butter
- 2 tablespoons butter, at room temperature
- 2 large eggs
- 1 teaspoon vanilla extract

1. Preheat the oven to 350°F (180°C). Line a baking sheet with parchment paper and set aside. 2. In a bowl, combine the flour, sweetener, and baking soda, mixing to blend. 3. Add the peanut butter, butter, eggs, and vanilla, and mix well to incorporate. 4. Drop by even spoonfuls onto the prepared baking sheet to make 15 cookies. 5. Using the back of a fork, press the cookies down a little and make decorative criss-cross marks. 6. Cook for 7 to 8 minutes for soft cookies or 10 to 12 minutes for crispy cookies.

Per Serving:

1 cookie: calories: 70 | fat: 5g | protein: 3g | carbs: 3g | net carbs: 2g | fiber: 1g

Avocado Salsa

Prep time: 10 minutes | Cook time: 0 minutes | Serves 4

- 2 or 3 avocados, peeled, pitted, and diced
- ¼ red onion, diced
- 1 garlic clove, minced
- Zest of ½ lime
- Juice of 1 lime
- ¼ cup olive oil
- Salt and freshly ground black pepper, to taste
- ¼ cup chopped fresh cilantro

1. In a large bowl, gently toss together the diced avocados, onion, garlic, lime zest and juice, and olive oil. Season with salt and pepper. Cover and refrigerate in an airtight container for up to 4 days. Top with the cilantro before serving.

Per Serving:

calories: 450 | fat: 42g | protein: 3g | carbs: 15g | net carbs: 5g | fiber: 10g

Creamed Onion Spinach

Prep time: 3 minutes | Cook time: 5 minutes | Serves 6

- 4 tablespoons butter
- ¼ cup diced onion
- 8 ounces (227 g) cream cheese
- 1 (12 ounces / 340 g) bag frozen spinach
- ½ cup chicken broth
- 1 cup shredded whole-milk Mozzarella cheese

1. Press the Sauté button and add butter. Once butter is melted, add onion to Instant Pot and sauté for 2 minutes or until onion begins to turn translucent. 2. Break cream cheese into pieces and add to Instant Pot. Press the Cancel button. Add frozen spinach and broth. Click lid closed. Press the Manual button and adjust time for 5 minutes. When timer beeps, quick-release the pressure and stir in shredded Mozzarella. If mixture is too watery, press the Sauté button and reduce for additional 5 minutes, stirring constantly.

Per Serving:

calories: 273 | fat: 24g | protein: 9g | carbs: 5g | net carbs: 3g | fiber: 2g

Crab Salad–Stuffed Avocado

Prep time: 20 minutes | Cook time: 0 minutes | Serves 2

- 1 avocado, peeled, halved lengthwise, and pitted

- ½ teaspoon freshly squeezed lemon juice
- 4½ ounces Dungeness crabmeat
- ½ cup cream cheese
- ¼ cup chopped red bell pepper
- ¼ cup chopped, peeled English cucumber
- ½ scallion, chopped
- 1 teaspoon chopped cilantro
- Pinch sea salt
- Freshly ground black pepper

1. Brush the cut edges of the avocado with the lemon juice and set the halves aside on a plate. 2. In a medium bowl, stir together the crabmeat, cream cheese, red pepper, cucumber, scallion, cilantro, salt, and pepper until well mixed. 3. Divide the crab mixture between the avocado halves and store them, covered with plastic wrap, in the refrigerator until you want to serve them, up to 2 days.

Per Serving:

calories: 389 | fat: 31g | protein: 19g | carbs: 10g | net carbs: 5g | fiber: 5g

Warm Herbed Olives

Prep time: 5 minutes | Cook time: 4 minutes | Serves 4

- ¼ cup good-quality olive oil
- 4 ounces green olives
- 4 ounces Kalamata olives
- ½ teaspoon dried thyme
- ¼ teaspoon fennel seeds
- Pinch red pepper flakes

1. Sauté the olives. In a large skillet over medium heat, warm the olive oil. Sauté the olives, thyme, fennel seeds, and red pepper flakes until the olives start to brown, 3 to 4 minutes. 2. Serve. Put the olives into a bowl and serve them warm.

Per Serving:

calories: 165 | fat: 17g | protein: 1g | carbs: 3g | net carbs: 2g | fiber: 1g

Parmesan Artichoke

Prep time: 1 minute | Cook time: 30 minutes | Serves 2

1 large artichoke

1 cup water

¼ cup grated Parmesan cheese

¼ teaspoon salt

¼ teaspoon red pepper flakes

1. Trim artichoke. Remove stem, outer leaves and top. Gently spread leaves. 2. Add water to Instant Pot and place steam rack on bottom. Place artichoke on steam rack and sprinkle with Parmesan, salt, and red pepper flakes. Click lid closed. Press the Steam button and adjust time for 30 minutes. 3. When timer beeps, allow a 15-minute natural release and then quick-release the remaining pressure. Enjoy warm topped with additional Parmesan.

Per Serving:

calories: 90 | fat: 3g | protein: 6g | carbs: 10g | net carbs: 6g | fiber: 4g

Bacon-Stuffed Mushrooms

Prep time: 20 minutes | Cook time: 40 minutes | Makes 16 stuffed mushrooms

- 16 large white mushrooms (1½ to 2 inches in diameter)
- 1 tablespoon avocado oil
- 8 slices bacon, diced
- ¼ cup finely chopped green onions
- 1 clove garlic, minced
- 1 (8 ounces) package cream cheese, cubed
- Sliced green onions, for garnish (optional)

1. Preheat the oven to 350°F. Line a sheet pan with parchment paper. 2. Clean the mushrooms and pat them dry. Remove the stems and chop them; set aside. Set the mushroom caps on the lined sheet pan, stem side up. 3. Heat the oil in a medium-sized skillet over medium heat. Add the bacon, chopped mushroom stems, green onions, and garlic and cook until the bacon is crispy and the mushroom stems are tender. Reduce the heat to low. 4. Add the cream cheese to the skillet and stir until melted and well incorporated into the other ingredients. Remove the skillet from the heat. 5. Fill each mushroom with a spoonful of the cream cheese mixture and place on the lined sheet pan. 6. Bake the stuffed mushrooms for 30 minutes, or until tender and slightly browned on top. This could take less time depending on how large your mushrooms are. Garnish with sliced green onions before

serving, if desired.

Per Serving:

calories: 305 | fat: 25g | protein: 14g | carbs: 5g | net carbs: 4g | fiber: 1g

Chinese Spare Ribs

Prep time: 3 minutes | Cook time: 24 minutes | Serves 6

- ➤ 1½ pounds (680 g) spare ribs
- ➤ Salt and ground black pepper, to taste
- ➤ 2 tablespoons sesame oil
- ➤ ½ cup chopped green onions
- ➤ ½ cup chicken stock
- ➤ 2 tomatoes, crushed
- ➤ 2 tablespoons sherry
- ➤ 1 tablespoon coconut aminos
- ➤ 1 teaspoon ginger-garlic paste
- ➤ ½ teaspoon crushed red pepper flakes
- ➤ ½ teaspoon dried parsley
- ➤ 2 tablespoons sesame seeds, for serving

1. Season the spare ribs with salt and black pepper to taste. 2. Set your Instant Pot to Sauté and heat the sesame oil. 3. Add the seasoned spare ribs and sear each side for about 3 minutes. 4. Add the remaining ingredients except the sesame seeds to the Instant Pot and stir well. 5. Secure the lid. Select the Meat/Stew mode and set the cooking time for 18 minutes at High Pressure. 6. When the timer beeps, perform a natural pressure release for 10 minutes, then release any remaining pressure. Carefully remove the lid. 7. Serve topped with the sesame seeds.

Per Serving:

calories: 336 | fat: 16g | protein: 43g | carbs: 3g | net carbs: 2g | fiber: 1g

CHAPTER 6 Vegetarian Mains

Three-Cheese Zucchini Boats

Prep time: 15 minutes | Cook time: 20 minutes | Serves 2

- 2 medium zucchini
- 1 tablespoon avocado oil
- ¼ cup low-carb, no-sugar-added pasta sauce
- ¼ cup full-fat ricotta cheese
- ¼ cup shredded Mozzarella cheese
- ¼ teaspoon dried oregano
- ¼ teaspoon garlic powder
- ½ teaspoon dried parsley
- 2 tablespoons grated vegetarian Parmesan cheese

1. Cut off 1 inch from the top and bottom of each zucchini. Slice zucchini in half lengthwise and use a spoon to scoop out a bit of the inside, making room for filling. Brush with oil and spoon 2 tablespoons pasta sauce into each shell. 2. In a medium bowl, mix ricotta, Mozzarella, oregano, garlic powder, and parsley. Spoon the mixture into each zucchini shell. Place stuffed zucchini shells into the air fryer basket. 3. Adjust the temperature to 350°F (177°C) and air fry for 20 minutes. 4. To remove from the basket, use tongs or a spatula and carefully lift out. Top with Parmesan. Serve immediately.

Per Serving:

calories: 245 | fat: 18g | protein: 12g | carbs: 9g | net carbs: 7g | fiber: 2g

Almond-Cauliflower Gnocchi

Prep time: 5 minutes | Cook time: 25 to 30 minutes | Serves 4

- 5 cups cauliflower florets
- ⅔ cup almond flour
- ½ teaspoon salt
- ¼ cup unsalted butter, melted
- ¼ cup grated Parmesan cheese

1. In a food processor fitted with a metal blade, pulse the cauliflower until finely chopped. Transfer the cauliflower to a large microwave-safe bowl and cover it with a paper towel. Microwave for 5 minutes. Spread the cauliflower on a towel to cool. 2. When cool enough to handle, draw up the sides of the towel and squeeze tightly over a sink to remove the excess moisture. Return the cauliflower to the food processor and whirl until creamy. Sprinkle in the flour and salt and pulse until a sticky dough comes together. 3. Transfer the dough to a workspace lightly floured with almond flour. Shape the dough into a ball and divide into 4 equal sections. Roll each section into a rope 1 inch thick. Slice the dough into squares with a sharp knife. 4. Preheat the air fryer to 400°F (204°C). 5. Working in batches if necessary, place the gnocchi in a single layer in the basket of the air fryer and spray generously with olive oil. Pausing halfway through the cooking time to turn the gnocchi, air fry for 25 to 30 minutes until golden brown and crispy on the edges. Transfer to a large bowl and toss with the melted butter and Parmesan cheese.

Per Serving:

calories: 220 | fat: 20g | protein: 7g | carbs: 8g | net carbs: 5g | fiber: 3g

Crispy Tofu

Prep time: 30 minutes | Cook time: 15 to 20 minutes | Serves 4

- 1 (16-ounce / 454-g) block extra-firm tofu
- 2 tablespoons coconut aminos
- 1 tablespoon toasted sesame oil
- 1 tablespoon olive oil
- 1 tablespoon chili-garlic sauce
- 1½ teaspoons black sesame seeds
- 1 scallion, thinly sliced

1. Press the tofu for at least 15 minutes by wrapping it in paper towels and setting a heavy pan on top so that the moisture drains. 2. Slice the tofu into bite-size cubes and transfer to a bowl. Drizzle with the coconut aminos, sesame oil, olive oil, and chili-garlic sauce. Cover and refrigerate for 1 hour or up to overnight. 3. Preheat the air fryer to 400°F (204°C). 4. Arrange the tofu in a single layer in the air fryer basket. Pausing to shake the pan halfway through the cooking time, air fry for 15 to 20 minutes until crisp. Serve with any juices that accumulate in the bottom of the air fryer, sprinkled with the sesame seeds and sliced scallion.

Per Serving:

calories: 186 | fat: 14g | protein: 12g | carbs: 4g | net carbs: 3g | fiber: 1g

Spinach Cheese Casserole

Prep time: 15 minutes | Cook time: 15 minutes | Serves 4

- ➤ 1 tablespoon salted butter, melted
- ➤ ¼ cup diced yellow onion
- ➤ 8 ounces (227 g) full-fat cream cheese, softened
- ➤ ⅓ cup full-fat mayonnaise
- ➤ ⅓ cup full-fat sour cream
- ➤ ¼ cup chopped pickled jalapeños
- ➤ 2 cups fresh spinach, chopped
- ➤ 2 cups cauliflower florets, chopped
- ➤ 1 cup artichoke hearts, chopped

1. In a large bowl, mix butter, onion, cream cheese, mayonnaise, and sour cream. Fold in jalapeños, spinach, cauliflower, and artichokes. 2. Pour the mixture into a round baking dish. Cover with foil and place into the air fryer basket. 3. Adjust the temperature to 370ºF (188ºC) and set the timer for 15 minutes. In the last 2 minutes of cooking, remove the foil to brown the top. Serve warm.

Per Serving:

calories: 490 | fat: 46g | protein: 9g | carbs: 12g | net carbs: 8g | fiber: 4g

Cheesy Broccoli Casserole

Prep time: 10 minutes | Cook time: 35 minutes | Serves 4

- ➤ 2 tablespoons butter
- ➤ ¼ white onion, diced
- ➤ 1 garlic clove, minced
- ➤ 1 pound (454 g) broccoli florets, roughly chopped
- ➤ Salt, to taste
- ➤ Freshly ground black pepper, to taste
- ➤ 4 ounces (113 g) cream cheese, at room temperature
- ➤ 1 cup shredded Cheddar cheese, divided
- ➤ ½ cup heavy (whipping) cream
- ➤ 2 eggs

1. Preheat the oven to 350ºF (180ºC). 2. In a large skillet over medium heat, melt the butter. 3. Add the onion and garlic. Sauté for 5 to 7 minutes until the onion is softened and translucent. 4. Add the broccoli. Season with salt and pepper. Cook for 4 to 5 minutes until just softened. Transfer to a 7-by-11-inch baking dish. 5. In a medium bowl, stir together the cream cheese, ½ cup of Cheddar, the cream, and eggs. Pour over the broccoli. Season with more salt and pepper, and top with the remaining ½ cup of Cheddar. Bake for 20 minutes. Refrigerate leftovers in an airtight container for up to 1 week.

Per Serving:

calories: 440 | fat: 39g | protein: 16g | carbs: 11g | net carbs: 8g | fiber: 3g

Stuffed Eggplant

Prep time: 20 minutes | Cook time: 1 hour | Serves 2 to 4

- ➤ 1 small eggplant, halved lengthwise
- ➤ 3 tablespoons olive, avocado, or macadamia nut oil
- ➤ 1 onion, diced
- ➤ 12 asparagus spears or green beans, diced
- ➤ 1 red bell pepper, diced
- ➤ 1 large tomato, chopped
- ➤ 2 garlic cloves, minced
- ➤ ½ block (8 ounces / 227 g) extra-firm tofu (optional)
- ➤ 3 tablespoons chopped fresh basil leaves
- ➤ Salt and freshly ground black pepper, to taste
- ➤ ¼ cup water
- ➤ 2 eggs
- ➤ Chopped fresh parsley, for garnish (optional)
- ➤ Shredded cheese, for garnish (optional)

1. Preheat the oven to 350ºF (180ºC). 2. Scoop out the flesh from the halved eggplant and chop it into cubes. Reserve the eggplant skin. 3. In a sauté pan with a lid, heat the oil over medium-high heat. Add the eggplant, onion, asparagus, bell pepper, tomato, garlic, and tofu (if using) and stir. Stir in the basil, season with salt and pepper, and cook for about 5 minutes. 4. Add the water, cover the pan, reduce the heat to medium, and cook for about 15 minutes longer. 5. Put the eggplant "boats" (the reserved skin) on a baking sheet. Scoop some of the cooked eggplant mixture into each boat (you may have some filling left over, which is fine—you can roast it alongside the eggplant). 6. Crack an egg into each eggplant boat, on top of the filling, then bake for about 40 minutes, or until desired doneness. 7. Remove the

eggplant from the oven and, if desired, sprinkle parsley and cheese over the top. Let the cheese melt and cool for about 5 minutes, then serve them up!

Per Serving:

calories: 380 | fat: 26g | protein: 12g | carbs: 25g | net carbs: 15g | fiber: 10g

Cheesy Garden Veggie Crustless Quiche

Prep time: 5 minutes | Cook time: 25 minutes | Serves 4

- ➤ 1 tablespoon grass-fed butter, divided
- ➤ 6 eggs
- ➤ ¾ cup heavy (whipping) cream
- ➤ 3 ounces goat cheese, divided
- ➤ ½ cup sliced mushrooms, chopped
- ➤ 1 scallion, white and green parts, chopped
- ➤ 1 cup shredded fresh spinach
- ➤ 10 cherry tomatoes, cut in half

1. Preheat the oven. Set the oven temperature to 350°F. Grease a 9-inch pie plate with ½ teaspoon of the butter and set it aside. 2. Mix the quiche base. In a medium bowl, whisk the eggs, cream, and 2 ounces of the cheese until it's all well blended. Set it aside. 3. Sauté the vegetables. In a small skillet over medium-high heat, melt the remaining butter. Add the mushrooms and scallion and sauté them until they've softened, about 2 minutes. Add the spinach and sauté until it's wilted, about 2 minutes. 4. Assemble and bake. Spread the vegetable mixture in the bottom of the pie plate and pour the egg-and-cream mixture over the vegetables. Scatter the cherry tomatoes and the remaining 1 ounce of goat cheese on top. Bake for 20 to 25 minutes until the quiche is cooked through, puffed, and lightly browned. 5. Serve. Cut the quiche into wedges and divide it between four plates. Serve it warm or cold.

Per Serving:

calories: 355 | fat: 30g | protein: 18g | carbs: 5g | net carbs: 4g | fiber: 1g

Buffalo Cauliflower Bites with Blue Cheese

Prep time: 10 minutes | Cook time: 8 to 10 minutes | Serves 4

- ➤ 1 large head cauliflower, chopped into florets

- ➤ 1 tablespoon olive oil
- ➤ Salt and freshly ground black pepper, to taste
- ➤ ¼ cup unsalted butter, melted
- ➤ ¼ cup hot sauce
- ➤ Garlic Blue Cheese Dip:
- ➤ ½ cup mayonnaise
- ➤ ¼ cup sour cream
- ➤ 2 tablespoons heavy cream
- ➤ 1 tablespoon fresh lemon juice
- ➤ 1 clove garlic, minced
- ➤ ¼ cup crumbled blue cheese
- ➤ Salt and freshly ground black pepper, to taste

1. Preheat the air fryer to 400ºF (204ºC). 2. In a large bowl, combine the cauliflower and olive oil. Season to taste with salt and black pepper. Toss until the vegetables are thoroughly coated. 3. Working in batches, place half of the cauliflower in the air fryer basket. Pausing halfway through the cooking time to shake the basket, air fry for 8 to 10 minutes until the cauliflower is evenly browned. Transfer to a large bowl and repeat with the remaining cauliflower. 4. In a small bowl, whisk together the melted butter and hot sauce. 5. To make the dip: In a small bowl, combine the mayonnaise, sour cream, heavy cream, lemon juice, garlic, and blue cheese. Season to taste with salt and freshly ground black pepper. 6. Just before serving, pour the butter mixture over the cauliflower and toss gently until thoroughly coated. Serve with the dip on the side.

Per Serving:

calories: 420 | fat: 39g | protein: 9g | carbs: 14g | net carbs: 11g | fiber: 3g

Italian Baked Egg and Veggies

Prep time: 10 minutes | Cook time: 10 minutes | Serves 2

- ➤ 2 tablespoons salted butter
- ➤ 1 small zucchini, sliced lengthwise and quartered
- ➤ ½ medium green bell pepper, seeded and diced
- ➤ 1 cup fresh spinach, chopped
- ➤ 1 medium Roma tomato, diced
- ➤ 2 large eggs
- ➤ ¼ teaspoon onion powder
- ➤ ¼ teaspoon garlic powder
- ➤ ½ teaspoon dried basil

- 1/4 teaspoon dried oregano

1. Grease two ramekins with 1 tablespoon butter each. 2. In a large bowl, toss zucchini, bell pepper, spinach, and tomatoes. Divide the mixture in two and place half in each ramekin. 3. Crack an egg on top of each ramekin and sprinkle with onion powder, garlic powder, basil, and oregano. Place into the air fryer basket. 4. Adjust the temperature to 330°F (166°C) and bake for 10 minutes. 5. Serve immediately.

Per Serving:

calories: 260 | fat: 21g | protein: 10g | carbs: 8g | net carbs: 5g | fiber: 3g

Crustless Spanakopita

Prep time: 15 minutes | Cook time: 45 minutes | Serves 6

- 12 tablespoons extra-virgin olive oil, divided
- 1 small yellow onion, diced
- 1 (32-ounce / 907-g) bag frozen chopped spinach, thawed, fully drained, and patted dry (about 4 cups)
- 4 garlic cloves, minced
- 1/2 teaspoon salt
- 1/2 teaspoon freshly ground black pepper
- 1 cup whole-milk ricotta cheese
- 4 large eggs
- 3/4 cup crumbled traditional feta cheese
- 1/4 cup pine nuts

1. Preheat the oven to 375°F (190°C). 2. In a large skillet, heat 4 tablespoons olive oil over medium-high heat. Add the onion and sauté until softened, 6 to 8 minutes. 3. Add the spinach, garlic, salt, and pepper and sauté another 5 minutes. Remove from the heat and allow to cool slightly. 4. In a medium bowl, whisk together the ricotta and eggs. Add to the cooled spinach and stir to combine. 5. Pour 4 tablespoons olive oil in the bottom of a 9-by-13-inch glass baking dish and swirl to coat the bottom and sides. Add the spinach-ricotta mixture and spread into an even layer. 6. Bake for 20 minutes or until the mixture begins to set. Remove from the oven and crumble the feta evenly across the top of the spinach. Add the pine nuts and drizzle with the remaining 4 tablespoons olive oil. Return to the oven and bake for an additional 15 to 20 minutes, or until the spinach is fully set and the top is starting to turn golden brown. Allow to cool slightly before cutting to serve.

Per Serving:

calories: 440 | fat: 38g | protein: 17g | carbs: 9g | net carbs: 8g | fiber: 1g

Mediterranean Pan Pizza

Prep time: 5 minutes | Cook time: 8 minutes | Serves 2

- 1 cup shredded Mozzarella cheese
- 1/4 medium red bell pepper, seeded and chopped
- 1/2 cup chopped fresh spinach leaves
- 2 tablespoons chopped black olives
- 2 tablespoons crumbled feta cheese

1. Sprinkle Mozzarella into an ungreased round nonstick baking dish in an even layer. Add remaining ingredients on top. 2. Place dish into air fryer basket. Adjust the temperature to 350°F (177°C) and bake for 8 minutes, checking halfway through to avoid burning. Top of pizza will be golden brown and the cheese melted when done. 3. Remove dish from fryer and let cool 5 minutes before slicing and serving.

Per Serving:

calories: 239 | fat: 17g | protein: 17g | carbs: 6g | net carbs: 5g | fiber: 1g

Tangy Asparagus and Broccoli

Prep time: 25 minutes | Cook time: 22 minutes | Serves 4

- 1/2 pound (227 g) asparagus, cut into 1 1/2-inch pieces
- 1/2 pound (227 g) broccoli, cut into 1 1/2-inch pieces
- 2 tablespoons olive oil
- Salt and white pepper, to taste
- 1/2 cup vegetable broth
- 2 tablespoons apple cider vinegar

1. Place the vegetables in a single layer in the lightly greased air fryer basket. Drizzle the olive oil over the vegetables. 2. Sprinkle with salt and white pepper. 3. Cook at 380°F (193°C) for 15 minutes, shaking the basket halfway through the cooking time. 4. Add 1/2 cup of vegetable broth to a saucepan; bring to a rapid boil and add the vinegar. Cook for 5 to 7 minutes or until the sauce has reduced by half. 5. Spoon the sauce over the warm vegetables and serve immediately. Bon appétit!

Per Serving:

calories: 89 | fat: 7g | protein: 3g | carbs: 7g | net carbs: 4g | fiber: 3g

Broccoli Crust Pizza

Prep time: 15 minutes | Cook time: 12 minutes | Serves 4

➢ 3 cups riced broccoli, steamed and drained well
➢ 1 large egg
➢ ½ cup grated vegetarian Parmesan cheese
➢ 3 tablespoons low-carb Alfredo sauce
➢ ½ cup shredded Mozzarella cheese

1. In a large bowl, mix broccoli, egg, and Parmesan. 2. Cut a piece of parchment to fit your air fryer basket. Press out the pizza mixture to fit on the parchment, working in two batches if necessary. Place into the air fryer basket. 3. Adjust the temperature to 370ºF (188ºC) and air fry for 5 minutes. 4. The crust should be firm enough to flip. If not, add 2 additional minutes. Flip crust. 5. Top with Alfredo sauce and Mozzarella. Return to the air fryer basket and cook an additional 7 minutes or until cheese is golden and bubbling. Serve warm.

Per Serving:

calories: 178 | fat: 11g | protein: 15g | carbs: 10g | net carbs: 4g | fiber: 6g

Eggplant Parmesan

Prep time: 15 minutes | Cook time: 17 minutes | Serves 4

➢ 1 medium eggplant, ends trimmed, sliced into ½-inch rounds
➢ ¼ teaspoon salt
➢ 2 tablespoons coconut oil
➢ ½ cup grated Parmesan cheese
➢ 1 ounce (28 g) 100% cheese crisps, finely crushed
➢ ½ cup low-carb marinara sauce
➢ ½ cup shredded Mozzarella cheese

1. Sprinkle eggplant rounds with salt on both sides and wrap in a kitchen towel for 30 minutes. Press to remove excess water, then drizzle rounds with coconut oil on both sides. 2. In a medium bowl, mix Parmesan and cheese crisps. Press each eggplant slice into mixture to coat both sides. 3. Place rounds into ungreased air fryer basket. Adjust the temperature to 350ºF (177ºC) and air fry for 15 minutes, turning rounds halfway through cooking. They will be crispy around the edges when done. 4. Spoon marinara over rounds and sprinkle with Mozzarella. Continue cooking an additional 2 minutes at 350ºF (177ºC) until cheese is melted. Serve warm.

Per Serving:

calories: 330 | fat: 24g | protein: 18g | carbs: 13g | net carbs: 9g | fiber: 4g

Roasted Veggie Bowl

Prep time: 10 minutes | Cook time: 15 minutes | Serves 2

➢ 1 cup broccoli florets
➢ 1 cup quartered Brussels sprouts
➢ ½ cup cauliflower florets
➢ ¼ medium white onion, peeled and sliced ¼ inch thick
➢ ½ medium green bell pepper, seeded and sliced ¼ inch thick
➢ 1 tablespoon coconut oil
➢ 2 teaspoons chili powder
➢ ½ teaspoon garlic powder
➢ ½ teaspoon cumin

1. Toss all ingredients together in a large bowl until vegetables are fully coated with oil and seasoning. 2. Pour vegetables into the air fryer basket. 3. Adjust the temperature to 360ºF (182ºC) and roast for 15 minutes. 4. Shake two or three times during cooking. Serve warm.

Per Serving:

calories: 168 | fat: 11g | protein: 4g | carbs: 15g | net carbs: 9g | fiber: 6g

Eggplant and Zucchini Bites

Prep time: 30 minutes | Cook time: 30 minutes | Serves 8

➢ 2 teaspoons fresh mint leaves, chopped
➢ 1½ teaspoons red pepper chili flakes
➢ 2 tablespoons melted butter
➢ 1 pound (454 g) eggplant, peeled and cubed
➢ 1 pound (454 g) zucchini, peeled and cubed
➢ 3 tablespoons olive oil

1. Toss all the above ingredients in a large-sized mixing dish. 2. Roast the eggplant and zucchini bites for 30 minutes at 325ºF (163ºC) in your air fryer, turning once or twice. 3. Serve with a homemade dipping sauce.

Per Serving:

calories: 140 | fat: 12g | protein: 2g | carbs: 8g | net carbs: 6g | fiber: 2g

Quiche-Stuffed Peppers

Prep time: 5 minutes | Cook time: 15 minutes | Serves 2

- ➢ 2 medium green bell peppers
- ➢ 3 large eggs
- ➢ ¼ cup full-fat ricotta cheese
- ➢ ¼ cup diced yellow onion
- ➢ ½ cup chopped broccoli
- ➢ ½ cup shredded medium Cheddar cheese

1. Cut the tops off of the peppers and remove the seeds and white membranes with a small knife. 2. In a medium bowl, whisk eggs and ricotta. 3. Add onion and broccoli. Pour the egg and vegetable mixture evenly into each pepper. Top with Cheddar. Place peppers into a 4-cup round baking dish and place into the air fryer basket. 4. Adjust the temperature to 350ºF (177ºC) and bake for 15 minutes. 5. Eggs will be mostly firm and peppers tender when fully cooked. Serve immediately.

Per Serving:

calories: 382 | fat: 27g | protein: 24g | carbs: 11g | net carbs: 7g | fiber: 4g

Vegetarian Chili with Avocado and Sour Cream

Prep time: 10 minutes | Cook time: 25 minutes | Serves 8

- ➢ 2 tablespoons good-quality olive oil
- ➢ ½ onion, finely chopped
- ➢ 1 red bell pepper, diced
- ➢ 2 jalapeño peppers, chopped
- ➢ 1 tablespoon minced garlic
- ➢ 2 tablespoons chili powder
- ➢ 1 teaspoon ground cumin
- ➢ 4 cups canned diced tomatoes
- ➢ 2 cups pecans, chopped
- ➢ 1 cup sour cream
- ➢ 1 avocado, diced
- ➢ 2 tablespoons chopped fresh cilantro

1. Sauté the vegetables. In a large pot over medium-high heat, warm the olive oil. Add the onion, red bell pepper, jalapeño peppers, and garlic and sauté until they've softened, about 4 minutes. Stir in the chili powder and cumin, stirring to coat the vegetables with the spices. 2. Cook the chili. Stir in the tomatoes and pecans and bring the chili to a boil, then reduce the heat to low and simmer until the vegetables are soft and the flavors mellow, about 20 minutes. 3. Serve. Ladle the chili into bowls and serve it with the sour cream, avocado, and cilantro.

Per Serving:

calories: 332 | fat: 32g | protein: 5g | carbs: 11g | net carbs: 5g | fiber: 6g

Spaghetti Squash Alfredo

Prep time: 10 minutes | Cook time: 15 minutes | Serves 2

- ➢ ½ large cooked spaghetti squash
- ➢ 2 tablespoons salted butter, melted
- ➢ ½ cup low-carb Alfredo sauce
- ➢ ¼ cup grated vegetarian Parmesan cheese
- ➢ ½ teaspoon garlic powder
- ➢ 1 teaspoon dried parsley
- ➢ ¼ teaspoon ground peppercorn
- ➢ ½ cup shredded Italian blend cheese

1. Using a fork, remove the strands of spaghetti squash from the shell. Place into a large bowl with butter and Alfredo sauce. Sprinkle with Parmesan, garlic powder, parsley, and peppercorn. 2. Pour into a 4-cup round baking dish and top with shredded cheese. Place dish into the air fryer basket. 3. Adjust the temperature to 320ºF (160ºC) and bake for 15 minutes. When finished, cheese will be golden and bubbling. Serve immediately.

Per Serving:

calories: 383 | fat: 30g | protein: 14g | carbs: 14g | net carbs: 11g | fiber: 3g

Caprese Eggplant Stacks

Prep time: 5 minutes | Cook time: 12 minutes | Serves 4

- ➢ 1 medium eggplant, cut into ¼-inch slices
- ➢ 2 large tomatoes, cut into ¼-inch slices
- ➢ 4 ounces (113 g) fresh Mozzarella, cut into ½-ounce / 14-g slices
- ➢ 2 tablespoons olive oil

➤ ¼ cup fresh basil, sliced

1. In a baking dish, place four slices of eggplant on the bottom. Place a slice of tomato on top of each eggplant round, then Mozzarella, then eggplant. Repeat as necessary. 2. Drizzle with olive oil. Cover dish with foil and place dish into the air fryer basket. 3. Adjust the temperature to 350ºF (177ºC) and bake for 12 minutes. 4. When done, eggplant will be tender. Garnish with fresh basil to serve.

Per Serving:

calories: 203 | fat: 16g | protein: 8g | carbs: 10g | net carbs: 7g | fiber: 3g

Broccoli with Garlic Sauce

Prep time: 19 minutes | Cook time: 15 minutes | Serves 4

➤ 2 tablespoons olive oil

➤ Kosher salt and freshly ground black pepper, to taste

➤ 1 pound (454 g) broccoli florets

➤ Dipping Sauce:

➤ 2 teaspoons dried rosemary, crushed

➤ 3 garlic cloves, minced

➤ ⅓ teaspoon dried marjoram, crushed

➤ ¼ cup sour cream

➤ ⅓ cup mayonnaise

1. Lightly grease your broccoli with a thin layer of olive oil. Season with salt and ground black pepper. 2. Arrange the seasoned broccoli in the air fryer basket. Bake at 395ºF (202ºC) for 15 minutes, shaking once or twice. In the meantime, prepare the dipping sauce by mixing all the sauce ingredients. Serve warm broccoli with the dipping sauce and enjoy!

Per Serving:

calories: 250 | fat: 23g | protein: 3g | carbs: 10g | net carbs: 9g | fiber: 1g

Whole Roasted Lemon Cauliflower

Prep time: 5 minutes | Cook time: 15 minutes | Serves 4

➤ 1 medium head cauliflower

➤ 2 tablespoons salted butter, melted

➤ 1 medium lemon

➤ ½ teaspoon garlic powder

➤ 1 teaspoon dried parsley

1. Remove the leaves from the head of cauliflower and brush it with melted butter. Cut the lemon in half and zest one half onto the cauliflower. Squeeze the juice of the zested lemon half and pour it over the cauliflower. 2. Sprinkle with garlic powder and parsley. Place cauliflower head into the air fryer basket. 3. Adjust the temperature to 350ºF (177ºC) and air fry for 15 minutes. 4. Check cauliflower every 5 minutes to avoid overcooking. It should be fork tender. 5. To serve, squeeze juice from other lemon half over cauliflower. Serve immediately.

Per Serving:

calories: 90 | fat: 7g | protein: 3g | carbs: 6g | net carbs: 4g | fiber: 2g

Garlic White Zucchini Rolls

Prep time: 20 minutes | Cook time: 20 minutes | Serves 4

➤ 2 medium zucchini

➤ 2 tablespoons unsalted butter

➤ ¼ white onion, peeled and diced

➤ ½ teaspoon finely minced roasted garlic

➤ ¼ cup heavy cream

➤ 2 tablespoons vegetable broth

➤ ⅛ teaspoon xanthan gum

➤ ½ cup full-fat ricotta cheese

➤ ¼ teaspoon salt

➤ ½ teaspoon garlic powder

➤ ¼ teaspoon dried oregano

➤ 2 cups spinach, chopped

➤ ½ cup sliced baby portobello mushrooms

➤ ¾ cup shredded Mozzarella cheese, divided

1. Using a mandoline or sharp knife, slice zucchini into long strips lengthwise. Place strips between paper towels to absorb moisture. Set aside. 2. In a medium saucepan over medium heat, melt butter. Add onion and sauté until fragrant. Add garlic and sauté 30 seconds. 3. Pour in heavy cream, broth, and xanthan gum. Turn off heat and whisk mixture until it begins to thicken, about 3 minutes. 4. In a medium bowl, add ricotta, salt, garlic powder, and oregano and mix well. Fold in spinach, mushrooms, and ½ cup Mozzarella. 5. Pour half of the sauce into a round baking pan. To assemble the rolls, place two strips of zucchini on a work surface. Spoon 2 tablespoons of ricotta mixture onto the slices and roll up. Place seam side down on top of sauce. Repeat with remaining ingredients. 6. Pour remaining sauce

over the rolls and sprinkle with remaining Mozzarella. Cover with foil and place into the air fryer basket. 7. Adjust the temperature to 350ºF (177ºC) and bake for 20 minutes. 8. In the last 5 minutes, remove the foil to brown the cheese. Serve immediately.

Per Serving:

calories: 270 | fat: 21g | protein: 14g | carbs: 7g | net carbs: 5g | fiber: 2g

Zucchini and Spinach Croquettes

Prep time: 9 minutes | Cook time: 7 minutes | Serves 6

➢ 4 eggs, slightly beaten
➢ ½ cup almond flour
➢ ½ cup goat cheese, crumbled
➢ 1 teaspoon fine sea salt
➢ 4 garlic cloves, minced
➢ 1 cup baby spinach
➢ ½ cup Parmesan cheese, grated
➢ ⅓ teaspoon red pepper flakes
➢ 1 pound (454 g) zucchini, peeled and grated
➢ ⅓ teaspoon dried dill weed

1. Thoroughly combine all ingredients in a bowl. Now, roll the mixture to form small croquettes. 2. Air fry at 340ºF (171ºC) for 7 minutes or until golden. Tate, adjust for seasonings and serve warm.

Per Serving:

calories: 179 | fat: 12g | protein: 11g | carbs: 6g | net carbs: 3g | fiber: 3g

Cauliflower Rice-Stuffed Peppers

Prep time: 10 minutes | Cook time: 15 minutes | Serves 4

➢ 2 cups uncooked cauliflower rice
➢ ¾ cup drained canned petite diced tomatoes
➢ 2 tablespoons olive oil
➢ 1 cup shredded Mozzarella cheese
➢ ¼ teaspoon salt
➢ ¼ teaspoon ground black pepper
➢ 4 medium green bell peppers, tops removed, seeded

1. In a large bowl, mix all ingredients except bell peppers. Scoop mixture evenly into peppers. 2. Place peppers into ungreased air fryer basket. Adjust the temperature to 350ºF (177ºC) and air fry for 15 minutes. Peppers will be tender and cheese will be melted when done. Serve warm.

Per Serving:

calories: 309 | fat: 23g | protein: 16g | carbs: 11g | net carbs: 7g | fiber: 4g

Cauliflower Tikka Masala

Prep time: 10 minutes | Cook time: 20 minutes | Serves 4

➢ For The Cauliflower
➢ 1 head cauliflower, cut into small florets
➢ 1 tablespoon coconut oil, melted
➢ 1 teaspoon ground cumin
➢ ½ teaspoon ground coriander
➢ For The Sauce
➢ 2 tablespoons coconut oil
➢ ½ onion, chopped
➢ 1 tablespoon minced garlic
➢ 1 tablespoon grated ginger
➢ 2 tablespoons garam masala
➢ 1 tablespoon tomato paste
➢ ½ teaspoon salt
➢ 1 cup crushed tomatoes
➢ 1 cup heavy (whipping) cream
➢ 1 tablespoon chopped fresh cilantro

Make The Cauliflower: 1. Preheat the oven. Set the oven temperature to 425°F. Line a baking sheet with aluminum foil. 2. Prepare the cauliflower. In a large bowl, toss the cauliflower with the coconut oil, cumin, and coriander. Spread the cauliflower on the baking sheet in a single layer and bake it for 20 minutes, until the cauliflower is tender. Make The Sauce: 1. Sauté the vegetables. While the cauliflower is baking, in a large skillet over medium-high heat, warm the coconut oil. Add the onion, garlic, and ginger and sauté until they've softened, about 3 minutes. 2. Finish the sauce. Stir in the garam masala, tomato paste, and salt until the vegetables are coated. Stir in the crushed tomatoes and bring to a boil, then reduce the heat to low and simmer the sauce for 10 minutes, stirring it often. Remove the skillet from the heat and stir in the cream and cilantro. 3. Assemble and serve. Add the cauliflower to the sauce, stirring to combine everything. Divide the mixture between four bowls and serve it hot.

Per Serving:

calories: 372 | fat: 32g | protein: 8g | carbs: 17g | net carbs: 10g | fiber:

7g

Crispy Eggplant Rounds

Prep time: 15 minutes | Cook time: 10 minutes | Serves 4

- ➤ 1 large eggplant, ends trimmed, cut into ½-inch slices
- ➤ ½ teaspoon salt
- ➤ 2 ounces (57 g) Parmesan 100% cheese crisps, finely ground
- ➤ ½ teaspoon paprika
- ➤ ¼ teaspoon garlic powder
- ➤ 1 large egg

1. Sprinkle eggplant rounds with salt. Place rounds on a kitchen towel for 30 minutes to draw out excess water. Pat rounds dry. 2. In a medium bowl, mix cheese crisps, paprika, and garlic powder. In a separate medium bowl, whisk egg. Dip each eggplant round in egg, then gently press into cheese crisps to coat both sides. 3. Place eggplant rounds into ungreased air fryer basket. Adjust the temperature to 400ºF (204ºC) and air fry for 10 minutes, turning rounds halfway through cooking. Eggplant will be golden and crispy when done. Serve warm.

Per Serving:

calories: 133 | fat: 8g | protein: 10g | carbs: 6g | net carbs: 4g | fiber: 3g

Greek Stuffed Eggplant

Prep time: 15 minutes | Cook time: 20 minutes | Serves 2

- ➤ 1 large eggplant
- ➤ 2 tablespoons unsalted butter
- ➤ ¼ medium yellow onion, diced
- ➤ ¼ cup chopped artichoke hearts
- ➤ 1 cup fresh spinach
- ➤ 2 tablespoons diced red bell pepper
- ➤ ½ cup crumbled feta

1. Slice eggplant in half lengthwise and scoop out flesh, leaving enough inside for shell to remain intact. Take eggplant that was scooped out, chop it, and set aside. 2. In a medium skillet over medium heat, add butter and onion. Sauté until onions begin to soften, about 3 to 5 minutes. Add chopped eggplant, artichokes, spinach, and bell pepper. Continue cooking 5 minutes until peppers soften and

spinach wilts. Remove from the heat and gently fold in the feta. 3. Place filling into each eggplant shell and place into the air fryer basket. 4. Adjust the temperature to 320ºF (160ºC) and air fry for 20 minutes. 5. Eggplant will be tender when done. Serve warm.

Per Serving:

calories: 275 | fat: 20g | protein: 9g | carbs: 17g | net carbs: 13g | fiber: 4g

Pesto Vegetable Skewers

Prep time: 30 minutes | Cook time: 8 minutes | Makes 8 skewers

- ➤ 1 medium zucchini, trimmed and cut into ½-inch slices
- ➤ ½ medium yellow onion, peeled and cut into 1-inch squares
- ➤ 1 medium red bell pepper, seeded and cut into 1-inch squares
- ➤ 16 whole cremini mushrooms
- ➤ ⅓ cup basil pesto
- ➤ ½ teaspoon salt
- ➤ ¼ teaspoon ground black pepper

1. Divide zucchini slices, onion, and bell pepper into eight even portions. Place on 6-inch skewers for a total of eight kebabs. Add 2 mushrooms to each skewer and brush kebabs generously with pesto. 2. Sprinkle each kebab with salt and black pepper on all sides, then place into ungreased air fryer basket. Adjust the temperature to 375ºF (191ºC) and air fry for 8 minutes, turning kebabs halfway through cooking. Vegetables will be browned at the edges and tender-crisp when done. Serve warm.

Per Serving:

calories: 50 | fat: 4g | protein: 2g | carbs: 4g | net carbs: 3g | fiber: 1g

Loaded Cauliflower Steak

Prep time: 5 minutes | Cook time: 7 minutes | Serves 4

- ➤ 1 medium head cauliflower
- ➤ ¼ cup hot sauce
- ➤ 2 tablespoons salted butter, melted
- ➤ ¼ cup blue cheese crumbles
- ➤ ¼ cup full-fat ranch dressing

1. Remove cauliflower leaves. Slice the head in ½-inch-thick slices. 2. In a small bowl, mix hot sauce and butter. Brush the mixture over the

cauliflower. 3. Place each cauliflower steak into the air fryer, working in batches if necessary. 4. Adjust the temperature to 400°F (204°C) and air fry for 7 minutes. 5. When cooked, edges will begin turning dark and caramelized. 6. To serve, sprinkle steaks with crumbled blue cheese. Drizzle with ranch dressing.

Per Serving:

calories: 140 | fat: 12g | protein: 5g | carbs: 6g | net carbs: 5g | fiber: 1g

Parmesan Artichokes

Prep time: 10 minutes | Cook time: 10 minutes | Serves 4

- ➤ 2 medium artichokes, trimmed and quartered, center removed
- ➤ 2 tablespoons coconut oil
- ➤ 1 large egg, beaten
- ➤ ½ cup grated vegetarian Parmesan cheese
- ➤ ¼ cup blanched finely ground almond flour
- ➤ ½ teaspoon crushed red pepper flakes

1. In a large bowl, toss artichokes in coconut oil and then dip each piece into the egg. 2. Mix the Parmesan and almond flour in a large bowl. Add artichoke pieces and toss to cover as completely as possible, sprinkle with pepper flakes. Place into the air fryer basket. 3. Adjust the temperature to 400°F (204°C) and air fry for 10 minutes. 4. Toss the basket two times during cooking. Serve warm.

Per Serving:

calories: 220 | fat: 18g | protein: 10g | carbs: 9g | net carbs: 4g | fiber: 5g

Greek Vegetable Briam

Prep time: 10 minutes | Cook time: 30 minutes | Serves 4

- ➤ ⅓ cup good-quality olive oil, divided
- ➤ 1 onion, thinly sliced
- ➤ 1 tablespoon minced garlic
- ➤ ¾ small eggplant, diced
- ➤ 2 zucchini, diced
- ➤ 2 cups chopped cauliflower
- ➤ 1 red bell pepper, diced
- ➤ 2 cups diced tomatoes

- ➤ 2 tablespoons chopped fresh parsley
- ➤ 2 tablespoons chopped fresh oregano
- ➤ Sea salt, for seasoning
- ➤ Freshly ground black pepper, for seasoning
- ➤ 1½ cups crumbled feta cheese
- ➤ ¼ cup pumpkin seeds

1. Preheat the oven. Set the oven to broil and lightly grease a 9-by-13-inch casserole dish with olive oil. 2. Sauté the aromatics. In a medium stockpot over medium heat, warm 3 tablespoons of the olive oil. Add the onion and garlic and sauté until they've softened, about 3 minutes. 3. Sauté the vegetables. Stir in the eggplant and cook for 5 minutes, stirring occasionally. Add the zucchini, cauliflower, and red bell pepper and cook for 5 minutes. Stir in the tomatoes, parsley, and oregano and cook, giving it a stir from time to time, until the vegetables are tender, about 10 minutes. Season it with salt and pepper. 4. Broil. Transfer the vegetable mixture to the casserole dish and top with the crumbled feta. Broil for about 4 minutes until the cheese is golden. 5. Serve. Divide the casserole between four plates and top it with the pumpkin seeds. Drizzle with the remaining olive oil.

Per Serving:

calories: 356 | fat: 28g | protein: 11g | carbs: 18g | net carbs: 11g | fiber: 7g

Basic Spaghetti Squash

Prep time: 10 minutes | Cook time: 45 minutes | Serves 2

- ➤ ½ large spaghetti squash
- ➤ 1 tablespoon coconut oil
- ➤ 2 tablespoons salted butter, melted
- ➤ ½ teaspoon garlic powder
- ➤ 1 teaspoon dried parsley

1. Brush shell of spaghetti squash with coconut oil. Place the skin side down and brush the inside with butter. Sprinkle with garlic powder and parsley. 2. Place squash with the skin side down into the air fryer basket. 3. Adjust the temperature to 350°F (177°C) and air fry for 30 minutes. 4. Flip the squash so skin side is up and cook an additional 15 minutes or until fork tender. Serve warm.

Per Serving:

calories: 180 | fat: 17g | protein: 1g | carbs: 8g | net carbs: 5g | fiber: 3g

CHAPTER 7 Stews and Soups

"Dolla Store" Pumpkin Soup

Prep time: 15 minutes | Cook time: 25 minutes | Serves 8

- 2 (9 ounces) packages soy chorizo
- 6 cups chicken bone broth
- ½ (15 ounces) can pure pumpkin
- 2 cups cooked riced cauliflower
- 1 cup unsweetened coconut milk
- 1 teaspoon garlic powder
- 1 teaspoon ground cinnamon
- 1 teaspoon ground ginger
- 1 teaspoon ground nutmeg
- 1 teaspoon paprika
- ⅛ teaspoon salt
- ⅛ teaspoon black pepper

1. Place a medium soup pot over medium heat and add all ingredients. Bring to boil while stirring regularly (5 to 10 minutes). 2. Reduce heat. Let simmer 15 minutes, stirring regularly until desired consistency achieved. 3. Remove from heat, let cool 5 minutes, and serve.

Per Serving:

calories: 237| fat: 15g | protein: 17g | carbs: 13g | net carbs: 8g | fiber: 5g

Slow Cooker Beer Soup with Cheddar & Sausage

Prep time: 15 minutes | Cook time: 8 hours | Serves 8

- 1 cup heavy cream
- 10 ounces sausages, sliced
- 1 cup celery, chopped
- 1 cup carrots, chopped
- 4 garlic cloves, minced
- 8 ounces cream cheese
- 1 teaspoon red pepper flakes
- 6 ounces beer
- 16 ounces beef stock
- 1 onion, diced
- 1 cup cheddar cheese, grated

- Salt and black pepper, to taste
- Fresh cilantro, chopped, to garnish

1. Turn on the slow cooker. Add beef stock, beer, sausages, carrots, onion, garlic, celery, salt, red pepper flakes, and black pepper, and stir to combine. Pour in enough water to cover all the ingredients by roughly 2 inches. Close the lid and cook for 6 hours on Low. 2. Open the lid and stir in the heavy cream, cheddar, and cream cheese, and cook for 2 more hours. Ladle the soup into bowls and garnish with cilantro before serving. Yummy!

Per Serving:

calories: 387| fat: 28g | protein: 24g | carbs: 12g | net carbs: 9g | fiber: 2g

Beef Meatball Minestrone

Prep time: 5 minutes | Cook time: 35 minutes | Serves 6

- 1 pound (454 g) ground beef
- 1 large egg
- 1½ tablespoons golden flaxseed meal
- ⅓ cup shredded Mozzarella cheese
- ¼ cup unsweetened tomato purée
- 1½ tablespoons Italian seasoning, divided
- 1½ teaspoons garlic powder, divided
- 1½ teaspoons sea salt, divided
- 1 tablespoon olive oil
- 2 garlic cloves, minced
- ½ medium yellow onion, minced
- ¼ cup pancetta, diced
- 1 cup sliced yellow squash
- 1 cup sliced zucchini
- ½ cup sliced turnips
- 4 cups beef broth
- 14 ounces (397 g) can diced tomatoes
- ½ teaspoon ground black pepper
- 3 tablespoons shredded Parmesan cheese

1. Preheat the oven to 400°F (205°C) and line a large baking sheet with aluminum foil. 2. In a large bowl, combine the ground beef, egg, flaxseed meal, Mozzarella, unsweetened tomato purée, ½ tablespoon of Italian seasoning, ½ teaspoon of garlic powder, and ½ teaspoon of

sea salt. Mix the ingredients until well combined. 3. Make the meatballs by shaping 1 heaping tablespoon of the ground beef mixture into a meatball. Repeat with the remaining mixture and then transfer the meatballs to the prepared baking sheet. 4. Place the meatballs in the oven and bake for 15 minutes. When the baking time is complete, remove from the oven and set aside. 5. Select Sauté mode of the Instant Pot. Once the pot is hot, add the olive oil, garlic, onion, and pancetta. Sauté for 2 minutes or until the garlic becomes fragrant and the onions begin to soften. 6. Add the yellow squash, zucchini, and turnips to the pot. Sauté for 3 more minutes. 7. Add the beef broth, diced tomatoes, black pepper, and remaining garlic powder, sea salt, and Italian seasoning to the pot. Stir to combine and then add the meatballs. 8. Lock the lid. Select Manual mode and set cooking time for 15 minutes on High Pressure. 9. When cooking is complete, allow the pressure to release naturally for 10 minutes and then release the remaining pressure. 10. Open the lid and gently stir the soup. Ladle into serving bowls and top with Parmesan. Serve hot.

Per Serving:

calories: 373 | fat: 19g | protein: 35g | carbs: 15g | net carbs: 11g | fiber: 4g

Shrimp Chowder

Prep time: 10 minutes | Cook time: 40 minutes | Serves 6

- ¼ cup (60 ml) refined avocado oil or melted ghee (if tolerated)
- 1⅓ cups (140 g) diced mushrooms
- ⅓ cup (55 g) diced yellow onions
- 10½ ounces (300 g) small raw shrimp, shelled and deveined
- 1 can (13½ ounces/400 ml) full-fat coconut milk
- ⅓ cup (80 ml) chicken bone broth
- 2 tablespoons apple cider vinegar
- 1 teaspoon onion powder
- 1 teaspoon paprika
- 1 bay leaf
- ¾ teaspoon finely ground gray sea salt
- ½ teaspoon dried oregano leaves
- ¼ teaspoon ground black pepper
- 12 radishes (about 6 ounces/170 g), cubed
- 1 medium zucchini (about 7 ounces/200 g), cubed

1. Heat the avocado oil in a large saucepan on medium for a couple of minutes, then add the mushrooms and onions. Sauté for 8 to 10 minutes, until the onions are translucent and mushrooms are beginning to brown. 2. Add the remaining ingredients, except the radishes and zucchini. Cover and bring to a boil, then reduce the heat to low and simmer for 20 minutes. 3. After 20 minutes, add the radishes and zucchini. Continue to cook for 10 minutes, until the vegetables are fork-tender. 4. Remove the bay leaf, divide among 6 small soup bowls, and enjoy.

Per Serving:

calories: 301 | fat: 23g | protein: 14g | carbs: 7g | net carbs: 5g | fiber: 2g

Bacon Cheddar Cauliflower Soup

Prep time: 15 minutes | Cook time: 30 minutes | Serves 6

- 1 large head cauliflower, chopped into florets
- ¼ cup olive oil
- Salt and freshly ground black pepper, to taste
- 12 ounces (340 g) bacon, chopped
- ½ onion, roughly chopped
- 2 garlic cloves, minced
- 2 cups chicken broth, or vegetable broth, plus more as needed
- 2 cups heavy (whipping) cream, plus more as needed
- ½ cup shredded Cheddar cheese, plus more for topping
- Sliced scallion, green parts only, or fresh chives, for garnish

1. Preheat the oven to 400ºF (205ºC). 2. On a large rimmed baking sheet, toss the cauliflower with the olive oil and season with salt and pepper. Bake for 25 to 30 minutes or until slightly browned. 3. While the cauliflower roasts, in a large saucepan over medium heat, cook the bacon for 5 to 7 minutes until crispy. Transfer the bacon to a paper towel-lined plate to drain; leave the bacon fat in the pan. 4. Return the pan to medium heat and add the onion and garlic. Stir well to combine and sauté for 5 to 7 minutes until the onion is softened and translucent. Season with salt and pepper. 5. Remove the cauliflower from the oven and add it to the pan with the onion and garlic. Stir in the broth and bring the liquid to a simmer. Reduce the heat to low.

Cook for 5 to 7 minutes. Remove from the heat. With an immersion blender, carefully blend the soup. Alternatively, transfer the soup to a regular blender (working in batches if necessary), blend until smooth, and return the soup to the pan. 6. Stir in the cream. You may need to add a bit more broth or cream, depending on how thick you like your soup. Add the Cheddar and stir until melted and combined. Spoon the soup into bowls and top with bacon and more Cheddar. Garnish with scallion.

Per Serving:

1 cup: calories: 545 | fat: 49g | protein: 15g | carbs: 11g | net carbs: 7g | fiber: 4g

Beef and Cauliflower Soup

Prep time: 10 minutes | Cook time: 14 minutes | Serves 4

- 1 cup ground beef
- ½ cup cauliflower, shredded
- 1 teaspoon unsweetened tomato purée
- ¼ cup coconut milk
- 1 teaspoon minced garlic
- 1 teaspoon dried oregano
- ½ teaspoon salt
- 4 cups water

1. Put all ingredients in the Instant Pot and stir well. 2. Close the lid. Select Manual mode and set cooking time for 14 minutes on High Pressure. 3. When timer beeps, make a quick pressure release and open the lid. 4. Blend with an immersion blender until smooth. 5. Serve warm.

Per Serving:

calories: 106 | fat: 8g | protein: 7g | carbs: 2g | net carbs: 1g | fiber: 1g

Chicken Enchilada Soup

Prep time: 10 minutes | Cook time: 40 minutes | Serves 6

- 2 (6-ounce / 170-g) boneless, skinless chicken breasts
- ½ tablespoon chili powder
- ½ teaspoon salt
- ½ teaspoon garlic powder
- ¼ teaspoon pepper
- ½ cup red enchilada sauce
- ½ medium onion, diced

- 1 (4-ounce / 113-g) can green chilies
- 2 cups chicken broth
- ⅛ cup pickled jalapeños
- 4 ounces (113 g) cream cheese
- 1 cup uncooked cauliflower rice
- 1 avocado, diced
- 1 cup shredded mild Cheddar cheese
- ½ cup sour cream

1. Sprinkle seasoning over chicken breasts and set aside. Pour enchilada sauce into Instant Pot and place chicken on top. 2. Add onion, chilies, broth, and jalapeños to the pot, then place cream cheese on top of chicken breasts. Click lid closed. Adjust time for 25 minutes. When timer beeps, quick-release the pressure and shred chicken with forks. 3. Mix soup together and add cauliflower rice, with pot on Keep Warm setting. Replace lid and let pot sit for 15 minutes, still on Keep Warm. This will cook cauliflower rice. Serve with avocado, Cheddar, and sour cream.

Per Serving:

calories: 318 | fat: 19g | protein: 21g | carbs: 10g | net carbs: 7g | fiber: 3g

Bacon Soup

Prep time: 10 minutes | Cook time: 1 hour 20 minutes | Serves 6

- ⅓ cup (69 g) lard
- 1 pound (455 g) pork stewing pieces
- ¾ cup (110 g) sliced shallots

10 strips bacon (about 10 ounces/285 g), cut into about ½-inch (1.25-cm) pieces

- 1¾ cups (415 ml) chicken bone broth
- 3 medium turnips (about 12½ ounces/355 g), cubed
- ¼ cup (60 ml) white wine, such as Pinot Grigio, Sauvignon Blanc, or
- unoaked Chardonnay
- 1 tablespoon prepared yellow mustard
- 4 sprigs fresh thyme
- ½ cup (120 ml) full-fat coconut milk
- 2 tablespoons apple cider vinegar
- 2 tablespoons unflavored gelatin
- 1 tablespoon dried tarragon leaves

1. Melt the lard in a large saucepan over medium heat. Once the lard

has melted, add the pork pieces and cook for 8 minutes, or until lightly browned on the outside. 2. Add the sliced shallots and bacon pieces. Sauté for an additional 5 minutes or until the shallots become fragrant. 3. Add the bone broth, turnips, wine, mustard, and thyme sprigs. Cover and bring to a boil, then reduce the heat to medium-low and cook until the meat and turnips are fork-tender, about 1 hour. 4. Remove the thyme sprigs and add the coconut milk, vinegar, gelatin, and tarragon. Increase the heat to medium and boil, covered, for another 10 minutes. 5. Divide the soup among 6 small bowls and serve.

Per Serving:

calories: 571 | fat: 41g | protein: 40g | carbs: 10g | net carbs: 9g | fiber: 1g

Chicken Poblano Pepper Soup

Prep time: 10 minutes | Cook time: 20 minutes | Serves 8

- ➢ 1 cup diced onion
- ➢ 3 poblano peppers, chopped
- ➢ 5 garlic cloves
- ➢ 2 cups diced cauliflower
- ➢ 1½ pounds (680 g) chicken breast, cut into large chunks
- ➢ ¼ cup chopped fresh cilantro
- ➢ 1 teaspoon ground coriander
- ➢ 1 teaspoon ground cumin
- ➢ 1 to 2 teaspoons salt
- ➢ 2 cups water
- ➢ 2 ounces (57 g) cream cheese, cut into small chunks
- ➢ 1 cup sour cream

1. To the inner cooking pot of the Instant Pot, add the onion, poblanos, garlic, cauliflower, chicken, cilantro, coriander, cumin, salt, and water. 2. Lock the lid into place. Select Manual and adjust the pressure to High. Cook for 15 minutes. When the cooking is complete, let the pressure release naturally for 10 minutes, then quick-release any remaining pressure. Unlock the lid. 3. Remove the chicken with tongs and place in a bowl. 4. Tilting the pot, use an immersion blender to roughly purée the vegetable mixture. It should still be slightly chunky. 5. Turn the Instant Pot to Sauté and adjust to high heat. When the broth is hot and bubbling, add the cream cheese and stir until it melts. Use a whisk to blend in the cream cheese if needed. 6. Shred the

chicken and stir it back into the pot. Once it is heated through, serve, topped with sour cream, and enjoy.

Per Serving:

calories: 202 | fat: 10g | protein: 20g | carbs: 8g | net carbs: 5g | fiber: 3g

Spicy Sausage and Chicken Stew

Prep time: 10 minutes | Cook time: 25 minutes | Serves 10

- ➢ 1 tablespoon coconut oil
- ➢ 2 pounds (907 g) bulk Italian sausage
- ➢ 2 boneless, skinless chicken thighs, cut into ½-inch pieces
- ➢ ½ cup chopped onions
- ➢ 1 (28 ounces / 794 g) can whole peeled tomatoes, drained
- ➢ 1 cup sugar-free tomato sauce
- ➢ 1 (4½ ounces / 128 g) can green chilies
- ➢ 3 tablespoons minced garlic
- ➢ 2 tablespoons smoked paprika
- ➢ 1 tablespoon ground cumin
- ➢ 1 tablespoon dried oregano leaves
- ➢ 2 teaspoons fine sea salt
- ➢ 1 teaspoon cayenne pepper
- ➢ 1 cup chicken broth
- ➢ 1 ounce (28 g) unsweetened baking chocolate, chopped
- ➢ ¼ cup lime juice
- ➢ Chopped fresh cilantro leaves, for garnish
- ➢ Red pepper flakes, for garnish

1. Place the coconut oil in the Instant Pot and press Sauté. Once melted, add the sausage, chicken, and onions and cook, stirring to break up the sausage, until the sausage is starting to cook through and the onions are soft, about 5 minutes. 2. Meanwhile, make the tomato purée: Place the tomatoes, tomato sauce, and chilies in a food processor and process until smooth. 3. Add the garlic, paprika, cumin, oregano, salt, and cayenne pepper to the Instant Pot and stir to combine. Then add the tomato purée, broth, and chocolate and stir well. Press Cancel to stop the Sauté. 4. Seal the lid, press Manual, and set the timer for 20 minutes. Once finished, let the pressure release naturally. 5. Just before serving, stir in the lime juice. Ladle the stew into bowls and garnish with cilantro and red pepper flakes.

Per Serving:

calories: 341 | fat: 23g | protein: 21g | carbs: 10g | net carbs: 8g | fiber: 2g

Summer Vegetable Soup

Prep time: 10 minutes | Cook time: 6 minutes | Serves 6

- 3 cups finely sliced leeks
- 6 cups chopped rainbow chard, stems and leaves separated
- 1 cup chopped celery
- 2 tablespoons minced garlic, divided
- 1 teaspoon dried oregano
- 1 teaspoon salt
- 2 teaspoons freshly ground black pepper
- 3 cups chicken broth, plus more as needed
- 2 cups sliced yellow summer squash, ½-inch slices
- ¼ cup chopped fresh parsley
- ¾ cup heavy (whipping) cream
- 4 to 6 tablespoons grated Parmesan cheese

1. Put the leeks, chard, celery, 1 tablespoon of garlic, oregano, salt, pepper, and broth into the inner cooking pot of the Instant Pot. 2. Lock the lid into place. Select Manual and adjust the pressure to High. Cook for 3 minutes. When the cooking is complete, quick-release the pressure. Unlock the lid. 3. Add more broth if needed. 4. Turn the pot to Sauté and adjust the heat to high. Add the yellow squash, parsley, and remaining 1 tablespoon of garlic. 5. Allow the soup to cook for 2 to 3 minutes, or until the squash is softened and cooked through. 6. Stir in the cream and ladle the soup into bowls. Sprinkle with the Parmesan cheese and serve.

Per Serving:

calories: 210 | fat: 14g | protein: 10g | carbs: 12g | net carbs: 8g | fiber: 4g

Cabbage Roll Soup

Prep time: 10 minutes | Cook time: 8 minutes | Serves 4

- ½ pound (227 g) 84% lean ground pork
- ½ pound (227 g) 85% lean ground beef
- ½ medium onion, diced
- ½ medium head cabbage, thinly sliced

- 2 tablespoons sugar-free tomato paste
- ½ cup diced tomatoes
- 2 cups chicken broth
- 1 teaspoon salt
- ½ teaspoon thyme
- ½ teaspoon garlic powder
- ¼ teaspoon pepper

1. Press the Sauté button and add beef and pork to Instant Pot. Brown meat until no pink remains. Add onion and continue cooking until onions are fragrant and soft. Press the Cancel button. 2. Add remaining ingredients to Instant Pot. Press the Manual button and adjust time for 8 minutes. 3. When timer beeps, allow a 15-minute natural release and then quick-release the remaining pressure. Serve warm.

Per Serving:

calories: 304 | fat: 16g | protein: 24g | carbs: 12g | net carbs: 8g | fiber: 4g

Swiss Chard and Chicken Soup

Prep time: 10 minutes | Cook time: 5 minutes | Serves 4

- 1 onion, chopped
- 6 garlic cloves, peeled
- 1 (2-inch) piece fresh ginger, chopped
- 1 (10-ounce / 283-g) can tomatoes with chiles
- 1½ cups full-fat coconut milk, divided
- 1 tablespoon powdered chicken broth base
- 1 pound (454 g) boneless chicken thighs, cut into large bite-size pieces
- 1½ cups chopped celery
- 2 cups chopped Swiss chard
- 1 teaspoon ground turmeric

1. To a blender jar, add the onion, garlic, ginger, tomatoes, ½ cup of coconut milk, and chicken broth base. Purée the ingredients into a sauce. 2. Pour the mixture into the inner cooking pot of the Instant Pot. Add the chicken, celery, and chard. 3. Lock the lid into place. Select Manual and adjust the pressure to High. Cook for 5 minutes. When the cooking is complete, let the pressure release naturally for 10 minutes, then quick-release any remaining pressure. 4. Unlock the lid and add the remaining 1 cup of coconut milk and turmeric. Stir to heat through and serve.

Per Serving:

calories: 338 | fat: 22g | protein: 25g | carbs: 10g | net carbs: 7g | fiber: 3g

Beef and Eggplant Tagine

Prep time: 15 minutes | Cook time: 25 minutes | Serves 6

- ➤ 1 pound (454 g) beef fillet, chopped
- ➤ 1 eggplant, chopped
- ➤ 6 ounces (170 g) scallions, chopped
- ➤ 4 cups beef broth
- ➤ 1 teaspoon ground allspices
- ➤ 1 teaspoon erythritol
- ➤ 1 teaspoon coconut oil

1. Put all ingredients in the Instant Pot. Stir to mix well. 2. Close the lid. Select Manual mode and set cooking time for 25 minutes on High Pressure. 3. When timer beeps, use a natural pressure release for 15 minutes, then release any remaining pressure. Open the lid. 4. Serve warm.

Per Serving:

calories: 158 | fat: 5g | protein: 21g | carbs: 8g | net carbs: 5g | fiber: 4g

Cream of Mushroom Soup

Prep time: 10 minutes | Cook time: 10 minutes | Serves 4

- ➤ 1 pound (454 g) sliced button mushrooms
- ➤ 3 tablespoons butter
- ➤ 2 tablespoons diced onion
- ➤ 2 cloves garlic, minced
- ➤ 2 cups chicken broth
- ➤ ½ teaspoon salt
- ➤ ¼ teaspoon pepper
- ➤ ½ cup heavy cream
- ➤ ¼ teaspoon xanthan gum

1. Press the Sauté button and then press the Adjust button to set heat to Less. Add mushrooms, butter, and onion to pot. Sauté for 5 to 8 minutes or until onions and mushrooms begin to brown. Add garlic and sauté until fragrant. Press the Cancel button. 2. Add broth, salt, and pepper. Click lid closed. Press the Manual button and adjust time for 3 minutes. When timer beeps, quick-release the pressure. Stir in heavy cream and xanthan gum. Allow a few minutes to thicken and serve warm.

Per Serving:

calories: 220 | fat: 19g | protein: 5g | carbs: 6g | net carbs: 5g | fiber: 1g

Easy Chili

Prep time: 10 minutes | Cook time: 35 minutes | Serves 6 to 8

- ➤ 2 pounds ground beef
- ➤ 2 tablespoons dried minced onions
- ➤ 2 teaspoons minced garlic
- ➤ 1 (15 ounces) can tomato sauce
- ➤ 1 (14½ ounces) can petite diced tomatoes
- ➤ 1 cup water
- ➤ 2 tablespoons chili powder
- ➤ 1 tablespoon ground cumin
- ➤ ½ teaspoon salt
- ➤ ½ teaspoon ground black pepper
- ➤ Suggested Toppings:
- ➤ Sour cream
- ➤ Sliced green onions or chopped white onions
- ➤ Shredded cheddar cheese

1. Cook the ground beef, onions, and garlic in a stockpot over medium heat, crumbling the meat with a large spoon as it cooks, until the meat is browned, about 10 minutes. Drain the fat, if necessary. 2. Add the tomato sauce, tomatoes, water, chili powder, cumin, salt, and pepper to the pot. Bring to a boil, then reduce the heat to low and simmer for 20 minutes to allow the flavors to develop and the chili to thicken slightly. 3. Garnish with the chili topping(s) of your choice and serve. Leftovers can be stored in an airtight container in the refrigerator for up to 5 days.

Per Serving:

calories: 429 | fat: 31g | protein: 27g | carbs: 9g | net carbs: 6g | fiber: 3g

Loaded Cauliflower Soup

Prep time: 5 minutes | Cook time: 25 minutes | Serves 3

- ➤ 2 bacon strips, roughly chopped
- ➤ ¼ medium onion, chopped
- ➤ 1½ cups chicken broth
- ➤ 1½ cups chopped cauliflower florets
- ➤ ½ teaspoon pink Himalayan sea salt

- ➤ ½ teaspoon freshly ground black pepper
- ➤ ¼ teaspoon garlic powder
- ➤ 1 cup heavy (whipping) cream
- ➤ 1 cup shredded Cheddar cheese
- ➤ 3 tablespoons sour cream
- ➤ 2 tablespoons chopped fresh chives

1. In a medium saucepan, cook the bacon over medium-high heat for 8 to 10 minutes, until crispy. Transfer the bacon to a paper towel-lined plate. 2. Add the onion to the saucepan and cook for 8 to 10 minutes, until tender. 3. Add the broth, cauliflower, salt, pepper, and garlic powder. Bring to a simmer and cook for about 5 minutes, until the cauliflower is tender. 4. Reduce the heat and stir in the cream. Slowly stir in the cheese. 5. Divide the soup among 3 serving bowls. Top each bowl with 1 tablespoon of sour cream and equal portions of the bacon crumbles and chives.

Per Serving:

calories: 510 | fat: 48g | protein: 15g | carbs: 7g | net carbs: 6g | fiber: 1g

Slow Cooker Taco Bell Soup

Prep time: 20 minutes | Cook time: 2 hours 20 minutes | Serves 8

- ➤ 2 pounds lean ground beef
- ➤ 1 medium onion, peeled and chopped
- ➤ 2 cloves garlic, peeled and minced
- ➤ 6 cups beef broth
- ➤ 2 cups water
- ➤ 8 ounces full-fat cream cheese, cubed
- ➤ ½ cup finely chopped cilantro
- ➤ 2 (4-ounce) cans diced green chilies, drained
- ➤ 2 tablespoons taco seasoning

1. In a medium skillet over medium heat, brown ground beef 10–15 minutes while stirring. Drain fat. Add onion and garlic. Sauté 5 minutes. 2. Add meat mixture to slow cooker along with rest of ingredients. 3. Cover with lid and cook 2 hours on high or 4 hours on low. 4. Let cool 10 minutes and then serve.

Per Serving:

calories: 307| fat: 16g | protein: 26g | carbs: 6g | net carbs: 4g | fiber: 2g

New England Clam Chowder

Prep time: 10 minutes | Cook time: 30

minutes | Serves 8

- ➤ ¼ pound uncured bacon, chopped
- ➤ 2 tablespoons grass-fed butter
- ➤ ½ onion, finely chopped
- ➤ 1 celery stalk, chopped
- ➤ 2 teaspoons minced garlic
- ➤ 2 tablespoons arrowroot
- ➤ 4 cups fish or chicken stock
- ➤ 1 teaspoon chopped fresh thyme
- ➤ 2 bay leaves
- ➤ 3 (6½-ounce) cans clams, drained
- ➤ 1½ cups heavy (whipping) cream
- ➤ Sea salt, for seasoning
- ➤ Freshly ground black pepper, for seasoning
- ➤ 2 tablespoons chopped fresh parsley

1. Cook the bacon. In a medium stockpot over medium-high heat, fry the bacon until it's crispy. Transfer the bacon with a slotted spoon to a plate and set it aside. 2. Sauté the vegetables. Melt the butter in the stockpot, add the onion, celery, and garlic and sauté them until they've softened, about 3 minutes. Whisk in the arrowroot and cook for 1 minute. Add the stock, thyme, and bay leaves and bring the soup to just before it boils. Then reduce the heat to medium-low and simmer until the soup thickens, about 10 minutes. 3. Finish the soup. Stir in the clams and cream and simmer the soup until it's heated through, about 5 minutes. Find and throw out the bay leaves. 4. Serve. Season the chowder with salt and pepper. Ladle it into bowls, garnish with the parsley, and crumbles of the bacon, then serve.

Per Serving:

calories: 384 | fat: 28g | protein: 23g | carbs: 6g | net carbs: 6g | fiber: 2g

Kale Curry Soup

Prep time: 10 minutes | Cook time: 15 minutes | Serves 3

- ➤ 2 cups kale
- ➤ 1 teaspoon almond butter
- ➤ 1 tablespoon fresh cilantro
- ➤ ½ cup ground chicken
- ➤ 1 teaspoon curry paste
- ➤ ½ cup heavy cream
- ➤ 1 cup chicken stock
- ➤ ½ teaspoon salt

1. Put the kale in the Instant Pot. 2. Add the almond butter, cilantro, and ground chicken. Sauté the mixture for 5 minutes. 3. Meanwhile, mix the curry paste and heavy cream in the Instant Pot until creamy. 4. Add chicken stock and salt, and close the lid. 5. Select Manual mode and set cooking time for 10 minutes on High Pressure. 6. When timer beeps, make a quick pressure release. Open the lid. 7. Serve warm.

Per Serving:

calories: 183 | fat: 13g | protein: 10g | carbs: 7g | net carbs: 6g | fiber: 1g

Cauliflower Soup

Prep time: 10 minutes | Cook time: 6 minutes | Serves 4

➢ 2 cups chopped cauliflower
➢ 2 tablespoons fresh cilantro
➢ 1 cup coconut cream
➢ 2 cups beef broth
➢ 3 ounces (85 g) Provolone cheese, chopped

1. Put cauliflower, cilantro, coconut cream, beef broth, and cheese in the Instant Pot. Stir to mix well. 2. Select Manual mode and set cooking time for 6 minutes on High Pressure. 3. When timer beeps, allow a natural pressure release for 4 minutes, then release any remaining pressure. Open the lid. 4. Blend the soup and ladle in bowls to serve.

Per Serving:

calories: 244 | fat: 21g | protein: 10g | carbs: 7g | net carbs: 4g | fiber: 3g

Creamy Cauliflower Soup with Bacon Chips

Prep time: 10 minutes | Cook time: 20 minutes | Serves 4

➢ 2 tablespoon ghee
➢ 1 onion, chopped
➢ 2 head cauliflower, cut into florets
➢ 2 cups water
➢ Salt and black pepper to taste
➢ 3 cups almond milk
➢ 1 cup shredded white cheddar cheese
➢ 3 bacon strips

1. Melt the ghee in a saucepan over medium heat and sauté the onion for 3 minutes until fragrant. 2. Include the cauli florets, sauté for 3

minutes to slightly soften, add the water, and season with salt and black pepper. Bring to a boil, and then reduce the heat to low. Cover and cook for 10 minutes. Puree cauliflower with an immersion blender until the ingredients are evenly combined and stir in the almond milk and cheese until the cheese melts. Adjust taste with salt and black pepper. 3. In a non-stick skillet over high heat, fry the bacon, until crispy. Divide soup between serving bowls, top with crispy bacon, and serve hot.

Per Serving:

calories: 413 | fat: 32g | protein: 17g | carbs: 20g | net carbs: 15g | fiber: 7g

Vegan Pho

Prep time: 10 minutes | Cook time: 20 minutes | serves 8

➢ 8 cups vegetable broth
➢ 1-inch knob fresh ginger, peeled and chopped
➢ 2 tablespoons tamari
➢ 3 cups shredded fresh spinach
➢ 2 cups chopped broccoli
➢ 1 cup sliced mushrooms
➢ ½ cup chopped carrots
➢ ⅓ cup chopped scallions
➢ 1 (8-ounce) package shirataki noodles
➢ 2 cups shredded cabbage
➢ 2 cups mung bean sprouts
➢ Fresh Thai basil leaves, for garnish
➢ Fresh cilantro leaves, for garnish
➢ Fresh mint leaves, for garnish
➢ 1 lime, cut into 8 wedges, for garnish

1. In a large stockpot over medium-high heat, bring the vegetable broth to a simmer with the ginger and tamari. 2. Once the broth is hot, add the spinach, broccoli, mushrooms, carrots, and scallions, and simmer for a few minutes, just until the vegetables start to become tender. 3. Stir in the shirataki noodles, then remove the pot from the heat and divide the soup among serving bowls. 4. Top each bowl with cabbage, sprouts, basil, cilantro, mint, and a lime wedge.

Per Serving:

calories: 47 | fat: 0g | protein: 3g | carbs: 10g | net carbs: 7g | fiber: 3g

Creamy Cauliflower Soup with Chorizo Sausage

Prep time: 15 minutes | Cook time: 35 minutes | Serves 4

- ➤ 1 cauliflower head, chopped
- ➤ 1 turnip, chopped
- ➤ 3 tablespoons butter
- ➤ 1 chorizo sausage, sliced
- ➤ 2 cups chicken broth
- ➤ 1 small onion, chopped
- ➤ 2 cups water
- ➤ Salt and black pepper, to taste

1. Melt 2 tablespoons of the butter in a large pot over medium heat. Stir in onion and cook until soft and golden, about 3 to 4 minutes. Add cauliflower and turnip, and cook for another 5 minutes. Pour the broth and water over. 2.Bring to a boil, simmer covered, and cook for about 20 minutes until the vegetables are tender. Remove from heat. Melt the remaining butter in a skillet. Add the chorizo sausage and cook for 5 minutes until crispy. Puree the soup with a hand blender until smooth. Taste and adjust the seasonings. Serve the soup in deep bowls topped with the chorizo sausage.

Per Serving:

calories: 135| fat: 11g | protein: 4g | carbs: 9g | net carbs: 6g | fiber: 3g

Broc Obama Cheese Soup

Prep time: 25 minutes | Cook time: 25 minutes | Serves 8

- ➤ 8 cups chicken broth
- ➤ 2 large heads broccoli, chopped into bite-sized florets
- ➤ 1 clove garlic, peeled and minced
- ➤ ¼ cup heavy whipping cream
- ➤ ¼ cup shredded Cheddar cheese
- ➤ ⅛ teaspoon salt
- ➤ ⅛ teaspoon black pepper

1. In a medium pot over medium heat, add broth and bring to boil (about 5 minutes). Add broccoli and garlic. Reduce heat to low, cover pot, and simmer until vegetables are fully softened, about 15 minutes. 2. Remove from heat and blend using a hand immersion blender to desired consistency while still in pot. Leave some chunks of varying sizes for variety. 3. Return pot to medium heat and add cream and cheese. Stir 3 to 5 minutes until fully blended. Add salt and pepper. 4.

Remove from heat, let cool 10 minutes, and serve.

Per Serving:

calories: 82 | fat: 4g | protein: 5g | carbs: 8g | net carbs: 5g | fiber: 3g

Thai Tum Yum Soup

Prep time: 10 minutes | Cook time: 20 minutes | serves 8

- ➤ 8 cups vegetable broth
- ➤ 1-inch knob fresh ginger, peeled and diced
- ➤ 2 garlic cloves, diced
- ➤ 1 teaspoon galangal
- ➤ 2 kefir lime leaves
- ➤ 1 cup coconut cream
- ➤ 1 cup sliced mushrooms
- ➤ 1 Roma tomato, coarsely chopped
- ➤ ½ yellow onion, coarsely chopped
- ➤ 1 cup coarsely chopped broccoli
- ➤ 1 cup coarsely chopped cauliflower
- ➤ 1 cup chopped fresh cilantro, for garnish
- ➤ 1 lime, cut into wedges, for garnish

1. In a large stockpot over medium heat, bring the broth to a simmer with the ginger, garlic, galangal, and lime leaves. 2. Pour in the coconut cream, followed by the mushrooms, tomato, onion, broccoli, and cauliflower. Simmer until tender. 3. Remove the pot from the heat and serve the soup garnished with the cilantro and a lime slice.

Per Serving:

calories: 97 | fat: 7g | protein: 1g | carbs: 9g | net carbs: 6g | fiber: 3g

Coconut Curry Broccoli Soup

Prep time: 10 minutes | Cook time: 20 minutes | Serves 4

- ➤ 4 tablespoons butter
- ➤ 1 celery stalk, diced
- ➤ 1 carrot, diced
- ➤ ½ onion, diced
- ➤ 1 garlic clove, minced
- ➤ 2 tablespoons curry powder
- ➤ 1 teaspoon red pepper flakes
- ➤ 3 cups chicken broth
- ➤ 2 cups broccoli florets
- ➤ 1 cup canned coconut cream
- ➤ Salt and freshly ground black pepper, to taste

1. In a large saucepan over medium heat, melt the butter. 2. Add the celery, carrot, onion, garlic, curry powder, and red pepper flakes. Stir to combine. Sauté for 5 to 7 minutes until the vegetables soften. 3. Stir in the chicken broth and bring to a simmer. 4. Add the broccoli and simmer for 5 to 7 minutes. 5. Stir in the coconut cream and simmer for 5 to 10 minutes more until the broccoli is cooked. Season well with salt and pepper and serve hot. Refrigerate leftovers in an airtight container for up to 1 week.

Per Serving:

calories: 274 | fat: 25g | protein: 7g | carbs: 11g | net carbs: 8g | fiber: 3g

Chicken Creamy Soup

Prep time: 5 minutes | Cook time: 10 minutes | Serves 4

➤ 2cups cooked and shredded chicken

➤ 3 tablespoons butter, melted

➤ 4 cups chicken broth

➤ 4 tablespoons chopped cilantro

➤ ⅓ cup buffalo sauce

➤ ½ cup cream cheese

➤ Salt and black pepper, to taste

1. Blend the butter, buffalo sauce, and cream cheese, in a food processor, until smooth. Transfer to a pot, add chicken broth and heat until hot but do not bring to a boil. Stir in chicken, salt, black pepper and cook until heated through. When ready, remove to soup bowls and serve garnished with cilantro.

Per Serving:

calories: 480 | fat: 41g | protein: 16g | carbs: 13g | net carbs: 12g | fiber: 1g

CHAPTER 8 Desserts

Double Chocolate Brownies

Prep time: 5 minutes | Cook time: 15 to 20 minutes | Serves 8

- ➤ 1 cup almond flour
- ➤ ½ cup unsweetened cocoa powder
- ➤ ½ teaspoon baking powder
- ➤ ⅓ cup Swerve
- ➤ ¼ teaspoon salt
- ➤ ½ cup unsalted butter, melted and cooled
- ➤ 3 eggs
- ➤ 1 teaspoon vanilla extract
- ➤ 2 tablespoons mini semisweet chocolate chips

1. Preheat the air fryer to 350°F (177°C). Line a cake pan with parchment paper and brush with oil. 2. In a large bowl, combine the almond flour, cocoa powder, baking powder, Swerve, and salt. Add the butter, eggs, and vanilla. Stir until thoroughly combined. (The batter will be thick.) Spread the batter into the prepared pan and scatter the chocolate chips on top. 3. Air fry for 15 to 20 minutes until the edges are set. (The center should still appear slightly undercooked.) Let cool completely before slicing. To store, cover and refrigerate the brownies for up to 3 days.

Per Serving:

calories: 191 | fat: 17g | protein: 6g | carbs: 7g | net carbs: 3g | fiber: 4g

Rich Chocolate Mug Cake

Prep time: 5 minutes | Cook time: 2 minutes | Serves 2

- ➤ ½ cup almond flour
- ➤ 2 tablespoons coconut flour
- ➤ 2 tablespoons cocoa powder
- ➤ 1¼ teaspoons baking powder
- ➤ 1 tablespoon monk fruit sweetener, granulated form
- ➤ ¼ cup melted grass-fed butter
- ➤ 2 eggs
- ➤ ½ teaspoon vanilla extract
- ➤ ½ cup keto-friendly chocolate chips like Lily's

Dark Chocolate Chips

1. Mix the dry ingredients. In a medium bowl, stir together the almond flour, coconut flour, cocoa powder, baking powder, and sweetener. 2. Finish the batter. Stir in the melted butter, eggs, and vanilla until everything is well combined. Stir in the chocolate chips. 3. Cook and serve. Divide the batter between two large mugs and microwave them on high for 90 seconds, or until the cakes are cooked. Serve them immediately.

Per Serving:

calories: 383 | fat: 35g | protein: 11g | carbs: 12g | net carbs: 5g | fiber: 7g

Fruit Pizza

Prep time: 15 minutes | Cook time: 14 minutes | serves 8

- ➤ Crust:
- ➤ 1¼ cups finely ground blanched almond flour
- ➤ ⅓ cup granular erythritol
- ➤ 1 teaspoon baking powder
- ➤ 1 large egg
- ➤ 5 tablespoons salted butter, softened
- ➤ 1 teaspoon vanilla extract
- ➤ Toppings:
- ➤ 5 ounces cream cheese (1/2 cup plus 2 tablespoons), softened
- ➤ 2 tablespoons granular erythritol
- ➤ 1 tablespoon heavy whipping cream
- ➤ ½ cup sliced fresh strawberries or whole raspberries
- ➤ ½ cup fresh blueberries

1. Preheat the oven to 350°F and grease the bottom of a 9-inch springform pan. 2. Make the crust: In a small bowl, whisk together the almond flour, erythritol, and baking powder. In a medium-sized bowl, whisk the egg, then stir in the butter and vanilla extract. Stir in the flour mixture, a little at a time, until well combined. 3. Spread the crust mixture evenly in the prepared pan and bake for 12 to 14 minutes, until lightly browned on top and around the edges. Allow the crust to cool completely before releasing it from the pan. 4. While the crust is cooling, prepare the toppings: In a small bowl, use a spoon to

beat the cream cheese, erythritol, and cream until completely combined. Spread evenly over the cooled crust. Garnish with fresh berries. 5. Cover and refrigerate the pizza for at least 2 hours before serving. Leftovers can be stored in an airtight container in the refrigerator for up to 2 days.

Per Serving:

calories: 230 | fat: 20g | protein: 6g | carbs: 5g | net carbs: 3g | fiber: 2g

Electrolyte Gummies

Prep time: 5 minutes | Cook time: 0 minutes | Makes 10 gummies

- ➤ 1 cup cold water
- ➤ 2 tablespoons unflavored gelatin
- ➤ 2 packets/scoops flavored electrolyte powder

Stovetop Directions 1. In a small saucepan, whisk together the water and gelatin until dissolved. Heat over medium heat for about 5 minutes until it just begins to simmer. Add your flavoring of choice and whisk until well combined. 2. Pour the mixture into silicone molds and refrigerate for 30 to 40 minutes or until set. 3. Pop the gummies out of the molds and enjoy! Microwave Directions 1. Pour the water into a small microwavable bowl or measuring cup (preferably with a spout). 2. Whisk in the gelatin until dissolved and then microwave for 2 minutes or until just starting to bubble. 3. Add your flavoring of choice and whisk until well combined. 4. Pour the mixture into silicone molds and refrigerate for 30 to 40 minutes or until set. 5. Pop the gummies out of the molds and enjoy! Store in an airtight container in the refrigerator for up to 3 weeks.

Per Serving:

1 gummy: calories: 4 | fat: 0g | protein: 1g | carbs: 0g | net carbs: 0g | fiber: 0g

Fried Cheesecake Bites

Prep time: 30 minutes | Cook time: 2 minutes | Makes 16 bites

- ➤ 8 ounces (227 g) cream cheese, softened
- ➤ ½ cup plus 2 tablespoons Swerve, divided
- ➤ 4 tablespoons heavy cream, divided
- ➤ ½ teaspoon vanilla extract
- ➤ ½ cup almond flour

1. In a stand mixer fitted with a paddle attachment, beat the cream cheese, ½ cup of the Swerve, 2 tablespoons of the heavy cream, and

the vanilla until smooth. Using a small ice-cream scoop, divide the mixture into 16 balls and arrange them on a rimmed baking sheet lined with parchment paper. Freeze for 45 minutes until firm. 2. Line the air fryer basket with parchment paper and preheat the air fryer to 350ºF (177ºC). 3. In a small shallow bowl, combine the almond flour with the remaining 2 tablespoons Swerve. 4. In another small shallow bowl, place the remaining 2 tablespoons cream. 5. One at a time, dip the frozen cheesecake balls into the cream and then roll in the almond flour mixture, pressing lightly to form an even coating. Arrange the balls in a single layer in the air fryer basket, leaving room between them. Air fry for 2 minutes until the coating is lightly browned.

Per Serving:

calories: 99 | fat: 9g | protein: 2g | carbs: 3g | net carbs: 2g | fiber: 1g

Strawberry Shortcake

Prep time: 10 minutes | Cook time: 25 minutes | Serves 6

- ➤ 2 tablespoons coconut oil
- ➤ 1 cup blanched finely ground almond flour
- ➤ 2 large eggs, whisked
- ➤ ½ cup granular erythritol
- ➤ 1 teaspoon baking powder
- ➤ 1 teaspoon vanilla extract
- ➤ 2 cups sugar-free whipped cream
- ➤ 6 medium fresh strawberries, hulled and sliced

1. In a large bowl, combine coconut oil, flour, eggs, erythritol, baking powder, and vanilla. Pour batter into an ungreased round nonstick baking dish. 2. Place dish into air fryer basket. Adjust the temperature to 300ºF (149ºC) and bake for 25 minutes. When done, shortcake should be golden and a toothpick inserted in the middle will come out clean. 3. Remove dish from fryer and let cool 1 hour. 4. Once cooled, top cake with whipped cream and strawberries to serve.

Per Serving:

calories: 344 | fat: 30g | protein: 8g | carbs: 10g | net carbs: 4g | fiber: 6g

Coffee Ice Pops

Prep time: 5 minutes | Cook time: 0 minutes | Serves 4

- ➤ 2 cups brewed coffee, cold
- ➤ ¾ cup coconut cream, ¾ cup unsweetened full-fat coconut milk, or ¾ cup heavy

(whipping) cream

- 2 teaspoons Swerve natural sweetener or 2 drops liquid stevia
- 2 tablespoons sugar-free chocolate chips (I use Lily's)

1. In a food processor (or blender), mix together the coffee, coconut cream, and sweetener until thoroughly blended. 2. Pour into ice pop molds, and drop a few chocolate chips into each mold. 3. Freeze for at least 2 hours before serving.

Per Serving:

calories: 105 | fat: 10g | protein: 1g | carbs: 7g | net carbs: 2g | fiber: 2g

Cinnamon Roll Cheesecake

Prep time: 15 minutes | Cook time: 35 minutes | Serves 12

- Crust:
- 3½ tablespoons unsalted butter or coconut oil
- 1½ ounces (43 g) unsweetened baking chocolate, chopped
- 1 large egg, beaten
- ⅓ cup Swerve
- 2 teaspoons ground cinnamon
- 1 teaspoon vanilla extract
- ¼ teaspoon fine sea salt
- Filling:
- 4 (8-ounce / 227-g) packages cream cheese, softened
- ¾ cup Swerve
- ½ cup unsweetened almond milk (or hemp milk for nut-free)
- 1 teaspoon vanilla extract
- ¼ teaspoon almond extract (omit for nut-free)
- ¼ teaspoon fine sea salt
- 3 large eggs
- Cinnamon Swirl:
- 6 tablespoons (¾ stick) unsalted butter (or butter flavored coconut oil for dairy-free)
- ½ cup Swerve
- Seeds scraped from ½ vanilla bean (about 8 inches long), or 1 teaspoon vanilla extract
- 1 tablespoon ground cinnamon

- ¼ teaspoon fine sea salt
- 1 cup cold water

1. Line a baking pan with two layers of aluminum foil. 2. Make the crust: Melt the butter in a pan over medium-low heat. Slowly add the chocolate and stir until melted. Stir in the egg, sweetener, cinnamon, vanilla extract, and salt. 3. Transfer the crust mixture to the prepared baking pan, spreading it with your hands to cover the bottom completely. 4. Make the filling: In the bowl of a stand mixer, add the cream cheese, sweetener, milk, extracts, and salt and mix until well blended. Add the eggs, one at a time, mixing on low speed after each addition just until blended. Then blend until the filling is smooth. Pour half of the filling over the crust. 5. Make the cinnamon swirl: Heat the butter over high heat in a pan until the butter froths and brown flecks appear, stirring occasionally. Stir in the sweetener, vanilla seeds, cinnamon, and salt. Remove from the heat and allow to cool slightly. 6. Spoon half of the cinnamon swirl on top of the cheesecake filling in the baking pan. Use a knife to cut the cinnamon swirl through the filling several times for a marbled effect. Top with the rest of the cheesecake filling and cinnamon swirl. Cut the cinnamon swirl through the cheesecake filling again several times. 7. Place a trivet in the bottom of the Instant Pot and pour in the water. Use a foil sling to lower the baking pan onto the trivet. Cover the cheesecake with 3 large sheets of paper towel to ensure that condensation doesn't leak onto it. Tuck in the sides of the sling. 8. Lock the lid. Select the Manual mode and set the cooking time for 26 minutes at High Pressure. 9. When the timer beeps, use a natural pressure release for 10 minutes. Carefully remove the lid. 10. Use the foil sling to lift the pan out of the Instant Pot. 11. Let the cheesecake cool, then place in the refrigerator for 4 hours to chill and set completely before slicing and serving.

Per Serving:

calories: 363 | fat: 34g | protein: 7g | carbs: 8g | net carbs: 6g | fiber: 1g

Pumpkin Pie Spice Pots De Crème

Prep time: 5 minutes | Cook time: 7 minutes | Serves 4

- 2 cups heavy cream (or full-fat coconut milk for dairy-free)
- 4 large egg yolks
- ¼ cup Swerve, or more to taste
- 2 teaspoons pumpkin pie spice

- ➤ 1 teaspoon vanilla extract
- ➤ Pinch of fine sea salt
- ➤ 1 cup cold water

1. Heat the cream in a pan over medium-high heat until hot, about 2 minutes. 2. Place the remaining ingredients except the water in a medium bowl and stir until smooth. 3. Slowly pour in the hot cream while stirring. Taste and adjust the sweetness to your liking. Scoop the mixture into four ramekins with a spatula. Cover the ramekins with aluminum foil. 4. Place a trivet in the Instant Pot and pour in the water. Place the ramekins on the trivet. 5. Lock the lid. Select the Manual mode and set the cooking time for 5 minutes at High Pressure. 6. When the timer beeps, use a quick pressure release. Carefully remove the lid. 7. Remove the foil and set the foil aside. Let the pots de crème cool for 15 minutes. Cover the ramekins with the foil again and place in the refrigerator to chill completely, about 2 hours. 8. Serve.

Per Serving:

calories: 289 | fat: 27g | protein: 8g | carbs: 4g | net carbs: 4g | fiber: 0g

After-Dinner Parfait

Prep time: 10 minutes | Cook time: 0 minutes | Serves 4

- ➤ 1 small (9-gram) package sugar-free Jell-O, any flavor
- ➤ 1 cup boiling water
- ➤ 1 cup cold water
- ➤ 4 ounces full-fat cream cheese, softened
- ➤ 2 tablespoons canned whipped cream
- ➤ 1 tablespoon crushed salty peanuts

1. In a medium bowl, add Jell-O to boiling water. Stir in cold water until mixture starts to thicken, 2–3 minutes. Refrigerate until firm, about 30 minutes. 2. Using a mixer in a medium mixing bowl, beat softened cream cheese until smooth. Going slowly at first, combine firm Jell-O with cream cheese. Gradually increase speed until desired consistency is reached. 3. Scoop into serving bowls and top with whipped cream and dusting of crushed peanuts.

Per Serving:

calories: 122 | fat: 10g | protein: 3g | carbs: 2g | net carbs: 2g | fiber: 0g

- ➤

Five-Minute Keto Cookie Dough

Prep time: 5 minutes | Cook time: 0 minutes | Makes 20 dough balls

- ➤ 8 ounces (227 g) cream cheese, at room temperature
- ➤ 6 tablespoons butter or ghee, at room temperature
- ➤ ½ cup peanut butter (or almond butter)
- ➤ ¼ cup granulated sweetener (such as erythritol)
- ➤ ½ teaspoon vanilla extract
- ➤ ½ to 1 teaspoon monk fruit or stevia, or more (optional)
- ➤ ¼ teaspoon sea salt
- ➤ ¼ cup stevia-sweetened chocolate chips (or >90% dark chocolate chunks)

1. In a large bowl, mix together the cream cheese and butter using an electric hand mixer. 2. Add the peanut butter, granulated sweetener, vanilla, monk fruit, and salt and mix again until well combined. Taste and adjust the sweetness to your liking. 3. Fold in the chocolate chips and then use a tablespoon or small scoop to form 20 dough balls. Arrange the dough balls on a plate or baking sheet. 4. Let chill in the refrigerator for 1 hour and store in an airtight container for up to 3 weeks.

Per Serving:

1 dough ball: calories: 123 | fat: 11g | protein: 2g | carbs: 4g | net carbs: 3g | fiber: 1g

Dairy-Free White Chocolate Bark

Prep time: 15 minutes | Cook time: 0 minutes | Makes 12 pieces of bark

- ➤ Nonstick cooking spray
- ➤ 6 ounces (170 g) coconut butter
- ➤ 1 ounce (28 g) coconut oil
- ➤ ¼ cup keto-approved protein powder
- ➤ ¼ cup powdered erythritol
- ➤ 2 tablespoons unsweetened coconut milk
- ➤ 1 teaspoon vanilla extract
- ➤ 1 teaspoon cookie/cake flavor extract (or more vanilla extract)
- ➤ 2 tablespoons sugar-free chocolate chips

1. Coat a small baking dish with nonstick spray. 2. In a blender,

combine the coconut butter, coconut oil, protein powder, erythritol, coconut milk, and vanilla and cookie/cake extracts. Blend until completely smooth. 3. Pour the contents of the blender evenly into the prepared baking dish. Sprinkle with the chocolate chips and freeze for at least 2 hours before cutting or breaking into pieces and digging in.

Per Serving:

calories: 176 | fat: 16g | protein: 3g | carbs: 5g | net carbs: 2g | fiber: 3g

Flourless Chocolate Cake

Prep time: 10 minutes | Cook time: 42 minutes | Makes one 9-inch cake

- ➢ 5 ounces unsweetened baking chocolate (100% cacao)
- ➢ ½ cup (1 stick) plus 2 tablespoons unsalted butter
- ➢ 5 large eggs
- ➢ 1 cup powdered erythritol
- ➢ ½ cup cocoa powder
- ➢ ½ teaspoon baking powder

1. Preheat the oven to 350°F and grease a 9-inch springform pan with coconut oil spray. 2. Put the chocolate and butter in a small microwave-safe bowl and microwave for 30 seconds. Stir and microwave for another 30 seconds, then stir again. If the chocolate is not fully melted, continue to microwave in 20- to 30-second intervals, stirring after each interval. Set aside. 3. Crack the eggs into a large bowl and mix with a hand mixer until frothy. Slowly pour in the melted chocolate as you keep mixing. Set aside. 4. Put the erythritol, cocoa powder, and baking powder in a small bowl and combine using a fork. In 2 batches, add the dry mixture to the wet mixture and combine using the mixer until you have a thick batter. 5. Pour the batter into the greased springform pan and bake for 40 minutes, or until a toothpick inserted in the center of the cake comes out clean. Allow to rest in the pan for 15 minutes prior to cutting and serving. To serve, run a knife around the edges to loosen the cake, then remove the rim of the springform pan and cut into 8 slices. 6. Store leftover cake in a sealed container or gallon-sized zip-top plastic bag for up to a week.

Per Serving:

calories: 296 | fat: 26g | protein: 7g | carbs: 8g | net carbs: 2g | fiber: 6g

Pine Nut Mousse

Prep time: 5 minutes | Cook time: 35 minutes | Serves 8

- ➢ 1 tablespoon butter
- ➢ 1¼ cups pine nuts
- ➢ 1¼ cups full-fat heavy cream
- ➢ 2 large eggs
- ➢ 1 teaspoon vanilla extract
- ➢ 1 cup Swerve, reserve 1 tablespoon
- ➢ 1 cup water
- ➢ 1 cup full-fat heavy whipping cream

1. Butter the bottom and the side of a pie pan and set aside. 2. In a food processor, blend the pine nuts and heavy cream. Add the eggs, vanilla extract and Swerve and pulse a few times to incorporate. 3. Pour the batter into the pan and loosely cover with aluminum foil. Pour the water in the Instant Pot and place the trivet inside. Place the pan on top of the trivet. 4. Close the lid. Select Manual mode and set the timer for 35 minutes on High pressure. 5. In a small mixing bowl, whisk the heavy whipping cream and 1 tablespoon of Swerve until a soft peak forms. 6. When timer beeps, use a natural pressure release for 15 minutes, then release any remaining pressure and open the lid. 7. Serve immediately with whipped cream on top.

Per Serving:

calories: 184 | fat: 19g | protein: 3g | carbs: 2g | net carbs: 2g | fiber: 0g

Cinnamon Churros

Prep time: 25 minutes | Cook time: 30 minutes | Serves 12

- ➢ Churros
- ➢ ⅔ cup unblanched almond flour
- ➢ ¼ cup coconut flour
- ➢ 1 tablespoon flaxseed meal
- ➢ 1 teaspoon xanthan gum
- ➢ 1 cup water
- ➢ ¼ cup unsalted butter
- ➢ 2 tablespoons 0g net carb sweetener
- ➢ ¼ teaspoon salt
- ➢ 2 large eggs, lightly beaten
- ➢ 1 teaspoon pure vanilla extract
- ➢ Garnish
- ➢ 1 tablespoon unsalted butter, melted

- ➢ 2 teaspoons ground cinnamon
- ➢ ¼ cup 0g net carb sweetener

1. Preheat oven to 350°F. Line a large baking sheet with parchment paper. 2. In a medium bowl, whisk together almond flour, coconut flour, flaxseed meal, and xanthan gum. 3. In a medium pot over medium heat, heat water almost to a boil and mix in ¼ cup butter, 2 tablespoons sweetener, and ¼ teaspoon salt until butter is melted and well blended. Add flour mix and keep stirring until a ball is formed. 4. Return dough to bowl and let cool for 5 minutes. Mix eggs and vanilla in with dough. 5. Let dough cool to room temperature, 10 to 15 minutes. Transfer dough into a pastry piping bag with star tip. Make twelve churros and place on baking sheet. 6. Bake 15 to 20 minutes until deep golden. 7. Remove from oven and brush with butter. Garnish with cinnamon and sweetener. Serve warm.

Per Serving:

calories: 100 | fat: 9g | protein: 3g | carbs: 6g | net carbs: 2g | fiber: 4g

Instant Protein Ice Cream

Prep time: 1 minutes | Cook time: 0 minutes | Serves 1

- ➢ 1 cup unsweetened almond milk
- ➢ 1 scoop flavored protein powder of choice
- ➢ ¼ teaspoon xanthan gum
- ➢ 1½ cups ice
- ➢ Ground cinnamon, for garnish (optional)

1. Put the milk in a blender. Add the protein powder, xanthan gum, and ice and puree on high until the mixture is smooth, 20 to 30 seconds. 2. Pour into a serving bowl and garnish with a dusting of cinnamon, if desired. Enjoy immediately.

Per Serving:

calories: 130 | fat: 5g | protein: 21g | carbs: 5g | net carbs: 3g | fiber: 2g

Southern Almond Pie

Prep time: 10 minutes | Cook time: 35 minutes | Serves 12

- ➢ 2 cups almond flour
- ➢ 1½ cups powdered erythritol
- ➢ 1 teaspoon baking powder
- ➢ Pinch of salt
- ➢ ½ cup sour cream
- ➢ 4 tablespoons butter, melted

- ➢ 1 egg
- ➢ 1 teaspoon vanilla extract
- ➢ Cooking spray
- ➢ 1½ teaspoons ground cinnamon
- ➢ 1½ teaspoons Swerve
- ➢ 1 cup water

1. In a large bowl, whisk together the almond flour, powdered erythritol, baking powder, and salt. 2. Add the sour cream, butter, egg, and vanilla and whisk until well combined. The batter will be very thick, almost like cookie dough. 3. Grease the baking dish with cooking spray. Line with parchment paper, if desired. 4. Transfer the batter to the dish and level with an offset spatula. 5. In a small bowl, combine the cinnamon and Swerve. Sprinkle over the top of the batter. 6. Cover the dish tightly with aluminum foil. Add the water to the pot. Set the dish on the trivet and carefully lower it into the pot. 7. Set the lid in place. Select the Manual mode and set the cooking time for 35 minutes on High Pressure. When the timer goes off, do a quick pressure release. Carefully open the lid. 8. Remove the trivet and pie from the pot. Remove the foil from the pan. The pie should be set but soft, and the top should be slightly cracked. 9. Cool completely before cutting.

Per Serving:

calories: 221 | fat: 19g | protein: 6g | carbs: 5g | net carbs: 2g | fiber: 2g

Golden Coconut Cream Pops

Prep time: 5 minutes | Cook time: 0 minutes | Makes 8 cream pops

- ➢ 1½ cups coconut cream
- ➢ ½ cup coconut milk
- ➢ 4 egg yolks
- ➢ 2 teaspoons ground turmeric
- ➢ 1 teaspoon ground ginger
- ➢ 1 teaspoon cinnamon
- ➢ 1 teaspoon vanilla powder or 1 tablespoon unsweetened vanilla extract
- ➢ ¼ teaspoon ground black pepper
- ➢ Optional: low-carb sweetener, to taste

1. Place all of the ingredients in a blender (including the optional sweetener) and process until well combined. Pour into eight ⅓-cup (80 ml) ice pop molds. Freeze until solid for 3 hours, or until set. 2. To easily remove the ice pops from the molds, fill a pot as tall as the

ice pops with warm (not hot) water and dip the ice pop molds in for 15 to 20 seconds. Remove the ice pops from the molds and then freeze again. Store in the freezer in a resealable bag for up to 3 months.

Per Serving:

calories: 281 | fat: 28g | protein: 4g | carbs: 5g | net carbs: 4g | fiber: 1g

No-Bake N'Oatmeal Chocolate Chip Cookies

Prep time: 20 minutes | Cook time: 0 minutes | Serves 14

➢ 1¼ cups (185 g) hulled hemp seeds
➢ ¼ cup (60 ml) melted coconut oil or cacao butter
➢ ½ teaspoon vanilla extract or powder
➢ ½ teaspoon ground cinnamon
➢ 2 drops liquid stevia
➢ ¼ cup (56 g) stevia-sweetened chocolate chips

1. Line a baking sheet with parchment paper or a silicone baking mat. 2. Put the hemp seeds, coconut oil, vanilla, cinnamon, and stevia in a medium-sized bowl. Stir to combine. 3. Transfer the mixture to a blender or food processor and pulse, just lightly, 1 second per pulse, three times. After the third pulse, pinch some dough with your fingers. If it holds together nicely, you're ready to move on. If not, pulse again until the dough holds together. 4. Fold the chocolate chips into the dough. 5. Using a round tablespoon (or a 1-tablespoon cookie scoop/melon baller), scoop up the dough, packing it firmly into the tablespoon. Transfer the scoop to the prepared baking sheet. Repeat with the remaining dough, making 14 cookies. 6. Chill for 30 minutes before consuming. These cookies are best served chilled, straight from the fridge.

Per Serving:

calories: 126 | fat: 11g | protein: 5g | carbs: 3g | net carbs: 1g | fiber: 2g

Keto Cheesecake with Pecan Almond Crust

Prep time: 20 minutes | Cook time: 1 hour 45 minutes | serves 16

➢ Crust:
➢ 1 cup finely ground blanched almond flour

➢ 1 cup raw pecan halves, finely crushed
➢ ½ cup granular erythritol
➢ ¼ cup (½ stick) salted butter, cubed
➢ Filling:
➢ 5 (8 ounces) packages cream cheese, softened
➢ 1½ cups confectioners'-style erythritol
➢ 4 large eggs
➢ 1 cup sour cream
➢ 1 tablespoon freshly squeezed lemon juice
➢ 1 teaspoon vanilla extract

Make The Crust: 1. Preheat the oven to 375°F. Grease the bottom and side of a 9- or 10-inch springform pan with butter, or line it with parchment paper cut to fit the bottom of the pan and grease the sides. 2. Place all the crust ingredients in a mixing bowl and mix with a fork until well combined. The mixture will be crumbly. Press the crust mixture into the prepared pan. 3. Par-bake the crust for 12 to 15 minutes, until brown around the edges. 4. Remove the crust from the oven and turn the oven temperature down to 325°F. Let the crust cool completely, then make the filling. Make The Filling: 1. Using a hand mixer, beat the cream cheese on medium speed until fluffy. 2. With the mixer still on medium speed, gradually blend in the erythritol. 3. Blend in the eggs one at a time, scraping down the bowl after each addition. 4. Beat in the sour cream, then add the lemon juice and vanilla extract. At this point, the batter will be very thick and creamy. To bake the cheesecake: 1. Wrap the bottom of the cooled springform pan in aluminum foil (this will protect the cake when it sits in the water bath). 2. Pour the filling over the cooled crust, then set the springform pan inside a roasting pan. 3. Pour hot water into the roasting pan so that it comes halfway up the side of the springform pan. 4. Bake the cheesecake for 1 hour 30 minutes or until the center is firm and the top is slightly browned. 5. Remove the springform pan from the water bath. Let the cheesecake cool completely, then refrigerate for at least 8 hours or overnight. 6. Before serving, run a knife around the rim of the pan to loosen the cake, then release the side of the pan. Leftovers can be stored in an airtight container in the refrigerator for up to 5 days.

Per Serving:

calories: 315 | fat: 28g | protein: 9g | carbs: 4g | net carbs: 2g | fiber: 1g

Strawberry Shake

Prep time: 10 minutes | Cook time: 0 minutes | Serves 2

- ¾ cup heavy (whipping) cream
- 2 ounces cream cheese, at room temperature
- 1 tablespoon Swerve natural sweetener
- ¼ teaspoon vanilla extract
- 6 strawberries, sliced
- 6 ice cubes

1. In a food processor (or blender), combine the heavy cream, cream cheese, sweetener, and vanilla. Mix on high to fully combine. 2. Add the strawberries and ice, and blend until smooth. 3. Pour into two tall glasses and serve.

Per Serving:

calories: 407 | fat: 42g | protein: 4g | carbs: 13g | net carbs: 6g | fiber: 1g

Vanilla Cream Pie

Prep time: 20 minutes | Cook time: 35 minutes | Serves 12

- 1 cup heavy cream
- 3 eggs, beaten
- 1 teaspoon vanilla extract
- ¼ cup erythritol
- 1 cup coconut flour
- 1 tablespoon butter, melted
- 1 cup water, for cooking

1. In the mixing bowl, mix up coconut flour, erythritol, vanilla extract, eggs, and heavy cream. 2. Grease the baking pan with melted butter. 3. Pour the coconut mixture in the baking pan. 4. Pour water and insert the steamer rack in the instant pot. 5. Place the pie on the rack. Close and seal the lid. 6. Cook the pie on Manual mode (High Pressure) for 35 minutes. 7. Allow the natural pressure release for 10 minutes.

Per Serving:

calories: 100 | fat: 7g | protein: 3g | carbs: 12g | net carbs: 8g | fiber: 4g

Thai Pandan Coconut Custard

Prep time: 10 minutes | Cook time: 30 minutes | Serves 4

- Nonstick cooking spray
- 1 cup unsweetened coconut milk
- 3 eggs
- ⅓ cup Swerve
- 3 to 4 drops pandan extract, or use vanilla

extract if you must

1. Grease a 6-inch heatproof bowl with the cooking spray. 2. In a large bowl, whisk together the coconut milk, eggs, Swerve, and pandan extract. Pour the mixture into the prepared bowl and cover it with aluminum foil. 3. Pour 2 cups of water into the inner cooking pot of the Instant Pot, then place a trivet in the pot. Place the bowl on the trivet. 4. Lock the lid into place. Select Manual and adjust the pressure to High. Cook for 30 minutes. When the cooking is complete, let the pressure release naturally. Unlock the lid. 5. Remove the bowl from the pot and remove the foil. A knife inserted into the custard should come out clean. Cool in the refrigerator for 6 to 8 hours, or until the custard is set.

Per Serving:

calories: 202 | fat: 18g | protein: 6g | carbs: 4g | net carbs: 3g | fiber: 1g

Lemon-Ricotta Cheesecake

Prep time: 10 minutes | Cook time: 30 minutes | Serves 6

- Unsalted butter or vegetable oil, for greasing the pan
- 8 ounces (227 g) cream cheese, at room temperature
- ¼ cup plus 1 teaspoon Swerve, plus more as needed
- ⅓ cup full-fat or part-skim ricotta cheese, at room temperature
- Zest of 1 lemon
- Juice of 1 lemon
- ½ teaspoon lemon extract
- 2 eggs, at room temperature
- 2 tablespoons sour cream

1. Grease a 6-inch springform pan extremely well. I find this easiest to do with a silicone basting brush so I can get into all the nooks and crannies. Alternatively, line the sides of the pan with parchment paper. 2. In the bowl of a stand mixer, beat the cream cheese, ¼ cup of Swerve, the ricotta, lemon zest, lemon juice, and lemon extract on high speed until you get a smooth mixture with no lumps. 3. Taste to ensure the sweetness is to your liking and adjust if needed. 4. Add the eggs, reduce the speed to low and gently blend until the eggs are just incorporated. Overbeating at this stage will result in a cracked crust. 5. Pour the mixture into the prepared pan and cover with aluminum foil

or a silicone lid. 6. Pour 2 cups of water into the inner cooking pot of the Instant Pot, then place a trivet in the pot. Place the covered pan on the trivet. 7. Lock the lid into place. Select Manual and adjust the pressure to High. Cook for 30 minutes. When the cooking is complete, let the pressure release naturally. Unlock the lid. 8. Carefully remove the pan from the pot, and remove the foil. 9. In a small bowl, mix together the sour cream and remaining 1 teaspoon of Swerve and spread this over the top of the warm cake. 10. Refrigerate the cheesecake for 6 to 8 hours. Do not be in a hurry! The cheesecake needs every bit of this time to be its best.

Per Serving:

calories: 217 | fat: 17g | protein: 6g | carbs: 10g | net carbs: 10g | fiber: 0g

Sweetened Condensed Coconut Milk

Prep time: 10 minutes | Cook time: 35 minutes | Serves 12

- ➢ 1 (13½ ounces/400 ml) can full-fat coconut milk
- ➢ 2 tablespoons confectioners'-style erythritol

1. Place all the ingredients in a small saucepan and bring to a rapid boil over medium-high heat. Reduce the heat and simmer lightly for 32 to 35 minutes, until the milk has thickened and reduced by about half. Use immediately in a recipe that calls for it, or let it cool and store in the fridge for later use.

Per Serving:

calories: 68 | fat: 7g | protein: 1g | carbs: 1g | net carbs: 1g | fiber: 0g

Butter Flax Cookies

Prep time: 25 minutes | Cook time: 20 minutes | Serves 4

- ➢ 8 ounces (227 g) almond meal
- ➢ 2 tablespoons flaxseed meal
- ➢ 1 ounce (28 g) monk fruit
- ➢ 1 teaspoon baking powder
- ➢ A pinch of grated nutmeg
- ➢ A pinch of coarse salt
- ➢ 1 large egg, room temperature.
- ➢ 1 stick butter, room temperature
- ➢ 1 teaspoon vanilla extract

1. Mix the almond meal, flaxseed meal, monk fruit, baking powder,

grated nutmeg, and salt in a bowl. 2. In a separate bowl, whisk the egg, butter, and vanilla extract. 3. Stir the egg mixture into dry mixture; mix to combine well or until it forms a nice, soft dough. 4. Roll your dough out and cut out with a cookie cutter of your choice. Bake in the preheated air fryer at 350ºF (177ºC) for 10 minutes. Decrease the temperature to 330ºF (166ºC) and cook for 10 minutes longer. Bon appétit!

Per Serving:

calories: 559 | fat: 51g | protein: 15g | carbs: 16g | net carbs: 5g | fiber: 11g

Blackberry "Cheesecake" Bites

Prep time: 5 minutes | Cook time: 0 minutes | serves 4

- ➢ 1½ cups almonds, soaked overnight
- ➢ 1 cup blackberries
- ➢ ⅓ cup coconut oil, melted
- ➢ ¼ cup full-fat coconut cream
- ➢ ⅓ cup monk fruit sweetener
- ➢ ¼ cup freshly squeezed lemon juice

1. Prepare a muffin tin by lining the cups with cupcake liners. Set aside. 2. In a high-powered blender, combine the soaked almonds, blackberries, melted coconut oil, coconut cream, monk fruit sweetener, and lemon juice. 3. Blend on high until the mixture is whipped and fluffy. 4. Divide the mixture equally among the muffin cups. 5. Place the muffin tin in the freezer for 90 minutes to allow the cheesecake bites to set.

Per Serving:

calories: 514 | fat: 48g | protein: 12g | carbs: 18g | net carbs: 9g | fiber: 9g

Strawberry Panna Cotta

Prep time: 10 minutes | Cook time: 10 minutes | Serves 4

- ➢ 2 tablespoons warm water
- ➢ 2 teaspoons gelatin powder
- ➢ 2 cups heavy cream
- ➢ 1 cup sliced strawberries, plus more for garnish
- ➢ 1 to 2 tablespoons sugar-free sweetener of choice (optional)
- ➢ 1½ teaspoons pure vanilla extract
- ➢ 4 to 6 fresh mint leaves, for garnish (optional)

1. Pour the warm water into a small bowl. Sprinkle the gelatin over the water and stir well to dissolve. Allow the mixture to sit for 10 minutes. 2. In a blender or a large bowl, if using an immersion blender, combine the cream, strawberries, sweetener (if using), and vanilla. Blend until the mixture is smooth and the strawberries are well puréed. 3. Transfer the mixture to a saucepan and heat over medium-low heat until just below a simmer. Remove from the heat and cool for 5 minutes. 4. Whisking constantly, add in the gelatin mixture until smooth. Divide the custard between ramekins or small glass bowls, cover and refrigerate until set, 4 to 6 hours. 5. Serve chilled, garnishing with additional sliced strawberries or mint leaves (if using).

Per Serving:

calories: 540 | fat: 57g | protein: 6g | carbs: 8g | net carbs: 7g | fiber: 1g

Crustless Cheesecake Bites

Prep time: 10 minutes | Cook time: 30 minutes | Serves 4

➢ 4 ounces cream cheese, at room temperature
➢ ¼ cup sour cream
➢ 2 large eggs
➢ ⅓ cup Swerve natural sweetener
➢ ¼ teaspoon vanilla extract

1. Preheat the oven to 350°F. 2. In a medium mixing bowl, use a hand mixer to beat the cream cheese, sour cream, eggs, sweetener, and vanilla until well mixed. 3. Place silicone liners (or cupcake paper liners) in the cups of a muffin tin. 4. Pour the cheesecake batter into the liners, and bake for 30 minutes. 5. Refrigerate until completely cooled before serving, about 3 hours. Store extra cheesecake bites in a zip-top bag in the freezer for up to 3 months.

Per Serving:

calories: 169 | fat: 15g | protein: 5g | carbs: 18g | net carbs: 2g | fiber: 0g

Almond Pie with Coconut

Prep time: 5 minutes | Cook time: 41 minutes | Serves 8

➢ 1 cup almond flour
➢ ½ cup coconut milk
➢ 1 teaspoon vanilla extract
➢ 2 tablespoons butter, softened
➢ 1 tablespoon Truvia
➢ ¼ cup shredded coconut
➢ 1 cup water

1. In the mixing bowl, mix up almond flour, coconut milk, vanilla extract, butter, Truvia, and shredded coconut. 2. When the mixture is smooth, transfer it in the baking pan and flatten. 3. Pour water and insert the trivet in the instant pot. 4. Put the baking pan with cake on the trivet. 5. Lock the lid. Select the Manual mode and set the cooking time for 41 minutes on High Pressure. Once the timer goes off, perform a natural pressure release for 10 minutes, then release any remaining pressure. Carefully open the lid. 6. Serve immediately.

Per Serving:

calories: 89 | fat: 9g | protein: 1g | carbs: 3g | net carbs: 2g | fiber: 1g

Appendix 1: 30 Days Keto Diet Meal Plan

DAYS	BREAKFAST	LUNCH	DINNER	SNACK/DESSERT
1	Cranberry-Orange Scones	Crack Chicken Breasts	Beef with Grilled Vegetables	Double Chocolate Brownies
2	Cinnamon Crunch Cereal	Basil Turkey Meatballs	Italian Beef Burgers	Fruit Pizza
3	Super Breakfast Combo	Turkey & Leek Soup	Creamy Pork Liver	Fried Cheesecake Bites
4	No-Crust Spinach Quiche	Jerk Chicken Kebabs	Ginger Beef Flank Steak	Strawberry Shortcake
5	Hashed Zucchini & Bacon Breakfast	Cajun Chicken	Beef Sausage Casserole	Coffee Ice Pops
6	Broccoli & Colby Cheese Frittata	Garlic Parmesan Drumsticks	Flounder Meuniere	After-Dinner Parfait
7	Sausage Breakfast Stacks	Thyme Chicken Thighs	Simple Lemon-Herb Whitefish	Flourless Chocolate Cake
8	Green Eggs and Ham	Duck & Vegetable Casserole	Salmon Fillets and Bok Choy	Pine Nut Mousse
9	Turkey Sausage Breakfast Pizza	Lemon-Dijon Boneless Chicken	Sardine Fritter Wraps	Cinnamon Churros
10	Turmeric Scrambled Eggs	Chicken Pesto Pizzas	Spicy Tuna Hand Rolls	Instant Protein Ice Cream
11	Cauliflower & Cheese Burgers	Lemon Thyme Roasted Chicken	Scallops & Mozza Broccoli Mash	Southern Almond Pie
12	Almond Flour Pancakes	Easy Marinated Chicken Thighs	Crab-Stuffed Avocado Boats	Strawberry Shake
13	Jerky Cookies	Coconut Curry Chicken	Lemon Pepper Shrimp	Vanilla Cream Pie
14	Diner Pancakes	Lemon Chicken	Parmesan Salmon Loaf	Butter Flax Cookies
15	Bacon Tomato Cups	Chicken Legs with Leeks	Almond Milk Curried Fish	Strawberry Panna Cotta
16	Quick Keto Blender Muffins	Buttered Duck Breast	Baked Lemon-Butter Fish	Crustless Cheesecake Bites
17	Classic Cinnamon Roll Coffee Cake	Chicken Enchilada Bowl	Red Cabbage Tilapia Taco Bowl	Rosemary Chicken Wings

18	Vegetable and Cheese Bake	Simple Shredded Chicken	Cucumber and Salmon Salad	Gourmet "Cheese" Balls
19	Cauliflower Avocado Toast	Cheddar Chicken Tenders	Winter Veal and Sauerkraut	Asiago Shishito Peppers
20	Bacon-Jalapeño Egg Cups	Chicken and Bacon Rolls	Ground Beef Stroganoff	Bone Broth Fat Bombs
21	Double-Dipped Mini Cinnamon Biscuits	Simple Chicken Masala	Garlic Beef Roast	Cauliflower Cheesy Garlic Bread
22	Jalapeño and Bacon Breakfast Pizza	Chicken Fajitas with Bell Peppers	Pork Larb Lettuce Wraps	Zucchini and Cheese Tots
23	Ham and Vegetable Frittata	Pork Chops with Pecan Crust	Barbacoa Beef Roast	Brussels Sprouts with Aioli Sauce
24	Bacon, Spinach, and Avocado Egg Wrap	Beef Stuffed Kale Rolls	Quick Shrimp Skewers	Finger Tacos
25	Bacon and Mushroom Quiche Lorraine	Chipotle-Spiced Meatball Subs	Lemony Fish and Asparagus	Lemon Pepper Wings
26	Chunky Cobb-Style Egg Salad	Steak with Tallow Herb Butter	Trout Casserole	Asparagus with Creamy Dip
27	Bacon Crackers	Classic Italian Bolognese Sauce	Cream Cheese and Berries	Devilish Eggs
28	Burger Skillet	Turmeric Pork Loin	Hangover Bacon-Wrapped Pickles	Snappy Bacon Asparagus
29	Spaghetti Squash Fritters	Rib Eye with Chimichurri Sauce	Pecan Ranch Cheese Ball	Buffalo Chicken Meatballs
30	Creamy Almond Coffee Smoothie	Beef Satay Skewers	Parmesan Chicken Balls with Chives	Rich Chocolate Mug Cake

Appendix 2: Measurement Conversion Chart

Volume Equivalents (Dry):	Temperature Equivalents:
1/8 teaspoon = 0.5 mL	225°F = 107°C
1/4 teaspoon = 1 mL	250°F = 121°C
1/2 teaspoon = 2 mL	275°F = 135°C
3/4 teaspoon = 4 mL	300°F = 149°C
1 teaspoon = 5 mL	325°F = 163°C
1 tablespoon = 15 mL	350°F = 177°C
1/4 cup = 59 mL	375°F = 191°C
1/2 cup = 118 mL	400°F = 204°C
3/4 cup = 177 mL	425°F = 218°C
1 cup = 235 mL	450°F = 232°C
2 cups (or 1 pint) = 475 mL	475°F = 246°C
4 cups (or 1 quart) = 1 L	500°F = 260°C

Weight Equivalents:	Volume Equivalents (Liquid):
1 ounce = 28 g	1/4 cup = 60 mL = 2 fl oz
2 ounces = 57 g	1/2 cup = 120 mL = 4 fl oz
5 ounces = 142 g	1 cup = 240 mL = 8 fl oz
10 ounces = 284 g	2 cups (or 1 pint) = 475 mL = 16 fl oz
15 ounces = 425 g	4 cups (or 1 quart) = 1 L = 32 fl oz
16 ounces (1 pound) = 455 g	1 gallon = 4 L = 128 fl oz
1.5 pounds = 680 g	
2 pounds = 907 g	

Appendix 3: Recipe Index

Made in United States
Troutdale, OR
07/14/2024

21219485R00060